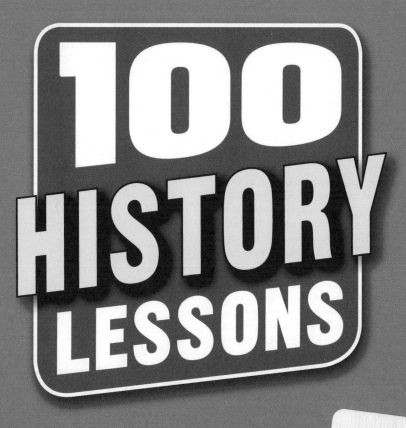

Terms and conditions

IMPORTANT – PERMITTED USE AND WARNINGS – READ CAREFULLY BEFORE USING

Copyright in the software contained in this CD-ROM and in its accompanying material belongs to Scholastic Limited. All rights reserved. © 2014 Scholastic Ltd.

Save for these purposes, or as expressly authorised in the accompanying materials, the software may not be copied, reproduced, used, sold, licensed, transferred, exchanged, hired, or exported in whole or in part or in any manner or form without the prior written consent of Scholastic Ltd. Any such unauthorised use or activities are prohibited and may give rise to civil liabilities and criminal prosecutions.

The material contained on this CD-ROM may only be used in the context for which it was intended in *100 History Lessons for the 2014 Curriculum*, and is for use only by the purchaser or purchasing institution that has purchased the book and CD-ROM. Permission to download images is given for purchasers only and not for users from any lending service. Any further use of the material contravenes Scholastic Ltd's copyright and that of other rights holders.

This CD-ROM has been tested for viruses at all stages of its production. However, we recommend that you run virus-checking software on your computer systems at all times. Scholastic Ltd cannot accept any responsibility for any loss, disruption or damage to your data or your computer system that may occur as a result of using either the CD-ROM or the data held on it.

IF YOU ACCEPT THE ABOVE CONDITIONS YOU MAY PROCEED TO USE THE CD-ROM.

Recommended system requirements:

- Windows: XP (Service Pack 3), Vista (Service Pack 2), Windows 7 or Windows 8 with 2.33GHz processor
- Mac: OS 10.6 to 10.8 with Intel Core™ Duo processor
- 1GB RAM (recommended)
- 1024 x 768 Screen resolution
- CD-ROM drive (24x speed recommended)
- 16-bit sound card
- Adobe Reader (version 9 recommended for Mac users)
- Broadband internet connections (for installation and updates)

For all technical support queries, please phone Scholastic Customer Services on 0845 6039091.

SCHOLASTIC

Book End, Range Road, Witney, Oxfordshire, OX29 0YD
www.scholastic.co.uk

© 2014, Scholastic Ltd

1 2 3 4 5 6 7 8 9   4 5 6 7 8 9 0 1 2 3

British Library Cataloguing-in-Publication Data
A catalogue record for this book is available from the
British Library.

ISBN 978-1407-12853-5
Printed by Bell & Bain Ltd, Glasgow

All rights reserved. This book is sold subject to the
condition that it shall not, by way of trade or otherwise,
be lent, hired out or otherwise circulated without the
publisher's prior consent in any form of binding or cover
other than that in which it is published and without a
similar condition, including this condition, being imposed
upon the subsequent purchaser.

No part of this publication may be reproduced, stored
in a retrieval system, or transmitted, in any form or
by any means, electronic, mechanical, photocopying,
recording or otherwise, other than for the purposes
described in the content of this product, without the
prior permission of the publisher. This product remains
in copyright, although permission is granted to copy
pages where indicated for classroom distribution and
use only in the school which has purchased the product,
or by the teacher who has purchased the product,
and in accordance with the CLA licensing agreement.
Photocopying permission is given only for purchasers
and not for borrowers of books from any lending
service.

Due to the nature of the web we cannot guarantee the
content or links of any site mentioned. We strongly
recommend that teachers check websites before using
them in the classroom.

Extracts from *The National Curriculum in English, History
Programme of Study* © Crown Copyright. Reproduced
under the terms of the Open Government Licence
(OGL). http://www.nationalarchives.gov.uk/doc/open-
government-licence/open-government-licence.htm

Author
Alison Milford

Editorial team
Jenny Wilcox, Rachel Morgan, Roanne Charles and
Kate Soar

Cover Design
Andrea Lewis

Design
Andrea Lewis

CD-ROM development
Hannah Barnett, Phil Crothers, MWA Technologies
Private Ltd

illustrations
Gemma Hastilow

Acknowledgements
Every effort has been made to trace copyright
holders for the works reproduced in this book,
and the publishers apologise for any inadvertent
omissions.

Contents

Introduction

The *100 History Lessons* series is designed to meet the requirements of the 2014 Curriculum, History Programmes of Study. There are three books in the series, Years 1–2, 3–4 and 5–6, and each book contains lesson plans, resources and ideas matched to the new curriculum. It can be a complex task to ensure that a progressive and appropriate curriculum is followed in all year groups; this series has been carefully structured to ensure that a progressive and appropriate curriculum is followed throughout.

About the new curriculum

The 2014 National Curriculum for Key Stages 1 and 2 explains the purpose and aims of history as follows:
A high-quality history education will help pupils gain a coherent knowledge and understanding of Britain's past and that of the wider world. It should inspire pupils' curiosity to know more about the past. Teaching should equip pupils to ask perceptive questions, think critically, weigh evidence, sift arguments, and develop perspective and judgement. History helps pupils to understand the complexity of people's lives, the process of change, the diversity of societies and relationships between different groups, as well as their own identity and the challenges of their time.

The National Curriculum for History aims to ensure that all children:
- *know and understand the history of these islands as a coherent, chronological narrative, from the earliest times to the present day: how people's lives have shaped this nation and how Britain has influenced and been influenced by the wider world*
- *know and understand significant aspects of the history of the wider world: the nature of ancient civilisations; the expansion and dissolution of empires; characteristic features of past non-European societies; achievements and follies of mankind*
- *gain and deploy a historically grounded understanding of abstract terms such as 'empire', 'civilisation', 'parliament' and 'peasantry'*
- *understand historical concepts such as continuity and change, cause and consequence, similarity, difference and significance, and use them to make connections, draw contrasts, analyse trends, frame historically valid questions and create their own structured accounts, including written narratives and analyses*
- *understand the methods of historical enquiry, including how evidence is used rigorously to make historical claims, and discern how and why contrasting arguments and interpretations of the past have been constructed*
- *gain historical perspective by placing their growing knowledge into different contexts, understanding the connections between local, regional, national and international history; between cultural, economic, military, political, religious and social history; and between short- and long-term timescales.*

The curriculum goes on to state that *children are expected to know, apply and understand the matters, skills and processes specified in the relevant Programme of Study.* There are two Programmes of Study in the primary history curriculum: one for Key Stage 1 and one for Key Stage 2. On its own, the content of the programmes of study is insufficient to create exciting and effective learning experiences. This series of books is designed to help provide guidance and support for schools and teachers, through a coherent, challenging, engaging and enjoyable scheme of work.

Terminology
- **Curriculum objectives:** These are the statutory programme of study statements or objectives.

■SCHOLASTIC
www.scholastic.co.uk

About the book

This book is divided into twelve chapters; six for each year group. Each chapter contains a half-term's work and is based around a topic or theme. Each chapter follows the same structure:

Chapter introduction

At the start of each chapter there is a summary of what is covered. This includes:

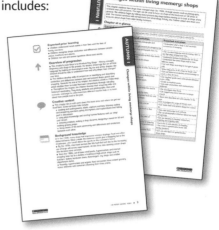

- **Introduction:** A description of what is covered in the chapter.
- **Chapter at a glance:** This is a table that summarises the content of each lesson, including: the curriculum objectives, a summary of the activities and the outcome.
- **Expected prior learning:** What the children are expected to know before starting the work in the chapter.
- **Overview of progression:** A brief explanation of how the children progress through the chapter.
- **Creative context:** How the chapter could link to other curriculum areas.
- **Background knowledge:** A section explaining grammatical terms and suchlike to enhance your subject knowledge, where required.

Lessons

Each chapter contains six weeks' of lessons, each week contains two lessons. At the start of each week there is an introduction about what is covered. The lesson plans then include the relevant combination of headings from below.

- **Lesson objectives:** Objectives that are based upon the Curriculum objectives, but are more specific broken-down steps to achieve them.
- **Expected outcomes:** What you should expect all, most and some children to know by the end of the lesson.
- **Resources:** What you require to teach the lesson.
- **Introduction:** A short and engaging activity to begin the lesson.
- **Whole-class work:** Working together as a class.
- **Group/Paired/Independent work:** Children working independently of the teacher in pairs, groups or alone.
- **Differentiation:** Ideas for how to support children who are struggling with a concept or how to extend those children who understand a concept without taking them onto new work.
- **Review:** A chance to review the children's learning and ensure the outcomes of the lesson have been achieved.

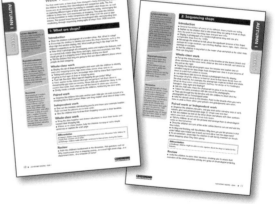

Assess and review

At the end of each chapter are activities for assessing and reviewing the children's understanding. These can be conducted at the end of the chapter or at a later date. They all follow the same format:

- **Curriculum objectives:** These are the areas of focus for the assess and review activity.
- **Resources:** What you require to conduct the activities.
- **Revise:** A series of short activities or one longer activity to revise and consolidate the children's learning and ensure they understand the concept(s).
- **Assess:** An assessment activity to provide a chance for the children to demonstrate their understanding and for you to check this.
- **Further practice:** Ideas for further practice on the focus, whether children are insecure in their learning or you want to provide extra practice or challenge.

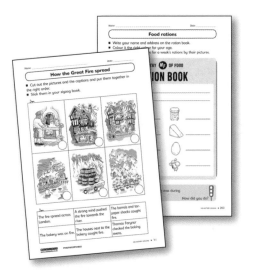

Photocopiable pages

At the end of each chapter are some photocopiable pages that will have been referred to in the lesson plans. These sheets are for the children to use. There is generally a title, an instruction, an activity and an 'I can' statement at the bottom. The children should be encouraged to complete the 'I can' statements by colouring in the traffic lights to say how they think they have done (red – not very well, amber – ok, green – very well).

These sheets are also provided on the CD-ROM alongside additional pages as referenced in the lessons (see page 7 About the CD-ROM).

■ SCHOLASTIC
www.scholastic.co.uk

About the CD-ROM

The CD-ROM contains:
- Printable versions of the photocopiable sheets from the book and additional photocopiable sheets as referenced in the lesson plans.
- Interactive activities for children to complete or to use on the whiteboard.
- Media resources to display.
- Printable versions of the lesson plans.
- Digital versions of the lesson plans with the relevant resources linked to them.

Getting started

Put the CD-ROM into your CD-ROM drive.
- For Windows users, the install wizard should autorun, if it fails to do so then navigate to your CD-ROM drive. Then follow the installation process.
- For Mac users, copy the disk image file to your hard drive. After it has finished copying double-click it to mount the disk image. Navigate to the mounted disk image and run the installer. After installation the disk image can be unmounted and the DMG can be deleted from the hard drive.
- To complete the installation of the program you need to open the program and click 'Update' in the pop-up. Please note – this CD-ROM is web-enabled and the content will be downloaded from the internet to your hard-drive to populate the CD-ROM with the relevant resources. This only needs to be done on first use, after this you will be able to use the CD-ROM without an internet connection. If at any point any content is updated you will receive another pop-up upon start up with an internet connection.

Navigating the CD-ROM

There are two options to navigate the CD-ROM either as a Child or as a Teacher.

Child
- Click on the 'Child' button on the first menu screen.
- In the second menu click on the relevant class (please note only the books installed on the machine or network will be accessible. You can also rename year groups to match your school's naming conventions via the Teacher > Settings > Rename books area).
- A list of interactive activities will be displayed, children need to locate the correct one and click 'Go' to launch it.
- There is the opportunity to print or save a PDF of the activity at the end.

Teacher
- Click on the Teacher button on the first menu screen and you will be taken to a screen showing which of the 100 History books you have purchased. From here, you can also access information about getting started and the credits.
- To enter the product click 'Next' in the bottom right.
- You then need to enter a password (the password is: login).
  - On first use: Enter as a Guest by clicking on the 'Guest' button.
  - If desired, create a profile for yourself by adding your name to the list of users. Profiles allow you to save favourites and to specify which year group(s) you wish to be able to view.

  - Go to 'Settings' to create a profile for yourself – click 'Add user' and enter your name. Then choose the year groups you wish to have access to (you can return to this screen to change this at any time). Click on 'Login' at the top of the screen to re-enter the disk under your new profile.
- On subsequent uses you can choose your name from the drop-down list. The 'Guest' option will always be available if you, or a colleague, wish to use this.
- You can search the CD-ROM using the tools or save favourites.

For more information about how to use the CD-ROM, please refer to the help file which can be found in the teacher area of the CD-ROM. It is a red button with a question mark on it on the right-hand side of the screen just underneath the 'Settings' tab.

Changes within living memory: shops

This chapter explores how shops have changed since the 1930s, through sources such as photographs, artefacts and oral accounts. The topic can be used to focus on shops in the local area or UK shops in general. The children begin by talking about present-day shops before moving on to look at shops of the past. The lessons continue with comparisons and chronology. Finally, the children collect and share oral accounts about shops from older family members.

Chapter at a glance

Curriculum objective

• Changes within living memory. Where appropriate, these should be used to reveal aspects of change in national life.

Week	Lesson	Summary of activities	Expected outcomes
1	1	• Children study shop photographs and share experiences. • They draw a simple recount of a shopping trip.	• Understand what a shop is and can share experiences of shopping.
	2	• Children order shop photographs from the 1930s to today.	• Can use time language and chronology skills to see that shops change over time.
2	1	• Children use photographs to find shop names and what was sold. • They match goods to the shops.	• Understand and use vocabulary for old shops. • Understand that some shops used to have different names. • Can sort shops according to the type of goods sold.
	2	• Children work together to make dioramas of old shops.	• Know why some of the shops no longer exist. • Can use historical vocabulary and knowledge to create a shop diorama.
3	1	• Children listen to a poem to find out that goods were home delivered. • They write their own list poem.	• Can say how goods were ordered and delivered in the 1930s. • Create a simple list poem. • Can make connections with modern home deliveries.
	2	• Groups investigate an old shop item and its modern version. • They draw and compare the items.	• Can investigate shop items. • Can suggest why some items are no longer around.
4	1	• Children learn about decorated food tins and sort examples by picture design.	• Know that decorative tins were popular in the past. • Can investigate the range of designs used.
	2	• Children design a picture for a tin lid.	• Can create their own picture design for a sweet tin.
5	1	• Children work as a team to create a class grocery shop.	• Can make shop props and artefacts. • Can use photographs to find out about the inside of a grocery.
	2	• Children talk about and try the roles of grocery staff and customers.	• Can use role play to develop comparison, enquiring and empathy skills.
6	1	• Children hear people's memories of shopping. • They work together to create a questionnaire for home.	• Can listen to oral accounts of shopping. • Can create a questionnaire to use with family members.
	2	• Children feed back the oral accounts from their families.	• Can use and report on questionnaires about shops.
Assess and review		• To review the half-term's work.	

Expected prior learning
- Children understand recent events in their lives and the lives of family members.
- Children recognise simple similarities and differences between people, places, traditions and objects.
- Children can ask and answer questions about past events.

Overview of progression
- This chapter's main focus is to introduce Key Stage I history concepts. Beginning with shops in the present, the lessons encourage the use of time language by looking at chronological order. By the end of the chapter, the children should be able to understand how and why shops have changed over time.
- The children develop skills of comparison in identifying and describing similarities and differences between past and present shops, goods and shopping. Towards the end of the chapter, the children create a 1930s shop, which enables them to make first-hand comparisons through role play.
- Throughout the chapter, the children develop their enquiring skills and historical vocabulary. They study artefacts and photographs, then oral accounts, and begin to understand how different sources help us to learn about how people lived in the past.

Creative context
- This chapter ties in with work about the local area and where we get our food from. Cross-curricular links include:
    - reading and writing poems, labels, captions and lists; listening; asking and answering questions; giving descriptions and explanations and taking part in discussions;
    - using place knowledge and naming human features such as 'shop' and 'street';
    - drawing artefacts, making a shop diorama, designing a sweet-tin lid and making grocery props;
    - being aware of the local community and differences and similarities between each other.

Background knowledge
- In the 1930s, many shops had impressive window displays. Food was often delivered home. Once a week, the customer would give a shopping list to the shopkeeper, who would deliver the goods to the customer's home.
- By the 1970s, most food services like this had died out due to the increasing use of large self-service supermarkets. At this time, late-opening corner shops also became more common.
- Since the 1990s, out-of-town retail parks, hypermarkets and internet shopping have led to a decline in traditional high-street shops such as butchers, bakers, hardware stores, fishmongers, toy shops and smaller department stores.
- Recently, supermarkets and organic food companies have revived grocery home deliveries with customers choosing their items online.

Week 1 lesson plans

The first week looks at how shops have changed in living memory and allows the children to develop their chronological and comparison skills. The first lesson acts as an introduction by helping to establish what shops are, as well as exploring different types of shop and how we shop today, encouraging the children to share their own experiences of shopping. This gives the children a strong foundation to make comparisons with shops from the past in later lessons. The second lesson focuses on chronological skills and extending time vocabulary, through sequencing photographs of shops from 1930 onwards.

1: What are shops?

Lesson objectives
● To use a wide vocabulary of everyday historical terms.
● To ask and answer questions, choosing stories and other sources to show that they know and understand key features of events.

Expected outcomes
● All children know what a shop is and share their experiences of shopping.
● Most children know that there are different types of place where people shop.
● Some children understand that there are different ways to shop, such as home shopping and shopping centres.

Resources
Photographs of a modern high-street shop and a shopping centre; a set of photographs of modern shops, such as a corner shop, supermarket, high-street shop, village shop, department store, post office, DIY store, a shop at a retail park, a market; A3 or A4 paper or thin card folded into an eight-page booklet for each child; a pre-drawn example booklet; colouring and writing pencils

Introduction
● Show the children a photograph of a modern shop. Ask: *What is a shop?*
● Encourage the children to identify and name the shop's features, such as the shop sign and window display. Ask: *What could you buy in the shop?* List the children's suggestions on the board.
● Now show a photograph of a shopping centre and explore the features, such as a central hall, indoor shop fronts and signs, stairs and escalators. Ask: *Why would you go to a shopping centre? What kinds of shop are there?*
● Tell the children that they are going to find out about different places where people do their shopping.

Whole-class work
● Display the set of shop photographs and work with the children to identify each one: shopping centre, high-street shop, corner shop, and so on.
● Taking each picture in turn, encourage each child to share their experiences of going to that type of shop or shopping place.
● Then ask the class: *Which type of shopping do you prefer? Why?*
● Next, explain to the children that you are going to tell them about a shopping trip you went on recently. Stress that you will tell the 'story' in the correct time order, from when you left the house to when you returned.
● Orally model a simple recount to the children, reinforcing the time order.

Paired work
● Organise the children into pairs and let each child give an oral recount of a shopping trip to their partner. Make sure they explain what kind of shop it was.

Independent work
● Give out the booklets and drawing pencils and show your example booklet. Point out that the pictures are in time order.
● Give the children time to draw their shopping recounts in their booklets.

Whole-class work
● Bring the class together and choose volunteers to show their books and recount their shopping trip.
● If time, or in a later session, help the children to copy or write simple sentences or captions for each page.

Differentiation
● Support: children may need gentle encouragement in class discussion; help children to ensure their recounts are in order.
● Challenge: children could add simple sentences to their pictures during the lesson.

Review
● Note the children's involvement in the discussion. Ask questions such as: *Why would people shop in shopping centres... in a small high-street shop... in a department store... at a computer at home?*

■SCHOLASTIC
www.scholastic.co.uk

Lesson objectives
● To develop an awareness of the past, using common words and phrases relating to the passing of time.
● To know where people and events they study fit within a chronological framework.
● To identify similarities and differences between ways of life in different periods.
● To use a wide vocabulary of everyday historical terms.
● To understand some of the ways in which we find out about the past.

Expected outcomes
● All children know that shops looked different in the past.
● Most children can use terms such as *oldest* and *newest* correctly.
● Some children can identify differences between older and newer shops.

Resources
Large photographs of shops from different periods; a long timeline on a display board or interactive whiteboard ready for the photographs to be added, or a string timeline with pegs; labels or word cards for the timeline with oldest and newest; date cards for each decade from 1930 to 2000 and present times; photocopiable page 23 'Shops now and then'; paper or card timelines; glue; scissors

2: Sequencing shops

Introduction
● Remind the children of some of the different shops people use today.
● Explain to the children that in this lesson they are going to look at shops from the past to see how they have changed over time.
● Display a photograph of a modern high-street shop and one of a comparable shop from the 1930s.
● Encourage the children to talk about the significant features of the shops; perhaps the large windows, eye-catching displays, doors, signs, steps, columns, awnings or canopies.
● Ask the children to say which is the newer shop and which is the older shop. How can they tell?

Whole-class work
● Put up the string timeline or point to the timeline on the board. Attach and draw attention to the word cards: *oldest* on the end at the left, and *newest* at the end on the right.
● Display the large photographs near the timeline and explain that an excellent way to see how shops have changed over time is to put pictures of them in order from oldest to newest.
● Let volunteers take turns to choose a photograph from the display. Encourage all of the children to look for clues to help them decide how old the shop could be. For example, the photograph might be in black and white. What do they notice about people's clothing, the design of the building(s), transport, shop signs and displays?
● Ask the child who chose the photograph to place it on the timeline.
● Follow the same procedure with the rest of the photographs.
● Then, go through the full timeline with the children to check that the photographs are in chronological order.
● Add the decade cards to the timeline. Point to the decade when you were born as well as those when your parents and grandparents were born.

Paired work or Independent work
● Organise the children into pairs, and give each child a timeline strip of card, scissors, glue and photocopiable page 23 'Shops now and then'.
● Ask the children to look at the three shops and discuss with their partners which ones look old and which ones look newer.
● Tell the children to cut out the pictures and arrange them in chronological order on their timelines.
● Once the children are sure of the order, advise them to cut out and add the time labels.
● As they are finishing, ask the children: *Why have you put the pictures in that order? What clues helped you to work out how old or new the shops were?*
● As an extension, encourage the children to ask family members or friends about shopping when they were young.

Differentiation
● Challenge: children might be able to write captions about the shops or labels for the features.

Review
● Invite the children to share their timelines, enabling you to assess their execution of the photocopiable activity and grasp of chronological ordering.

Lesson objectives
● To develop an awareness of the past, using common words and phrases relating to the passing of time.
● To know where people and events they study fit within a chronological framework.
● To identify similarities and differences between ways of life in different periods.
● To answer and ask questions, choosing stories and other sources to show that they know and understand key features of events.
● To use a wide vocabulary of everyday historical terms.
● To understand some of the ways in which we find out about the past.

Expected outcomes
● All children know that some 1930s shops had names and uses different from those of present-day shops.
● Most children use the names of 1930s shops correctly and match the goods to the shops.
● Some children understand why some of the shops of the past are not popular any more.

Resources
Photographs of a 1930s butcher's shop and a modern-day butcher's shop; interactive activity 'What shop am I?' on the CD-ROM; photocopiable pages 'Old shop fronts' (on A3 paper) and 'Where do the goods go?' from the CD-ROM; scissors; glue; colouring pencils

Week 2 lesson plans

This week focuses on the different types of shop that existed in the 1930s and the goods they sold. The lesson builds on their historical vocabulary by introducing historical items and shop names, including some that are no longer used or are not well known. This is reinforced by a sorting activity, where the children match 1930s items with their shops. The children discuss what has happened to some of the shops and why, for example, different names or big stores are now common. The second lesson extends vocabulary and knowledge through the creation of dioramas of 1930s shop fronts.

1: What are shops?

Introduction
● Show the children a photograph of a butcher's shop from the 1930s. Look for clues to work out what the shop sold. Elicit or explain that a shop that specialises in meat and meat products is a butcher's shop.
● Now display a photograph of a present-day butcher's alongside the old one. Ask: *Which is the older shop and which is the newer shop?*
● Discuss where else people buy meat today, for example at the supermarket.

Whole-class work
● Tell the children that they are going to look at some different shops from the past and sort out the goods that they sold.
● Use interactive activity 'What shop am I?' on the CD-ROM to show different examples of 1930s shop fronts. Help the children to look closely at a particular shop's features to work out what it might have sold. Draw attention to details such as the window arrangements, goods displayed outside, signage, plaques or posters.
● Once the children have made their suggestions, read the selection of captions. Ask children to help you click and drag the right caption into place and then add the shop name to the sign.
● Reiterate what each shop is called and what it sells: for example, a draper's sells fabric (or material) to make things such as clothes and curtains.

Paired work
● Organise mixed-ability pairs and give each child photocopiable pages 'Old shop fronts' (on A3 paper) and 'Where do the goods go?' from the CD-ROM.
● Look at the shop fronts and read out the names with the children. Explain that they need to cut out the goods from 'Where do the goods go?' and glue them in the right shop windows on 'Old shop fronts'.
● As the children work, ask, for example: *What is this item? Which shop would sell this item?*
● Let the children colour in the shops and draw more items in the windows.

> **Differentiation**
> ● Support: give extra clues for the sorting activity. Provide support when using scissors.
> ● Challenge: children could design their own shop signs, in freehand or on a computer.

Review
● Bring the children together and share the work. Ask: *Why do you think shops such as drapers and small hardware shops are not seen much today? Do shops like that have different names instead? For example, is a draper's now a fabric shop?*
● Assess children's contributions to the interactive activity and discussions. Check their execution and feedback of the sorting activity. Note how well they use shop names and understand what those shops sold.

■SCHOLASTIC
www.scholastic.co.uk

Lesson objectives
● To develop an awareness of the past, using common words and phrases relating to the passing of time.
● To use a wide vocabulary of everyday historical terms.
● To answer and ask questions, choosing stories and other sources to show that they know and understand key features of events.
● To understand some of the ways in which we find out about the past.

Expected outcomes
● All children can create the main features of an old-fashioned shop front.
● Most children can identify how shops from the past displayed their goods.
● Some children can make comparisons between old and new shop fronts.

Resources
Photographs of a modern high-street shop and a 1930s shop; shop fronts from photocopiable page 'Old shop fronts' from the CD-ROM; other photographs of shop fronts; vertical-standing boxes with front and top sides taken off; pre-made diorama example; pens; paints; paper; pre-drawn awning shapes; card and paper for pictures of shop-window items and signs; a range of material for 3D goods outside such as collage scraps, cloth, clay, tin foil, blunt sticks for tools such as spades and rakes, small cups for buckets, card or wood for tables, string; scissors; glue

2: Shop-front diorama

Introduction
● Display photocopiable page 'Old shop fronts' from the CD-ROM and recap on the different types of shops from the past. Revise what type of goods or services each shop offered.
● Explain that they are going to make a 2D diorama to bring one of the shop fronts to life.
● Show a pre-made diorama of a 1930s shop. Ask the children what the shop is and how they can tell (for example a grocer's with tins stacked in a pyramid shape, bags of sugar arranged).
● Point out the background and focus on the use of decorated pictures of goods stuck in the front windows. You could also include a small poster and decorated shop sign.
● Highlight the use of different materials to make the 3D items on display outside the shop, such as the table made from wood stuck with glue, coloured clay or play dough for fruit and vegetables on the table, a card awning.

Paired work or Independent work
● Discuss with the children what shop front diorama they would like to create and encourage different ideas for the 3D goods they could make, such as tools and hardware, clothes, rolls of material, cut-out shapes of clothes, miniature versions of toys.
● Display photographs of old shops for the children's reference.
● Let the children choose what shop front they would like to use for their diorama and give them the relevant enlarged shop front from photocopiable page 'Old shop fronts'.
● Suggest that the first stage in making the diorama is to decorate the shop front and use their own illustrations and collage materials of goods to stick in the shop windows.
● Once the shop backgrounds are completed, let the children stick them on the back of their diorama box.
● They can then work on the 3D displays outside the shop front. Advise them that they have a range of materials laid out for them to select and use.
● Use tape or glue to attach shop awning shapes if the children want to include them and strong card strips attached to the shop front, with short pieces of string for any hanging 3D goods such as meat or pots and pans.
● Once the 3D items are put together, let the children decorate the rest of the front of the diorama box as a high-street pavement.

Differentiation
● Support: help children who are less confident in cutting and making models.
● Challenge: ask children to make detailed models for their shop or include figures.

Review
● Once the children have created their dioramas, display them in the classroom in the form of an old high street and encourage the children to talk about their individual shop and what it sells.
● Check children's knowledge of old shops fronts and their goods while executing the practical activity.

Week 3 lesson plans

This week focuses on enquiry, comparison and communication skills, as well as extending historical vocabulary through poetry, oral accounts and handling old shop objects. In the first lesson, the children explore through poetry, photographs and oral accounts how and why many people in the past had their shopping delivered home. Then, through writing poetry, the children use vocabulary of the past themselves. In the second lesson, the children handle shop items and record their observations. Finally, they compare the items with modern versions.

1: A shop delivery list poem

Introduction

● Show the photograph of the 1930s grocer's shop from media resource 'Inside a grocer's shop' on the CD-ROM. Note that the items are on or behind the counter where the shopkeeper would stand. Point to the customer and explain that many people would leave their shopping list with the shopkeeper and then leave.
● Ask: *Why do you think the shoppers couldn't choose their own goods?* (The goods are behind the counter; goods needed weighing and packing.)

Whole-class work

● Pose the question that if the shoppers went home without their shopping, how did they get their goods? Tell the children to listen to a poem to work out the answer.
● Display photocopiable page 'My delivery list' from the CD-ROM. Explain what *delivery* means. Read the poem and then ask: *Who is talking in the poem? What is he doing? How does he move around?*
● Point to the illustrations of the delivery vans and bicycles around the poem and highlight the fact that these were often used to deliver goods.
● Ask the children if they have worked out how customers got their goods. (They were delivered home by van or bicycle.)
● Highlight some of the old-fashioned vocabulary such as *washing soap* and *loose tea*. Ask: *How do these words tell us that the poem is set in the past?* (We don't use or hear these terms much any more; items such as washing soap and loose tea are not used much today.)

Paired work or Independent work

● Give each child photocopiable page 24, 'My delivery list poem'. Read out the shopping items listed at the bottom of the sheet and then read the poem, pausing at the blank spaces.
● Working in pairs or independently, let the children add the missing goods to the poem. Advise them that the last describing words in each line, as well as what the item comes in, are clues to help them.

Whole-class work

● Explain that when supermarkets came along, home deliveries died out as people could choose the groceries themselves and drive them home.
● Suggest that home deliveries have come back into popularity and encourage the children to discuss why.

Differentiation
● Support: read the completed poem back to them.
● Challenge: children could write modern home-shopping list poems.

Review

● Share and enjoy the children's poems. Check that they understand what a delivery man or boy did and the types of goods they delivered.

Lesson objectives
● To develop an awareness of the past, using common words and phrases relating to the passing of time.
● To identify similarities and differences between ways of life in different periods.
● To use a wide vocabulary of everyday historical terms.
● To understand some of the ways in which we find out about the past.

Expected outcomes
● All children know that many goods were delivered to the door in the past.
● Most children know how and why goods were delivered to the door.
● Some children can make comparisons between home deliveries then and now.

Resources
Media resource 'Inside a grocer's shop' on the CD-ROM; photocopiable page 'My delivery list' from the CD-ROM; photocopiable page 24 'My delivery list poem'; colouring pencils

■SCHOLASTIC
www.scholastic.co.uk

2: Old and new shop objects

Lesson objectives
● To develop an awareness of the past, using common words and phrases relating to the passing of time.
● To identify similarities and differences between ways of life in different periods.
● To use a wide vocabulary of everyday historical terms.
● To answer and ask questions, choosing stories and other sources to show that they know and understand key features of events.
● To understand some of the ways in which we find out about the past.

Expected outcomes
● All children can describe and record old and modern shop objects.
● Most children can tell the difference between old and new shop objects.
● Some children understand why some objects are not used any more.

Resources
Photocopiable page 25 'Investigating old and new shop objects'; old shop items such as tea caddies, biscuit tins, sweet tins and soap flakes; brown paper; large boxes and bags; washboard; matching modern versions of the items (or catalogue pictures for large items, such as washing machine); camera

Introduction

● Before the lesson, parcel the old shop items in brown paper and put them in a wooden box. Put modern shop items in cardboard boxes or reusable 'bags for life'.
● Be prepared to organise the children into small mixed-ability groups.
● To introduce the lesson to the whole class, show the children the box of wrapped-up shop deliveries. Explain that the packages contain deliveries from a shop of the past.
● Hold up a reusable shopping bag or cardboard box that contains the equivalent un-parcelled modern shop items.
● Work with a volunteer to unwrap one of the 1930s parcels to reveal an object such as a washboard or tin of tea leaves.
● Ask the children to observe its features. Model on the board five questions about the object's shape, weight, size, material and colour. Ask: *What do you think it is?*
● Show the modern version and do the same investigation. Encourage the children to comment on the similarities and differences between the two objects.

Group work

● Give each child photocopiable page 25 'Investigating old and new shop objects' and give each group a 1930s shopping parcel. Ask the children to work together to investigate the object and draw it carefully on their sheets.
● Check that they are asking the five questions modelled on the board, and giving answers.
● Once they have completed the investigation, ask them to find the matching modern version from your display.
● Let the children take it back to their tables to investigate and draw it. Encourage them to compare the two objects they have drawn.

Whole-class work

● Afterwards, ask each group to tell the rest of the class about their shop object from the past and the modern-day object. Ask: *What features are similar and what are different? Which of the two objects do you find more interesting? Why?*
● Emphasise that historical objects like these help us to find out what shops sold in the past and why. Elicit, for example, that a washboard was bought because people didn't have washing machines.
● Take photographs of the objects and display them along with the children's investigation sheets. Encourage the children to label the photographs.

> **Differentiation**
> ● Support: mixed-ability groups should provide support in discussing the objects; some children may need help with label writing.
> ● Challenge: children could develop their written answers and use reference books.

Review

● Look at the completed display with the children and encourage them to talk about the information it presents. Ask, for example: *What does this washboard tell us about home life during the 1930s?*

Lesson objectives
- To develop an awareness of the past, using common words and phrases relating to the passing of time.
- To identify similarities and differences between ways of life in different periods.
- To use a wide vocabulary of everyday historical terms.
- To understand some of the ways in which we find out about the past.

Expected outcomes
- All children understand that most biscuits and many sweets were sold in decorated tins.
- Most children can sort tin styles and designs into groups.
- Some children understand why pictured tins were used.

Resources
Images of old-fashioned biscuit and sweet tins or actual artefact examples; a couple of modern tins of biscuits or sweets (source online); sets of images, one for each group, showing a variety of old-fashioned biscuit and sweet tins (source online); A3 paper; glue

Week 4 lesson plans

This week, the children find out about the past by looking at the colourful and eye-catching designs of biscuit and sweet tins. Lots of perishable goods, such as biscuits, were put in tins to keep them fresh. Biscuit and sweet manufacturers often produced beautiful tins to encourage people to buy their goods. The children look at old tins or photographs of them to explore the different styles before designing their own sweet tin. Then they get a chance to use their design to decorate the lids of their own sweet tins. The completed tins can be used in creating a 1930s shop in the following week.

1: Sorting old tin designs

Introduction
- Show the children a modern biscuit tin or sweet tin as well as a comparable plastic version. Ask the children if they have seen tins like these in the shops, for example during the Christmas period.
- Discuss when biscuit tins are often bought, for example, for special occasions, at large gatherings.

Whole-class work
- Show the children an example of an old-fashioned biscuit or sweet tin. Explain that in the past, tins were often for everyday use as well as special occasions and were good for keeping things fresh. Ask: *Why do you think plastic packets were not used?* (Plastics for such everyday use had not been developed.)
- Encourage the children to comment on the tin's features, such as its shape and picture design.
- Explain that many old-fashioned biscuit and sweet tins had special pictures on them. Introduce more examples showing patterns, pictures of the contents, pictures from the distant past, flowers, Christmas, animals, landscape views, fantasy images, and tins in the shape of an object such as a bus. Note that these are all hand-drawn illustrations, unlike today's which are usually more photographic – often of the contents inside the tin.

Group work
- Put the children into small mixed-ability groups, and explain that they are going to look at different tins and sort them into picture or design groups.
- Give out a set of pictures of the tins to each group and encourage the children to think about how they could sort the pictures or designs. Ask questions such as: *Should tins with flowers on them go with tins with pictures of a garden?*

Whole-class work
- Once the children have sorted their tin pictures, let each group describe one of their groups and the examples they have.
- Then encourage all the children to say which tin they like best and why.
- Ask: *Why do you think the biscuit or sweet makers made such nice tins?* (To present a good image and make people want to buy them.)

> **Differentiation**
> - Support: offer prompts and suggestions for the sorting exercise.

Review
- Note children's progress through their discussion and how well they are making distinctions between the tins and items. Assess understanding of change by asking, for example: *How do we get everyday biscuits and sweets today?* (In plastic wrappers.) *When do people buy tinned biscuits and sweets now?* (For special occasions.)

SCHOLASTIC
www.scholastic.co.uk

Lesson objectives
● To develop an awareness of the past, using common words and phrases relating to the passing of time.
● To identify similarities and differences between ways of life in different periods.
● To use a wide vocabulary of everyday historical terms.
● To understand some of the ways in which we find out about the past.

Expected outcomes
● All children can draw a picture for an old-fashioned sweet tin.
● Most children understand that the picture needs to be eye catching.
● Some children understand why old tins came in so many different designs.

Resources
A selection of old-fashioned biscuit and sweet tins, or photographs; images or real examples of old-fashioned sweets; photographs or picture books showing food tins; tins such as travel sweet, lozenge or mint tins; paper or card cut to size to stick onto the tin lids (or to form lids if photographs are being used), and sketch paper of the same size; drawing and colouring pencils and pens; paints; strong glue; self-adhesive plastic

2: An old sweet-tin picture

Introduction
● Show the children an example of an old-fashioned biscuit or sweet tin and remind them of the activity of sorting the tins according to their picture designs.
● Discuss how tins were used to store dry goods such as sweets, biscuits, crisps and tea leaves.
● Show some examples from the photographs used in the last lesson and discuss the types of picture used, for example, of people, fairy or folk stories, flowers, Christmas, castles, animals, landscapes, patterns, biscuit or sweet shapes.
● Ask: *Why do the tins have eye-catching, attractive pictures?* (So that people would want to buy them.)

Whole-class work
● Hold up a tin and explain to the children that they are going to draw their own picture to go on the lid of an old-fashioned sweet tin. Also show real examples or images of the types of sweet that were popular in the past, such as sherbet pips, lemon bon-bons, aniseed balls, pear drops, bullseyes, mints, barley sugars and jellied fruits. Discuss what they look like and what they might taste like.
● Discuss ideas: for example, flowers, a favourite animal, a scene such as the sea or a castle, a book or nursery-rhyme character, or patterns. The design doesn't need to relate to the contents of the tin. If possible, display old tins and photographs of tin designs for the children's reference.

Independent work
● Give each child lid-shaped blank paper and explain that they can use this to sketch their first ideas for their tin lid. Stress that most artists and designers sketch their pictures roughly first so that they can review and make changes; then the final picture will be what they want.
● Once the children have created their designs, encourage them to share their ideas with each other and why they think their picture would encourage people to buy the tin.
● When they are happy with their design, give the children the lid-shaped card to draw and decorate their 'best' picture.
● Use strong glue to stick the picture on the tin, and seal it with clear self-adhesive plastic.

Whole-class work
● Set up a class display of the children's tins along with photographs or artefact tins.

Differentiation
● Support: talk through design ideas to help children decide what to draw.
● Challenge: children could write a short advertising description of their tin and add labels to their design.

Review
● Encourage the children to tell the class about their tin: their ideas, designs and final picture and why they think people may want to buy their tin.
● Keep the designs as assessment, along with photographs of their final work. Ask questions such as: *Why do you think tins became less popular? Why are many old tins still around? Why were some kept, and not thrown away?*

Week 5 lesson plans

This week, the children will show their knowledge and understanding of how shops from the past worked by re-creating a 1930s grocery shop in a corner of the classroom and using it for a role-play lesson. Using ideas from photographic evidence, the children create artefacts and help to arrange the shop layout. The shop allows the children to role play shopping in the 1930s, using historical vocabulary they have learned over the weeks, and develop skills in comparison, empathy and enquiry.

1: Making a 1930s grocer's shop

Introduction

● Tell the children that you are going to work together to turn a corner of the classroom into a shop from long ago.
● Point out that the shop counter and shelving are already in their places, but the name of the shop and the other details need to be completed.
● Show the children a few photographs of the inside of a grocery from the 1930s and elicit what a grocer's sells. Identify the main features and objects in the scene.
● Sketch a possible plan on the board, to include items such as grocery tins, biscuit and sweet tins, packets and sacks of flour, a tub of sugar, baskets of fruit and vegetables, weighing scales, paper bags, counter bell, posters and the till.
● Ask the children to suggest what they could call their grocery. Write their suggestions on the board and agree on the name of the shop.

Group work

● Divide the children into groups. (This will need careful organisation, and additional adult support.) Discuss the tasks that need to be done to create the shop. Activities might include:
  ● making shop goods from card or clay
  ● decorating boxes and labels for tins, jars and bags
  ● using clay to make food, such as cheese, eggs and vegetables
  ● writing name and price labels for goods
  ● setting out artefacts and their tins from previous lessons
  ● collecting (or making) coins for the till and putting them in
  ● laying out parcel paper and string
  ● drawing and decorating posters
  ● painting or colouring in the name on the shop banner
  ● creating 'artefacts' or pictures of items that are unavailable or hazardous (such as glass bottles).
● When the shop is completed, ask the children to check if anything else is needed, such as role-play props, or if there is a modern-day item that should not be in an old shop.

Review

● Display photographs of modern and 1930s grocery shops near the class shop so that children can identify the similarities and differences.
● Ask the children how they felt about creating the shop elements. What did they find easy or difficult? Ask further questions that will show their understanding of the historical 'space' and encourage developed answers that explain their meanings and choices.

Lesson objectives
● To develop an awareness of the past, using common words and phrases relating to the passing of time.
● To identify similarities and differences between ways of life in different periods.
● To use a wide vocabulary of everyday historical terms.
● To understand some of the ways in which we find out about the past.

Expected outcomes
● All children know what a 1930s grocery shop looked like.
● Most children can talk about items that were sold in a 1930s grocery.
● Some children can identify differences between a 1930s grocery and a modern one.

Resources
Photographs of a 1930s and modern-day grocery interiors; shop counter (large table) and shelving set up; materials to make a shop banner; old-fashioned cash register or a card model of one; old-fashioned shopkeeper's apron; paints; crayons; modelling clay; boxes and tins; collected artefacts; children's tins from previous lesson; food scoop; parcel paper; string; baskets; 'old' money; brass counter bell; weighing scales and weights; brown overall

SCHOLASTIC
www.scholastic.co.uk

Lesson objectives

● To develop an awareness of the past, using common words and phrases relating to the passing of time.
● To use a wide vocabulary of everyday historical terms.
● To answer and ask questions, choosing stories and other sources to show that they know and understand key features of events.
● To understand some of the ways in which we find out about the past.

Expected outcomes

● All children can imagine what it was like to run or visit a grocer's shop in the past.
● Most children can take on different roles in the shop.
● Some children can identify differences between the roles of a shopkeeper and a customer.

Resources

Class grocery shop; shop items; props and costumes

2: Role playing in the 1930s shop

Introduction

● Focus the children's attention on the 1930s grocer shop they helped to create in the classroom in the previous lesson.
● Encourage the children to talk to you about the different features of the shop and their uses, such as the counter bell, the weighing scales, the brown paper and string.
● Discuss the different roles of the shopkeeper, shop assistant, delivery boy and the shoppers (customers).
● Demonstrate different actions that would take place in the shop, such as scooping out flour from a tub into bags; weighing and bagging some fruit; totalling up a bill; greeting and serving a customer; reading a list; putting groceries together in a box ready to be packaged.
● Encourage the children to share their thoughts about what the people would wear and have with them. For example, a customer might have a purse and a shopping list; the shopkeeper or assistant might wear an overall and have a ball of string in their pocket.

Group work

● Organise the children into small groups and, while the rest of the class is occupied with other activities on the topic, or in classroom 'free time', allow one group at a time to re-enact life in the 1930s shop, taking on the different roles with the costumes and props. You might want to let the children decide themselves what roles they will play, or allocate a role to a child and then suggest role changes.

Whole-class work

● Once each group has taken their turn in the shop, have a class discussion about their experiences and encourage them to ask any questions that might have arisen while they were role playing in the shop.

Differentiation
● Support: mixed-ability groups will be useful, so that less-confident learners can be prompted by ideas and talk from more-confident partners.

Review

● Discuss what other shops could be created. If possible, make plans over the subsequent weeks to change the grocery shop into another shop, such as a haberdashery, and to make further artefacts or props.
● Note the children's use of learned vocabulary appropriate to shops from the past as well as their knowledge and understanding of shopping through role play.
● Take note of those who are independently asking historical questions that arise from the role play or those who work out the answers to their own queries.

Week 6 lesson plans

This week, children are introduced to oral history and how it can help us find out about shops in the past. Listening to people's memories can give the past an immediacy and help the children realise that some shop changes were recent. The lessons also allow the children to involve their families. In the first lesson, children listen to recordings of people's memories. They then take a questionnaire home to ask family members about their shopping memories. Finally, the children report on what their families said and practise their listening skills to hear the other children's accounts.

1: Oral history project – shopping memories

Introduction

● Explain to the children that you are going to play a recording of someone who is talking about their memories of shops and shopping when they were young (source online).
● Play the recording to the children. Then review what the person said. Encourage the children to make connections with what they have learned over the past few weeks, or ask leading questions that arise from the recount to prompt the children's ideas.
● Explain that what they heard was an oral account, which means that it is a spoken memory. Ask the children why a spoken account like this is a good way of learning about the past. (Because it is first-hand information from someone who has experienced that time in the past.)

Whole-class work

● Encourage the children to identify the value of talking with older people like their grandparents and parents about the past. Explain to the children that they are going to collect oral accounts from their family members such as grandparents, aunts, uncles and older family friends.
● Work with the children to make a list of questions which they could ask family members about shops. For example:
  ● What kind of shops did you go to when you were young?
  ● What were the shops like inside?
  ● What do you remember about the kind of things you bought?
  ● How often did you go shopping?
  ● Did your shopping get delivered?
  ● Are the shops still there?
  ● What were the shopkeepers like?
● Type out the list of questions on the whiteboard and give each of the children a copy to take home along with a letter to parent. Explain to the children that their parents or grandparents will help them with writing down answers to the questions.

Differentiation
● Support: encourage less-confident learners to contribute to the discussion and suggest questions.
● Challenge: encourage children to write down some of the answers themselves, and/or add extra questions.

Review

● Check how well the children understand what oral accounts are and why they are useful.
● Ask them to imagine they have grown up and have children or grandchildren of their own. What would they be able to tell them about their own experiences of shopping as a child?

Lesson objectives
● To develop an awareness of the past, using common words and phrases relating to the passing of time.
● To know where people and events they study fit within a chronological framework.
● To use a wide vocabulary of everyday historical terms.
● To identify similarities and differences between ways of life in different periods.
● To answer and ask questions, choosing stories and other sources to show that they know and understand key features of events.
● To understand some of the ways in which we find out about the past.
● To identify different ways in which the past is represented.

Expected outcomes
● All children understand that a person can talk about their memories of the past.
● Most children can ask questions to a person about their memories.
● Some children understand how oral accounts help them to find out about the past.

Resources
Text and audio recordings of accounts of shopping memories (from the internet or through local history societies; paper; questionnaires and parent letters to explain the project and asking for support – in the letter, ask parents to either record their conversations with the children or write their answers down after they have talked)

■SCHOLASTIC
www.scholastic.co.uk

Lesson objectives
● To develop an awareness of the past, using common words and phrases relating to the passing of time.
● To know where people and events they study fit within a chronological framework.
● To use a wide vocabulary of everyday historical terms.
● To identify similarities and differences between ways of life in different periods.
● To answer and ask questions, choosing stories and other sources to show that they know and understand key features of events.
● To understand some of the ways in which we find out about the past.
● To identify different ways in which the past is represented.

Expected outcomes
● All children can recount the shopping memories of older family members.
● Most children can recount shopping memories and make links to what they already know.
● Some children understand that people can have different memories about shops.

Resources
Completed questionnaires or recordings from the children; quiet listening corner for all the children

2: Oral history project – family shopping memories

Introduction
● Collect in the completed questionnaires and recordings before the lesson.
● Settle the children in a quiet listening corner and explain that they are going to listen to each other speak.
● Remind the children about their oral history project in which they used their questionnaires to gather memories of shopping from older family members.
● Encourage the children to talk about how oral history helps them find out about the past. (It lets them know what different aspects of life were like from someone who lived at that time.)

Whole-class work
● Select a completed questionnaire or recording and ask the child if they would like to share their family member's memories with your help.
● Let the child talk about the memories they have collected, with cues from you as appropriate to remind them of what was said.
● Another option is to play a recording of a family member's memories after the child has introduced who that person is to them. For example: *These are the memories my gran told me about shopping when she was a girl.*
● After each account, let the other children ask questions for further discussion. Make a note of significant points on the board.
● Once all the oral accounts have been given, have a discussion of the memories and how they can be similar or quite different. Did different people of a similar age have different memories of going to the same type of shop?
● As an extension, create a class recording of all the oral accounts so that the children can listen to them whenever they want.
● Invite family members into class to give a talk about their shopping memories.

Differentiation
● Support: help children to read out their questionnaire answers, or give them memory cues when they talk to the group; do not press less confident learners to talk to the class if they do not want to; you could read out their accounts and check with them that you are correct.
● Challenge: children could make their completed questionnaire into a written report.

Review
● Review with the children what they have learned about shops and shopping in the past after listening to the oral accounts. Add it to the other information they have learned earlier in the topic using photographs and artefacts.
● Note how well the children feed back their oral accounts and any questions they asked to those who have just talked. Ask: *How does oral history help us to understand about the past?*

Curriculum objectives
● To develop an awareness of the past, using common words and phrases relating to the passing of time.
● To identify similarities and differences between ways of life in different periods.

Resources
Interactive activity 'Past or present-day shopping?' on the CD-ROM

Shops

Revise
● Working with the children as a class or within groups, draw a mind map on the board or flipchart. In the centre of the mind map, write the title 'Shops from the past'.
● Write subtitles around the mind map relating to the areas learned about shopping in the past: for example, shop fronts, shop names, features of an old grocer's shop, shopping habits.
● Help the children to focus on each area and draw out from the subtitles on the mind map to list what information they have learned about each one – for example, that in a grocer's, shoppers did not serve themselves.

Assess
● Set the children to work independently on interactive activity 'Past or present-day shopping?' on the CD-ROM.
● Explain to the children first that they need to study seven pictures of past and modern-day pictures of shops and shopping .
● They then need to drag each picture into the right box with the column heading 'Shops of the past' or 'Present-day shops'.
● As they work on the activity, ask the children to discuss their choices. Make a note of their answers.
● Once the activity has been completed, ask the children within the group or as a class to discuss any significant similarities between shops of the past and the shops of today.

Further practice
● Ask the children to focus on one type of shop from the past, such as a butcher, greengrocer, haberdashery or department store, and research its differences and similarities when compared with present-day versions.

Curriculum objectives
● To answer questions, choosing and using parts of stories and other sources to show that they know and understand key features of events.

Resources
Interactive activity 'Shop timeline' and 'Y1 Autumn 1 quiz' on the CD-ROM

Y1 Autumn 1 quiz

Revise
● Review the interactive activity 'Shop timeline' on the CD-ROM with the whole class.
● Challenge individual children to add shop names from their locality in the correct positions on the time line. Alternatively, ask them to add types of shops, such as drapers and ironmongers.
● Get children to complete a table headed 'Same' and 'Different'. Support them in writing similarities and differences between modern shops and those in the 1930s.

Assess
● Ask the children to complete interactive activity 'Y1 Autumn 1 quiz' on the CD-ROM. There are ten multiple-choice questions that test what the children have learned throughout the topic. They will need to read each question carefully before choosing the correct answer.
● Give the children a set length of time (such as 15 minutes) to answer the questions. This can be used as part of a formal assessment or as a fun challenge activity, giving children the opportunity to show what they have learned about the topic.

Further practice
● Review any common errors or misconceptions from the quiz. If time is available, move to the more recent past and compare their grandparent's experience of shopping with today. Use local shops, restaurants to draw out comparisons or the legacy of previous shopping practices for example, more ethnic foods, restaurants and so on.

Shops now and then

■ These shops are from different times. Cut them out and stick them in order on your timeline. Put the oldest first, and the newest last.

■ Cut out the dates below. Match them to the correct picture.

■ When you have got them right, stick them on your timeline with the shops.

1930s	1960s
2010s	

Name: _____ Date: _____

My delivery list poem

- The shopping words from this poem are missing.
- Put the words from the box below into the right places.

Good morning, good morning,
Good morning, Miss Jones.
Here is your shopping
Delivered by van.

There are

one large packet of smelly _____

two round tins of crunchy _____

three small bags of chewy _____

four glass bottles of creamy _____

five square tins of dark brown _____

six big boxes of soapy _____

| flakes | biscuits | tea leaves |
| cheese | milk | sweets |

I can say how goods were ordered and delivered in the 1930s.

How did you do?

24 ■ 100 HISTORY LESSONS

PHOTOCOPIABLE

SCHOLASTIC
www.scholastic.co.uk

Investigating old and new objects

- Look carefully at your two objects.
- Draw them in the boxes below.
- Colour them in with the right colours.
- Then write their names.

An object from an old shop

It is a _____

An object from a modern shop

It is a _____

I can investigate and compare shop items.

How did you do?

Events beyond living memory: the Great Fire of London

This chapter looks at a significant event in British history – the Great Fire of London in 1666. The chapter establishes when and where the fire started and puts the main events in sequence. The children study building features, firefighting methods and eyewitness accounts to consider how the fire happened and spread, what people did, and what the results were. The children find out how the diarists Samuel Pepys and John Evelyn tell us about the fire and about the contribution of architect Christopher Wren in rebuilding London. The topic ends by exploring how the fire was commemorated.

Chapter at a glance

Curriculum objective

• Events beyond living memory that are significant nationally or globally.

Week	Lesson	Summary of activities	Expected outcomes
1	1	• Children look at London landmarks and locate London on a map. • They study a pre-1666 London picture and a portrait of Charles II. • They put the fire on a timeline.	• Know when the Great Fire took place and understand what London was like in 1666. • Know who was king at the time of the fire. • Can locate the date of the fire on a UK timeline.
	2	• Children hear how the fire was thought to have started and why it got out of control. • They put the events of the fire in order in a zigzag book.	• Understand how and where the Great Fire started. • Understand why the fire spread so quickly.
2	1	• Children study, describe and label pictures of buildings used at the time of the fire.	• Can label the features of a timber-framed house and tar-paper shack. • Understand why many buildings were destroyed.
	2	• Children look at pictures of buildings used in 1666 and groups make a collage of the fire.	• Can use their knowledge to create models for a frieze of London during the fire.
3	1	• Children study pictures of 17th century firefighting. • They compare the equipment with today's.	• Can use a range of sources to find out how the Great Fire was fought. • Understand why firefighting methods failed to stop the fire.
	2	• Children sing a rhyme and find out that its origins are from the Great Fire. • They create and perform more verses.	• Can use their knowledge of 17th century fire equipment to create more lines for 'London's Burning'.
4	1	• Children learn what an eyewitness is. • They look at portraits of Pepys and Evelyn and learn about their diary accounts. • Groups complete diary entries of the fire.	• Know that Pepys and Evelyn were eyewitnesses to the fire. • Can find out how they experienced the fire. • Can write events in chronological order.
	2	• Groups use pictures and eyewitness accounts to help them act a short piece of drama.	• Can use pictures and eyewitness accounts to help them re-enact escaping the fire.
5	1	• Children put pictures of the fire in order. • They create a timeline of the main events.	• Can put the events of the Great Fire into order.
	2	• Children use pictures and a diary extract to find out about the camps set up for the homeless. • They design posters asking for aid for the homeless.	• Can use eyewitness accounts to find out about those made homeless by the fire. • Understand how homeless people might have felt and what they needed.
6	1	• Children learn how London was rebuilt. • They identify good and bad effects. • They study and draw a portrait of Christopher Wren and his role in rebuilding London.	• Understand how London was rebuilt after the fire. • Learn how the fire was good and bad for London. • Understand the role of Christopher Wren.
	2	• Children review their work and discuss what they have learned. • They learn about the Monument and design a new part.	• Can recall the causes and events of the fire and how people acted. • Can design a new top for the Monument to represent an important aspect of the fire.
Assess and review		• To review the half-term's work.	

■SCHOLASTIC
www.scholastic.co.uk

Expected prior learning

● Children can sequence specific events on a timeline and use common time words and phrases.
● Children can use pictures and oral accounts to find out about the past.
● Children can identify why some events happened and what happened as a result.

Overview of progression

● The children understand that the Great Fire was very long ago in the Stuart period. They put the date on a timeline and sequence the main events of the fire. Through studying portraits and comparing buildings and firefighting methods with modern-day versions, the children use words and phrases relating to the passing of time.
● The chapter explores London then and now to discover why the fire grew out of control and why it wouldn't happen today. They also see similarities in the situations of the refugees of the fire and today's disaster victims.
● The children find out how the past can be represented in different ways by listening to diary extracts and looking at visual sources. Through role play, their own diary accounts and new designs for the top of the Monument, the children make their own interpretation of the Great Fire.

Creative context

● This chapter works well with topics on buildings, fire and a local project on London. Cross-curricular links include:
  ● writing labels, captions, posters, diary recounts and rhymes; taking part in discussions, role play and performance;
  ● creating a 2D collage frieze of the Great Fire; making models of 17th century buildings; drawing and painting posters; illustrating events and diaries; creating a design for the Monument;
  ● designing an aid poster and selecting and using tools and materials for a collage;
  ● locating London on a UK map and identifying places and landmarks on old and new maps of London.

Background knowledge

● **Causes:** London had had a long hot summer; Wooden buildings were dry; firefighting equipment rotted in the heat. Wharfs were crammed with tar-paper shacks and warehouses were packed with flammable materials and gunpowder left from the Civil War. Timber-framed houses were built touching each other in long, narrow streets.
● **The fire:** the fire started in the early hours of 2 September 1666 in a bakery in Pudding Lane. Many thought that a spark from an oven lit straw on the floor. Some believed the fire was started as a political act of sabotage, but nothing was proved. The fire spread rapidly towards the Thames, where the flammable materials were stored. Permission was sought to demolish houses to create firebreaks, but the mayor was not keen, and the fire worsened. A high wind fanned it across the city. By Sunday afternoon, the city was in a fierce firestorm. Firefighting methods were useless.
● **Effects:** people fled their homes. By Thursday, with the help, eventually, of firebreaks and the wind dropping, the fire died down. The fire had destroyed St Paul's Cathedral, which was covered in wooden scaffolding for maintenance. The fire officially left six people dead and destroyed 13,200 homes, 87 churches and many official buildings. Over 100,000 people were left homeless in camps around London. Many died from injuries, illness and the cold of the coming winter.
● **Rebuilding:** Charles II set about rebuilding London with the help of Christopher Wren. The king wanted wider streets, parks and stone buildings. Tar-paper warehouses were forbidden along the river. Firefighting methods improved with the founding of a fire brigade with better equipment. New building work turned London into a place of wealth again, employing many during the renewal.

Week 1 lesson plans

In the first lesson, the children find out where London is and what it looks like now, before comparing it with the time of the Great Fire. By studying a portrait of Charles II, the children learn that the event happened a very long time ago and work out where to place it on a timeline. In the second lesson, the children hear how the fire might have started and why it spread so quickly. From this, they create a zigzag book of the fire.

1: London at the time of the Great Fire

Lesson objectives
● To develop an awareness of the past, using common words and phrases relating to the passing of time.
● To know where people and events they study fit within a chronological framework.
● To identify similarities and differences between ways of life in different periods.
● To answer and ask questions, choosing stories and other sources to show that they know and understand key features of events.

Expected outcomes
● All children recognise that the Great Fire took place a long time ago.
● Most children can place the Great Fire on a timeline.
● Some children recognise that the Great Fire took place in 1666 during the reign of Charles II.

Resources
Film clips or photographs of modern London; media resource 'The Great Fire' and interactive activity 'Timeline maker' on the CD-ROM; picture of London before the Great Fire, showing, for example, St Paul's Cathedral and the Thames (see the BBC history-interactive website and www.fireoflondon.org.uk); map of the UK; portrait of Charles II; if possible, set up a display that includes an old and a modern map of London, with panoramic pictures

Introduction
● Show some film footage or several photographs of London showing key landmarks. Ask the children if they know where these famous buildings are. Help them to identify the capital city of London.
● Show, or invite a volunteer to show you, where London is on a map of the UK. Compare this with the location of the children's school.
● Now show the picture of London just before the fire. Ask: *What can you see in the picture? Is it new or old?* Explain that the scene shows London a very long time ago, shortly before the time when there was a terrible fire which destroyed most of the city. Briefly look at the picture from the media resource 'The Great Fire' on the CD-ROM to help the children to understand this.

Whole-class work
● Draw the children's attention back to the picture of London before the fire. Ask the children to talk about the picture and pick out different features. Notice how close together the buildings are and the materials they might be made from. Ask: *What might happen if a fire broke out?*

Paired work
● Ask the children in pairs to examine the portrait of Charles II. Encourage them to think about: what sort of picture it is; who it shows; his clothes and hairstyle. Ask: *How can you identify the person as a king?*

Whole-class work
● Take the children's feedback about the portrait. Then confirm that it is Charles II, King of England at the time of the fire. Explain that the block of time when Charles' family – the Stuarts – were the kings of England is called the Stuart period.
● Open interactive activity 'Timeline maker' and invite volunteers to help you to locate the time of the Great Fire – 1666 – on the timeline.
● Note the children's birth years and the current year on the timeline to help the children get an idea of how long ago the Great Fire of London happened.

Review
● Look again at the pictures of London. Assess the children's ability to recognise the differences between old and new pictures of the city. Ask: *Did the Great Fire of London take place recently or long ago? Which period (block of time) did it happen in?* (The Stuart period.)

■SCHOLASTIC
www.scholastic.co.uk

2: The start of the fire

Introduction

- Display media resource 'The Great Fire' on the CD-ROM. Remind the children that the fire took place long ago and destroyed a large part of London.

Whole-class work

- Show the children an old map of London and highlight Pudding Lane. Explain that the fire was thought to have started here in a bakery. If possible, show pictures of what Pudding Lane and the bakery might have looked like.
- Introduce the children to the portrait of Thomas Farynor. Explain that he was King Charles II's baker. Ask: *What do you think he had to do?* Make the point that the bakery would have been very busy, with many ovens.
- Use photocopiable page 'How the fire began' from the CD-ROM to tell the story of how the fire started in the bakery in Pudding Lane and how and why it spread quickly out of control.
- Ask questions to check that the children understand how the fire got stronger, using vocabulary such as *straw, strong wind, dry wood, closely built houses, flammable materials.*

Paired work or Independent work

- Put the children into pairs and give each child a copy of photocopiable page 41 'How the Great Fire spread', a zigzag book, scissors, glue and colouring pencils.
- Explain that they are going to make a zigzag book to show how the fire started and spread. Point to the mixed-up pictures and captions on the sheet and read out the caption for each picture.
- Let the children work in their pairs, or independently, to recall the story and number the events in the correct order. Encourage the children to retell the events to you or each other before they cut out the pictures and captions.
- Allow the children to stick the pictures in order, one per zigzag page, and then colour them in. Remind the children to make sure the front page is left blank, as a cover.
- Then let the children draw a picture of the bakery on the front covers of their books.

Whole-class work

- Before the end of the lesson, ask volunteers to use their zigzag books to recall and retell the order of events of how the fire started.

Differentiation

- Support: children may need prompt questions to help in the sequencing of events and help with reading the captions.
- Challenge: children could write their own sentences to add to each page of the zigzag books.

Review

- Ask the children to suggest reasons why the fire burned so strongly so quickly. Encourage them to use their new historical vocabulary to explain causes and effects accurately.
- Check the children's ability to recall the order of events and how the fire started and spread.

Lesson objectives

- To develop an awareness of the past, using common words and phrases relating to the passing of time.
- To know where people and events they study fit within a chronological framework.
- To use a wide vocabulary of everyday historical terms.
- To answer and ask questions, choosing stories and other sources to show that they know and understand key features of events.

Expected outcomes

- All children know when and why the fire started and what happened.
- Most children can put the events of the fire in the right sequence.
- Some children understand why the fire spread so quickly.

Resources

Media resource 'The Great Fire' and photocopiable page 'How the fire began' from the CD-ROM; a roughly contemporary map of London showing Pudding Lane; a picture of a street like Pudding Lane before the fire and one of a 17th century bakery (if possible); portrait of Thomas Farynor; photocopiable page 41 'How the Great Fire spread'; a six-page zigzag book for each child; scissors; glue; colouring pencils

Week 2 lesson plans

Here the focus is on why so many buildings were destroyed in the fire and how they were a factor in why the fire spread and grew in strength. In the first lesson, the children study pictures of a timber house and tar-paper shack and discuss why they were fire hazards. They also use new historical vocabulary by learning about the different features of the buildings. In the second lesson, the children use their knowledge of the buildings to create a wall frieze of the Great Fire.

1: Houses during the Great Fire

Introduction

● Display the picture of a timber-framed house from photocopiable page 'Great Fire of London houses' from the CD-ROM. Explain that many of the houses in London before the fire looked like this and were called timber-framed houses. Elicit that timber is another word for *wood*.
● Discuss the features, such as the wooden construction, tall height, overhanging eaves, thatched roof, windows and plaster walls.

Whole-class work

● Now display the picture of the tar-paper shack alongside the timber house. Tell the children that some poor people lived in small shacks made from tar-paper. Explain tar-paper by asking the children if they have seen hot liquid tar used on road surfaces. Say that when it cools down, tar becomes very hard and waterproof. Tar-paper is made from thick paper soaked in liquid tar and left to harden. Ask: *Why would people use tar-paper for walls and roofs?* (It's cheap and waterproof.)
● Look again at the pictures and encourage the children to think about why both types of building would burn easily and contribute to the spread of the fire.

Group work

● Give groups of children the sets of word cards containing the key features of the timber-framed and tar-paper houses. Invite the children to work together to match the words to the pictures on display.
● Ask for volunteers to add the labels to the displayed pictures, reading out the words to the class.

Independent work

● Hand out copies of photocopiable sheet and let the children write in the correct labels from the word cards on display.

Differentiation
● Support: mixed-ability groups for the labelling activity would allow better readers to help children understand the word cards.
● Challenge: encourage children to draw, and, if possible, label, their own homes; ask them to consider how we protect our homes from catching fire today, for example with less-flammable materials, fitting smoke alarms, fixing guards over open fires, turning off heated appliances and so on.

Review

● At the end of the lesson, show a picture of timber-framed houses in a tight alley and note how close together they are. Ask: *Why don't we build houses that touch each other across a lane any more?* (To avoid the easy spread of a fire, better security against theft, greater privacy.)

Lesson objectives
● To develop an awareness of the past, using common words and phrases relating to the passing of time.
● To use a wide vocabulary of everyday historical terms.
● To answer and ask questions, choosing stories and other sources to show that they know and understand key features of events.
● To understand some of the ways in which we find out about the past.

Expected outcomes
● All children can identify features of a timber-framed house and tar-paper shack.
● Most children recognise how buildings in London during the Fire could easily burn.
● Some children recognise how the buildings contributed to the fire's spread.

Resources
Photocopiable page 'Great Fire of London houses' from the CD-ROM; word cards for labelling features of houses (tar-paper walls, plaster, wood frame, wood patterns, thatched roof, casement windows, jetty, wooden door frame); picture of a narrow street of timber-framed houses; drawing pencils

Lesson objectives

● To develop an awareness of the past, using common words and phrases relating to the passing of time.
● To use a wide vocabulary of everyday historical terms.
● To answer and ask questions, choosing stories and other sources to show that they know and understand key features of events.

Expected outcomes

● All children can draw and make 2D collage models of buildings from the fire.
● Most children can choose collage materials to show how buildings could easily catch fire.
● Some children understand why so many buildings burned during the fire.

Resources

Media resource 'The Great Fire' on the CD-ROM; the labelled pictures of the timber-framed house and the tar-paper house from the previous lesson; a picture of St Paul's Cathedral before the fire; a display area for the frieze with a black and orange backdrop and river at the bottom, small card shack outlines, card outline of old St Paul's Cathedral, linked card timber-framed house outlines; various wooden, fabric and paper collage materials for the buildings and flames; card to create jetties; glue; scissors; paints; coloured pens; adhesive tape

2: A Great Fire collage frieze

Introduction

● Display media resource 'The Great Fire' on the CD-ROM, which shows the buildings on fire in the city and by the river. Remind the children that many of the houses and places where people worked were destroyed in the fire.
● Show the children a picture of the old St Paul's Cathedral. Explain that although it was made of stone with a lead roof, its wooden spire and the wooden scaffolding put up around it for building work caught fire. The heat from this and nearby burning buildings was so strong that the stone split and the lead melted.

Whole-class work

● Explain to the children that to help in showing why the buildings caught fire, they are going to produce a large collage of London during the fire.
● Point to the display space, with the river at the bottom and the orange and black sky at the top.
● Show examples, including St Paul's Cathedral, of what the children can create, and discuss what materials they could use to produce a realistic effect. For example: card timber-framed house outlines linked together; materials for wood such as lollipop sticks, straws or brown pipe-cleaners and straw for the roofs; small boxes or card for jetties; smaller card shack shapes with small roofs from materials such as clay, and plaster of Paris dried onto hessian cloth to use as walls, or rough wood such as twigs for the shack frame.
● Finally, remind the children that the buildings are on fire and they need to show the flames by using, for example, paint, cellophane, coloured shiny paper, painted tissue or crêpe paper.

Group work

● Put the children into small groups and start them on their task, allocating certain buildings to certain groups. Point out to the children the pictures of the different buildings from the previous lesson for them to refer to while they are making their collages.
● Offer support with suggestions of suitable collage materials. Listen to the children's talk as they work, on the materials they have chosen and why the real materials would have so easily caught fire.
● If the children complete their buildings, encourage them to create extra items such as boats, barrels and people. Assess how well the children produce models that show some historical accuracy and distinct features.

Whole-class work

● Work together to fix the collage buildings to the frieze, around and in front of St Paul's. Remind them that the houses were built in close rows and that the shacks were packed tightly along the river.

> ### Differentiation
> ● Support: encourage children's ideas by helping them with choosing materials and fixings.
> ● Challenge: set further jobs to create more complicated or additional parts of the frieze.

Review

● Use the completed frieze to encourage the children to develop their understanding of why the buildings caught fire. Discuss the materials they have used and which real, often flammable, materials they represent, such as sticks for wooden beams.

Week 3 lesson plans

Now the children investigate firefighting during the Great Fire and why it was another factor in the spread of the fire. In the first lesson, the children look at 17th century firefighters, tools and methods, then compare them with firefighting today. Then, the children reinforce this knowledge as they add more lines to the rhyme 'London's Burning' and see the rhyme as an another example of how we find out about the past.

1: Old and new ways of fighting fires

Introduction

- Display media resource 'Firefighting long ago' on the CD-ROM. Ask the children: *How do we know that this is a scene from long ago?* (People's clothes, the buildings, the style of the picture, for example.)

Whole-class work

- Focus on the firefighters. Stress that there was no brigade of trained firefighters at this time. If a fire was spotted, a watchman would ring a warning on nearby church bells and local people would come to help. Limited firefighting equipment was stored in the churches.
- Study photographs of old firefighting equipment. Talk the children through the different items: for example, large hooks were used for pulling the roof thatch or to pull down a building, a hand-held water pump called a water squirt was used to pump water onto the fire and a leather bucket was used to throw water onto the fire. Evaluate how effective – or not – these methods would be for a large fire.
- Now look at present-day firefighters in action in photographs or on film footage. Explain that they are very well trained and well equipped. Ask: *What happens if someone sees a fire today?*
- Look at the different equipment used today and discuss what each one is used for and how it is used.

Paired work or Independent work

- Hand out a copy of photocopiable page 42 'Old and new firefighting tools' to each child. Explain that you want them to work in pairs to match the names of the firefighting tools to their correct pictures. Read through the words and ask: *Was this word used long ago or is it used today?*
- Afterwards, let the children work independently to draw a firefighting scene from the Great Fire on one half of their paper, and a present-day firefighting scene on the other.

Whole-class work

- Bring the children together and discuss their pictures and photocopiable sheet. Ask: *Which firefighting items from long ago are still used today? How have they changed?*
- Add that, during the Great Fire, many of the wooden ladders were rotten, buckets had holes and the heat of fire was too strong for people to pull down the buildings.

Lesson objectives

- To develop an awareness of the past, using common words and phrases relating to the passing of time.
- To identify similarities and differences between ways of life in different periods.
- To use a wide vocabulary of everyday historical terms.
- To answer and ask questions, choosing stories and other sources to show that they know and understand key features of events.

Expected outcomes

- All children recognise similarities and differences between 17th century and modern firefighting.
- Most children can describe how firefighting tools were used during the Great Fire.
- Some children understand why the firefighting methods were unable to stop the fire.

Resources

Media resource 'Firefighting long ago' on the CD-ROM; photographs or a film clip of modern firefighting (see www.london-fire.gov.uk); photocopiable page 42 'Old and new firefighting tools'; blank paper folded across the middle; colouring pens and pencils

---

Differentiation
- Support: support quieter or less confident learners with extra questions to encourage them to make observations and extend their thoughts.
- Challenge: children could write several report-style sentences to go with their comparison drawings.

Review

- Discuss old firefighting methods. Prompt the children to use their newly learned words to explain why the methods were useless against such a big fire.

Lesson objectives

● To develop an awareness of the past, using common words and phrases relating to the passing of time.
● To identify similarities and differences between ways of life in different periods.
● To use a wide vocabulary of everyday historical terms.
● To answer and ask questions, choosing stories and other sources to show that they know and understand key features of events.
● To understand some of the ways in which we find out about the past.

Expected outcomes

● All children know that the rhyme 'London's Burning' comes from long ago and is about the Great Fire.
● Most children recognise the names and uses of 17th century firefighting tools.
● Some children understand how we can use old rhymes to find out about the past.

Resources

Set of action word cards for display (pump, blow up, climb, chop, pull, throw); a bucket; set of old firefighting word cards (squirter, gunpowder, ladder, axe, long hook, bucket)

2: 'London's Burning', a class rhyme

Introduction

● Put the action word cards up on display before the lesson. Put the firefighting word cards in the bucket. Write the text of the rhyme 'London's Burning' on the board.
● Show the children the rhyme and sing it to the children, encouraging them to join in if they can. Ask the children if any of them have heard it before.
● Tell the children that it was first sung just after the Great Fire of London. Ask: *Is that long ago or in recent times?*
● Help the children to make the link between the words of the rhyme and firefighting attempts during the fire.
● Sing the rhyme together again, with actions, such as pouring on water from an imaginary bucket.

Whole-class work

● Tell the children that they are going to add new verses to the rhyme about firefighting in the Great Fire.
● Write the first and third lines of the rhyme on the board, keeping the second and fourth lines clear for new text.
● Hold up the bucket and explain that it contains the names of some old firefighting tools.
● Choose a child to pick out a name card and help them to read it out.
● With the class, discuss how the tool was used in the Great Fire.
● Point to the action word cards on display, and ask the children which one could be used with the tool.
● Then, using the rhyme's patterns, work with the children to create new lines using the tool and action word. For example:

London's burning, London's burning,
Fetch the long hook, Fetch the long hook,
Fire! Fire! Fire! Fire!
Pull the hay down, pull the hay down.

● Invite children to choose another tool from the bucket to create another verse. Do this until all the tool cards are used up.

Group work

● Organise mixed-ability groups and allocate them a verse each to enact. Ask them to discuss and decide together how to act out the actions for their verse.
● Let the groups have a practice and then bring them together.

Whole-class work

● Have a class performance of the new rhyme with all the children singing as each group acts their verse in turn.
● Ask: *Why do you think we still sing the old rhyme even though the Great Fire of London was so long ago?* If needed, ask further prompting questions such as: *Could it be because the fire was so terrible that people have remembered it over the years or do they just like the rhyme?*

Independent work

● As an extension, give each child a printout of the class rhyme for them to illustrate and practise reading.

Review

● Set a quick-fire challenge with the cards. Hold up and read out a firefighting word card at random for the children to mime the corresponding action.
● Take note of those children who understand how the old rhyme can offer information from the past. Ask: *What firefighting methods or tools will always be useful?*

Week 4 lesson plans

This week introduces Samuel Pepys and John Evelyn and examines their role as important witnesses to the Great Fire. The children learn how the diaries tell us about life during the fire and how Londoners reacted. The children write their own simple diary account of the fire. Then they use role play to explore the actions and feelings of people escaping the fire.

1: Eyewitness accounts

Introduction

● Display a picture of the Great Fire showing people watching it from afar. Discuss what is happening. Elicit that the people watching are eyewitnesses to the Great Fire and establish what an eyewitness is.
● Display the portraits of Samuel Pepys and John Evelyn and tell the children their names. Explain that they lived in London in 1666 and witnessed what happened during and after the fire.
● Look at the portraits and ask: *How do you think these men were able to tell us about the Great Fire?* (By writing down what they saw.) Confirm that both Pepys and Evelyn wrote diaries during the time of the fire.
● Let the children look at a modern diary, and identify what it is and how it is used.

Whole-class work

● Explain to the children that they are going to find out about the fire by hearing diary entries by Pepys and Evelyn. Display and read the extracts on photocopiable page 'Eyewitness accounts of the Great Fire' from the CD-ROM.
● Focus on different elements of the extracts to show how they give us particular information about what people did and what London was like. Note information that is the same in both accounts, and any notable differences. Do Pepys and Evelyn have different experiences or opinions of the same event?
● Write the diary dates on the board and list the main events under each date, such as *Sunday 2 September – Start of the fire; Monday 3 September – Streets on fire.*

Group work

● Arrange mixed-ability groups of six. Provide a copy of photocopiable page 'My Great Fire diary' from the CD-ROM to each group.
● Ask the children to imagine they are a boy or girl in London at the time of the Great Fire and to write a short diary entry for each day of the fire. Give each child in the group a different day.
● Use shared writing to start. For example: *I woke up in the night. I could smell burning.*
● Encourage the children to talk about what they are going to write before they work on their own entries.
● Once the sentences are written, ask the children to draw pictures to illustrate their days.

> #### Differentiation
> ● Support: act as a scribe or write children's oral sentences for them to copy.

Review

● Let the groups share their diaries and compare their experiences of the fire.
● Ask the children: *What is an eyewitness? How do the diaries of Samuel Pepys and John Evelyn give us information about the fire? Do they give us the same information?* Note those children who understand that the diaries describe different experiences of the same event.

Lesson objectives

● To develop an awareness of the past, using common words and phrases relating to the passing of time.
● To use a wide vocabulary of everyday historical terms.
● To answer and ask questions, choosing stories and other sources to show that they know and understand key features of events.
● To understand some of the ways in which we find out about the past.
● To identify different ways in which the past is represented.

Expected outcomes

● All children understand what an eyewitness is and that Pepys and Evelyn wrote about the fire.
● Most children understand that information about the fire can be found in contemporary accounts like Pepys' and Evelyn's diaries.
● Some children understand that witnesses can give different interpretations of the same event.

Resources

A picture of people watching the Great Fire (for example, *The Great Fire of London* by Philippe-Jacques de Loutherbourg), portraits of Samuel Pepys (for example, by John Hayls) and John Evelyn (for example, by Godfrey Kneller); a modern diary; photocopiable pages 'Eyewitness accounts of the Great Fire' and 'My Great Fire diary' from the CD-ROM; writing and drawing pencils

■ SCHOLASTIC
www.scholastic.co.uk

2: Escaping from the fire

Lesson objectives
- To use a wide vocabulary of everyday historical terms.
- To answer and ask questions, choosing stories and other sources to show that they know and understand key features of events.
- To understand some of the ways in which we find out about the past.

Expected outcomes
- All children know that people escaped to different places during the Great Fire.
- Most children understand how people might have felt during the fire.
- Some children can communicate in detail what people did and how they felt during the fire.

Resources
Media resource 'The Great Fire' on the CD-ROM; other pictures of people escaping the fire; photocopiable page 'Eyewitness accounts of the Great Fire' from the CD-ROM; fire word cards

Introduction
- Show the children media resource 'The Great Fire' on the CD-ROM, which shows the buildings burning all the way down to the River Thames and people escaping by boat on the river.
- Tell them to imagine that they were on or at the edge of the Thames at the time. Ask: *What can you hear? What can you see? What can you smell? How do you feel?*
- Discuss the children's responses, emphasising the smell of the smoke, the heat from the fire, the sounds of burning and falling wood and of people shouting, the light and colours from the flames and the expressions of worry and fear on people's faces.

Whole-class work
- Tell the children that they will be working in groups to plan and present a short role play about escaping from the fire.
- Using pictures, and extracts from the diary of Pepys on photocopiable page 'Eyewitness accounts of the Great Fire' from the CD-ROM, identify what actions people took when faced by the fire. List the children's responses, such as collecting together some possessions and escaping by walking, running, riding on a cart or getting onto a boat. Encourage speculation of other possible actions, for example, burying valuables in the garden or seeking shelter in a building less at risk, like a stone church.

Group work
- Organise the children into small groups and ask them to plan a short piece of drama showing people's actions during the fire. As a starting point, write their ideas on the board, and read and display a set of fire word cards to support the activity, for example: smoke, flames, boat, carry, cry, shout, scream, burning, cart, hurry, bury, crowds, belongings, river, water, Thames, heat, tired, scared, crashing.

> ### Differentiation
> - Support: children can share their skills and ideas in mixed-ability groups; groups will need to be individually guided to maintain focus; children may need help in structuring the role play to match the words with suitable actions.

Review
- Ask each group in turn to present their role plays. Encourage other groups to say what each role play tells them about the Great Fire.
- Afterwards, explain that, although the fire was a terrible thing, only a few people were killed. Can the children suggest why? (Perhaps because, although the fire spread quickly, most people were able to escape before it reached them.)
- Ask the children: *What would it feel like to be in London at the time of the fire? What would you do? How would you escape? Where would you go?*

Week 5 lesson plans

In the first lesson this week, the children develop their chronological understanding by creating a simple timeline of the Great Fire. As the fire lasted only a week, it is within the children's capabilities to show the events in chronological order and then relate what happened over that time. In the second lesson, the children learn through John Evelyn's diary accounts about the terrible aftermath of thousands of homeless people living in refugee camps. By comparing these camps with those of natural disasters today, the children can relate to the suffering of the homeless and create posters to encourage others to help.

1: A timeline of the fire

Lesson objectives
● To develop an awareness of the past, using common words and phrases relating to the passing of time.
● To know where people and events they study fit within a chronological framework.
● To answer and ask questions, choosing stories and other sources to show that they know and understand key features of events.

Expected outcomes
● All children can sequence the events of the Great Fire on a timeline.
● Most children can use a timeline to retell the story of the fire in order.
● Some children recognise the short length of the fire despite its devastation of London.

Resources
Images showing events at different stages of the fire; a Great Fire timeline marked from 2 September to 7 September; photocopiable page 'A timeline of the Great Fire' from the CD-ROM; scissors; glue

Introduction
● Look at a few pictures of events that took place during the Great Fire, ideally on the whiteboard. Ask the children to explain what they show and suggest a title or caption for each picture for you to write underneath, such as: *The fire starts at the bakery in Pudding Lane.* Ask the children to sequence the pictures chronologically.
● Introduce a timeline of the Great Fire, covering the period from Sunday 2 September to Friday 7 September 1666. Ask the children to say where the pictures should go on the timeline.
● Count how many days the fire lasted. Discuss whether it seems a long time or not. Highlight that six days might not seem very long considering how much of London was destroyed, but it was a long time for a fire to keep burning.
● Explain to the children that they will be making their own timeline, using pictures and text.

Paired work or Independent work
● Give out photocopiable page 'A timeline of the Great Fire' on the CD-ROM to each child. Ask the children to cut out the pictures, captions and dates.
● Let the children work in mixed-ability pairs to start with, discussing each picture and then arranging them in chronological sequence.
● Encourage the children to read the captions (or read the captions for them) and let them match the captions to the pictures.
● Once they have completed this part of the task in pairs, ask the children to work on their own timelines of the Great Fire. Ask them to stick the dates at the start and end of the timeline first and then glue on the pictures and captions in chronological order.
● Check the children's timelines as they work. Are they putting all the pictures and captions in the correct order?

Whole-class work
● Invite the children to retell the story of the Great Fire of London, using their timelines to help them. This will reinforce their knowledge of the significant events of the fire and also their understanding of chronological order.

Differentiation
● Challenge: children could be given additional pictures to add to their timelines.

Review
● Ask the children how long the fire lasted. (Six days.) Highlight the importance of time in history and the use of dates by which events can be sequenced. Briefly relate this focus on dates to the work using diaries and timelines in previous lessons.
● Use the children's timelines to assess their historical sequencing skills and knowledge of the events and development of the fire.

SCHOLASTIC
www.scholastic.co.uk

Lesson objectives
● To identify similarities and differences between ways of life in different periods.
● To use a wide vocabulary of everyday historical terms.
● To ask and answer questions, choosing and using parts of stories and other sources to show that they know and understand key features of events.
● To identify different ways in which the past is represented.

Expected outcomes
● All children understand that thousands of homeless people stayed in camps after the fire.
● Most children recognise that the homeless needed help to survive.
● Some children understand that many homeless people suffered badly for many months.

Resources
Pictures of London before and just after the fire; photocopiable page 'Eyewitness accounts of the Great Fire' from the CD-ROM; photograph of a modern-day refugee camp; A3 paper; writing and colouring pencils; word-processing ICT access (optional)

2: Aid posters for the Great Fire homeless

Introduction
● Show the children pictures of London before and after the Great Fire and encourage the children to make comparisons between the two.
● Remind the children that only six people were known to have died in the fire. Ask: *But what do you think happened to the many people who lived in the thousands of houses that were destroyed in the fire?* Note the children's ideas on the board.

Whole-class work
● Explain that we know what happened to many people from the diary accounts of John Evelyn. Read the extract photocopiable page on 'Eyewitness accounts of the Great Fire' from the CD-ROM. Note that the places where the camps were set up were just fields at the time of the fire.
● Compare the description of the camps with a photograph of a modern-day refugee camp set up after a natural disaster. Emphasise that many people today can still lose their homes through disasters such as earthquakes, tornados, fires and floods and face similar problems to those escaping the Great Fire of London.
● Encourage the children to share their thoughts about what it must have been like to be one of the homeless living in a flimsy tent or shack on an open field.

Paired work or Independent work
● Put the children into pairs and give them poster paper and pencils. Tell the children that they are going to work in their pairs to draw a poster to encourage people unaffected or less badly affected by the fire to help the people left homeless by the fire.
● Explain that King Charles II organised for bread to be brought into the camps to help feed the people. Discuss what else people might have needed, and list ideas on the board: perhaps other food such as meat, fruit and vegetables; milk; clean water; clothing; blankets; cooking, eating and washing equipment; bedding and toys. Let the pairs choose one of the areas to focus on for their poster.
● Before they start, write up an agreed slogan for the posters, such as *Help the Great Fire Homeless!* After they have designed and drawn their posters, the children can copy or use ICT to add the slogan to their posters.

Differentiation
● Support: put the children into mixed-ability pairs to help with ideas for the design of the poster and for writing the slogan. ICT can also help less-confident writers.
● Challenge: ask children to write a list of what the homeless people might need.

Review
● Bring the children together at the end of the lesson for the pairs to show their posters. Discuss the different ideas and check how consistently they relate to 17th century life.
● Emphasise that it took many months for new houses to be built and for people to be rehomed, and that some people died at the camps, from disease, injuries or the cold. Some people were encouraged to find homes away from London. Ask: *Would you want to live somewhere else or stay in London, probably in a camp, until a new house was built? Why?*

Week 6 lesson plans

In this final week, the children compare the improvements that the Great Fire brought with its bad effects. They learn about Sir Christopher Wren and his plans for rebuilding London and St Paul's Cathedral. The last lesson encourages the children to look back on their work on the fire and discuss the different ways they have found out about the past. Finally, they design a new part for the Monument to represent something important about the fire.

1: Good and bad effects of the Great Fire

Introduction

- Recap the events of the Great Fire and highlight that in just six days most of London had burned down.
- Recall that the fire left thousands of people homeless and that it took many years for London to be rebuilt.
- Discuss the fact that, although the fire was devastating, the lessons learned from it, in fact, made London a better place to live once it was rebuilt.

Whole-class work

- Explain to the children that they are going to investigate the bad and good effects of the Great Fire on London.
- Bring up interactive activity 'Good and bad effects of the Great Fire' on the CD-ROM. Point to the two columns, *Good effects* and *Bad effects* and the different descriptions at the bottom of the screen.
- Read out a label. Let the children discuss with their neighbours whether they think it is a good effect or bad effect.
- Use a show of hands to vote for a good or bad effect, encouraging the children to give reasons. Let a volunteer drag and drop the effect into the right place.
- Continue until all the effects are in their columns, then ask the children: *How did the Great Fire of London make life better?*

Independent work

- Now display the portrait of Sir Christopher Wren, and check the children's understanding of the word *portrait*. Explain that Wren was an architect who designed buildings, and he made plans for a new London with wider streets, stone buildings and open spaces and parks.
- Focus on the building at the back of the portrait. Ask: *What do you think the building is?* Elicit that it is the new St Paul's Cathedral. Ask: *Why would that be in Christopher Wren's portrait?* (He designed it.)
- Give out photocopiable page 43 'Sir Christopher Wren' and ask the children to draw his portrait. Point to the oval shape at the top of the frame where they can draw an example of what Wren rebuilt in London, such as a wider street, a stone building, a park or St Paul's Cathedral.
- The children should then complete the sentences underneath the portrait.

Lesson objectives
- To develop an awareness of the past, using common words and phrases relating to the passing of time.
- To use a wide vocabulary of everyday historical terms.
- To answer and ask questions, choosing stories and other sources to show that they know and understand key features of events.
- To understand some of the ways in which we find out about the past.
- To identify different ways in which the past is represented.

Expected outcomes
- All children understand that the fire had both good and bad effects on London.
- Most children recognise how the good effects of the fire made London a safer place to live.
- Some children recognise the role that Sir Christopher Wren had in rebuilding London.

Resources
Interactive activity 'Good and bad effects of the Great Fire' on the CD-ROM; portrait of Sir Christopher Wren with St Paul's Cathedral in the background; photocopiable page 43 'Sir Christopher Wren'; colouring pencils

Differentiation
- Support: children might need prompt questions when working on the interactive activity.
- Challenge: encourage children to find out more about Sir Christopher Wren.

Review

- At the end of the lesson, encourage volunteers to explain why they chose their example of Wren's work and how it made a difference to London life. Explain that a great many people were given jobs during the reconstruction, which helped people begin to be more prosperous.
- Ask: *Why did the good effects of the fire make a difference to the future of London?*

SCHOLASTIC
www.scholastic.co.uk

2: Remembering the Great Fire of London

Lesson objectives
● To develop an awareness of the past, using common words and phrases relating to the passing of time.
● To know where people and events they study fit within a chronological framework.
● To use a wide vocabulary of everyday historical terms.
● To answer and ask questions, choosing stories and other sources to show that they know and understand key features of events.
● To identify different ways in which the past is represented.

Expected outcomes
● All children can recall the events of the fire.
● Most children can design a memorial that reflects their knowledge of the fire.
● Some children recognise the devastating effects of the fire and why we still remember it.

Resources
All the children's work from the topic; photographs of the Monument (see www.themonument.info for reference); sheets of thin card; a card base and card tube 'monument' for each child; drawing and painting materials; glue and/or tape

Introduction
● Either give each child their topic work or have stations around the room that focus on different areas, such as the firefighting work, zigzag books, diaries or aid posters. The groups can then move from station to station.
● Put the children into small groups and explain that they are going to look back over their work on the Great Fire of London.

Group work
● Give the children time to share their work and discuss what they have learned about the Great Fire of London. Let them consider what else they would like to know about the fire.
● Move around to hear the children as they talk. Encourage the development of discussion, if needed, with open questions.

Whole-class work
● Bring the groups together to share their thoughts and queries. If appropriate, make a note of further research to do.
● Display a photograph of the Monument. Explain that Sir Christopher Wren designed it as a memorial to make sure people never forgot the Great Fire of London. Tell the children that it is positioned on a street corner very close to where the fire first started in what was then Pudding Lane. Ask: *Why is it important to remember the Great Fire?* Ask further prompt questions to encourage answers. For example: *What did many people lose in the fire? How much of London burned down? How terrible do you think it was for anyone trapped in the fire?*
● Show a close-up image of the top of the Monument. Ask the children to describe what they see. Use prompt questions such as: *Why is it is a golden colour? What do the long parts coming out of the urn represent? What do they look like?* (Flames.)

Independent work
● Give each child a small sheet of thin card and drawing materials. Ask them to draw and decorate something else that could sit on top of the Monument. Explain that their design must show something important they have learned about the fire. Discuss and note down the children's ideas, such as: a timber-framed house collapsing, firefighting equipment, people escaping in a boat, the camps, St Paul's Cathedral on fire.
● Once the children have drawn and painted their Monument design, let them add it to the top of painted card tubes (these can be painted before the lesson if necessary) and then stick the whole Monument onto a card base.

Review
● Encourage the children to show their Monuments and to explain their design and why they chose it.
● Ask the children if they can remember the different sources they used to find out about the fire, such as diaries, pictures and their own role playing.
● Note whether they understand the significance of the fire and how it affected the lives of people in London. Ask: *What was London like to live in after it had been rebuilt?*

Lesson objectives
● To ask and answer questions, choosing and using parts of stories and other sources to show that they know and understand key features of events.

Resources
Reference material on the Great Fire including books, pictures, access to websites, the children's own topic work

The Great Fire of London

Revise
● Tell the children that they will be taking part in a quiz about the Great Fire of London.
● Elicit that a list of questions is needed for a quiz and explain that they will be working in teams to come up with questions which can be then be put to other groups.
● Introduce the children to the resources, such as the books, websites and work completed in the lessons. Tell the children that you want them to work together to use the information to suggest some questions about the Great Fire. Encourage questions that are reasonably specific, rather than open-ended, such as: *In which street did the fire start? What did Samuel Pepys bury in his garden?*
● Split the class into small groups and start them on their research. Careful support and guidance will be necessary to ensure that they identify suitable questions and that they know the answers!
● Ask the groups to record their questions and answers, nominating a scribe if appropriate.

Assess
● Bring the class together and start the quiz. The format can vary depending on ability. For example, each group could ask two questions to the other teams who could then respond orally or in writing.
● It is important that the group asking a question has the opportunity to say whether the answer is correct and, if not, to say what the answer is.
● Use a score card to maintain interest and add a competitive element.

Further practice
● Ask each child to produce a coloured picture representing their view of the Great Fire.
● Discuss which parts of the topic they have enjoyed the most. Encourage good writers to label their drawings or add simple captions.

Lesson objectives
● To answer questions, choosing and using parts of stories and other sources to show that they know and understand key features of events.

Resources
Interactive activity 'Y1 Autumn 2 quiz' on the CD-ROM.

Y1 Autumn 2 quiz

Revise
● Invite the children in pairs or groups to design a newspaper front page about the Great Fire. The activity could be done on paper or on computer if available. Adult support might be required to scribe the text.

Assess
● Ask the children to complete interactive activity 'Y1 Autumn 2 quiz' on the CD-ROM. There are ten multiple choice questions that test what the children will have learned throughout the topic. They will need to read each question carefully before choosing the correct answer.
● Give children a set length of time (such as 15 minutes) to answer the questions. This can be used as part of a formal assessment or as a fun challenge activity, giving children the opportunity to show what they have learned about the topic.
● Less confident readers may need adult support to read the questions aloud.

Further practice
● Write out five facts they have learned about the Great Fire of London and three facts they have learned about Samuel Pepys from work in previous lessons.

■SCHOLASTIC
www.scholastic.co.uk

Name: _____   Date: _____

How the Great Fire spread

- Cut out the pictures and the captions and put them together in the right order.
- Stick them in your zigzag book.

The fire spread across London.	A strong wind pushed the fire towards the river.	The barrels and tar-paper shacks caught fire.
The bakery was on fire.	The houses next to the bakery caught fire.	Thomas Farynor checked the baking ovens.

Old and new firefighting tools

■ Match each word to the correct picture.

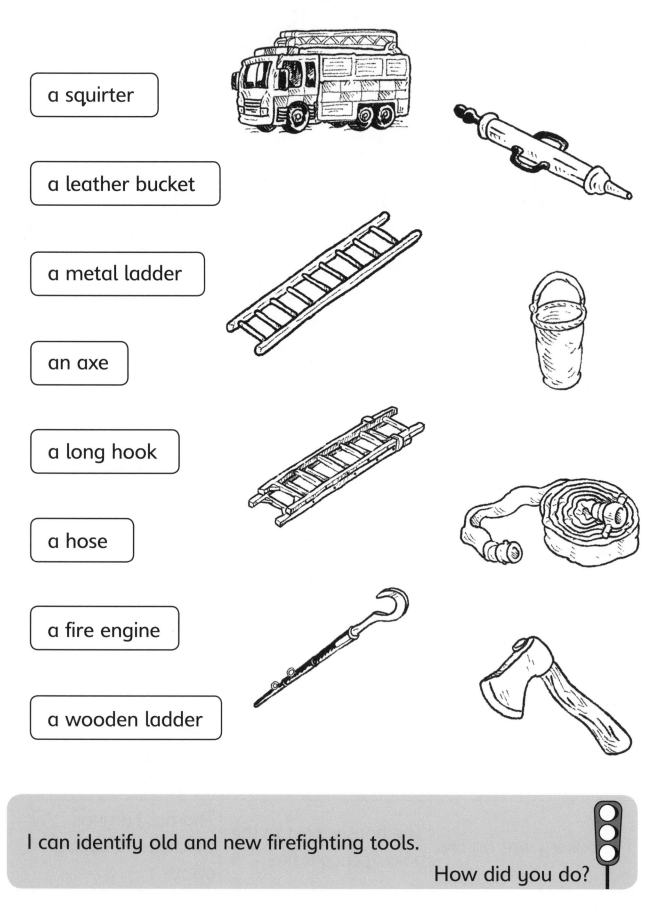

a squirter

a leather bucket

a metal ladder

an axe

a long hook

a hose

a fire engine

a wooden ladder

I can identify old and new firefighting tools.

How did you do?

PHOTOCOPIABLE

SCHOLASTIC
www.scholastic.co.uk

Sir Christopher Wren

■ Draw a portrait of Sir Christopher Wren.

■ Draw something that he built in the shape at the top of the picture.

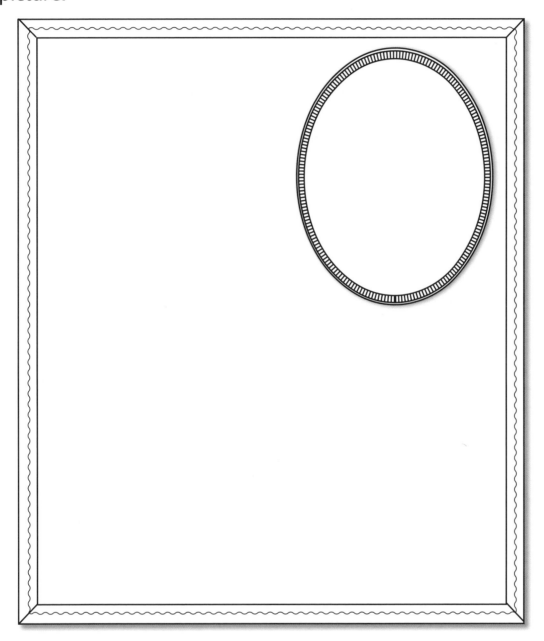

■ Write the missing words in the sentence.

Sir Christopher Wren helped rebuild _____
after the Great Fire.

I can understand how Christopher Wren helped to
rebuild London.

How did you do?

Lives of significant individuals: Pieter Bruegel the Elder and LS Lowry

This chapter looks at the lives and works of 16th century Flemish artist Pieter Bruegel and 20th century Lancashire artist LS Lowry. The children discover how paintings can help us to understand how people lived or what places looked like in the past. The chapter compares the two painters and the lives of people in their historical periods, and looks at changes that have happened between the two periods. The children show their understanding of Lowry's and Bruegel's paintings by creating their own artwork.

Chapter at a glance

Curriculum objectives

• The lives of significant individuals in the past who have contributed to national and international achievements. Some should be used to compare aspects of life in different periods.

Week	Lesson	Summary of activities	Expected outcomes
1	1	• Children study self-portraits to place the artists on a timeline. • They draw their own self-portraits.	• Can investigate self-portraits to find out when artists lived and who they were.
	2	• Children listen to a short narrative about Bruegel's life. • They compare and label pictures of the rich and poor in 16th century Netherlands.	• Can identify differences between rich and poor at Bruegel's time. • Can explain why Bruegel was called 'Peasant Bruegel'.
2	1	• Children examine Bruegel's *Children's Games*. • They record their favourite game from the painting.	• Can investigate the games in Bruegel's *Children's Games* and compare them with present-day games.
	2	• Children freeze into position for a photographic version of Bruegel's *Children's Games*.	• Can re-create Bruegel's *Children's Games* with modern games.
3	1	• Children listen to a mill worker's account of work in the mill and identify true and false sentences about the account.	• Understand that Lowry's paintings and the poor working conditions in mills were in recent times. • Understand what life was like for a mill worker.
	2	• Children study a photograph to identify a mill's features. • They use a checklist to locate the features on a Lowry painting.	• Can identify mill features and find the same features in a Lowry painting. • Can use historical language about a painting.
4	1	• Groups decorate cut-outs of Lowry-style buildings for a class mural of a Lowry or local landscape.	• Can study the way buildings are created in Lowry's paintings. • Can create Lowry-style buildings for a mural.
	2	• Children match name labels to buildings and draw in their missing features. • They draw their home or favourite building in a Lowry style.	• Can label and draw in the missing features of buildings. • Can draw a picture of their home in the style of LS Lowry.
5	1	• Children investigate how Lowry figures are painted and use finger paints to create their own figures for the class mural.	• Can study and re-create the painting style of Lowry's 'matchstick' people. • Know how people dressed in 1930s Lancashire.
	2	• Children listen to a song about Lowry's 'matchstick men'. • They draw their own matchstick person and write a few simple sentences about it.	• Can use their knowledge of Lowry's painting style and their learned vocabulary to draw their own matchstick person and write a simple description of it.
6	1	• Children investigate Bruegel's *Peasant Wedding* and give recounts as one of the characters. • They write a simple thank-you letter. • Children investigate Lowry's *VE Day* and create comic-strip recounts.	• Understand that *Peasant Wedding* was set long ago and that *VE Day* was within living memory. • Are aware that an event can be experienced and represented in different ways.
	2	• Children list similarities and differences between a Bruegel and a Lowry painting. • They draw a picture of their school as a historical resource for children of the future.	• Can use comparison skills and understand that the painters had similar ideas. • Can understand how we use paintings as a way to find out about the past.
Assess and review		• To review the half-term's work.	

■ SCHOLASTIC
www.scholastic.co.uk

Expected prior learning

● Children should be confident in asking and answering questions in detail, using visual sources such as photographs and paintings.
● Children have the skills to recognise similarities and differences between people, places, traditions and objects.
● Children should be confident in using common time words and phrases.

Overview of progression

● Children use time words and phrases from the beginning, to say which artist lived *long ago* and which lived in *recent times.*
● The children are aware of the big time gap between the two artists, but they come to see similarities of ideas and content. The paintings also allow comparisons of life in the distant past and recent past with life today.
● Open questions help the children to study a painting for clues about different historical ages, such as how people dressed, worked, celebrated and played. From this, the children create their own historical source for the future by drawing a picture of their school.
● The children come to appreciate that paintings are interpretations of a way of life. They also understand how one historical event can be seen in different ways by imagining the accounts of different characters in a painting.

Creative context

● This chapter works well with cross-curricular topics such as:
  ● an art focus on the works of Bruegel and Lowry and describing similarities and differences in their styles and content; using the techniques of Lowry with colour, line, shape and form;
  ● writing labels, captions and recounts as well as listening, asking and answering questions in detail, giving explanations and taking part in role play;
  ● using PE skills in playing games from the past and today; following rules for team games.

Background knowledge
Pieter Bruegel the Elder (1525–1569)

● Bruegel was a painter and printmaker who lived in the Netherlands and Belgium. He is famous for his paintings of landscapes and peasant life. It is believed he was given his nickname *Peasant Bruegel* because of his habit of dressing as a peasant to mingle anonymously at peasant celebrations to get inspiration for his paintings.
● Bruegel was one of the first artists in the Netherlands to focus on the lives of peasants as the main subjects of paintings. He also included people with disabilities. Art at this time mainly contained idealised scenes or portraits of town life and wealthy families. Bruegel's paintings are unique primary sources of how life was lived in 16th century Netherlands, including celebrations, weather, farming, games, clothing, traditions and food. His two sons were also artists; his eldest was Pieter Bruegel the Younger.

LS Lowry (1887–1976)

● Laurence Stephen Lowry was born in Stretford in Lancashire but grew up in the mill town of Pendlebury. In 1905, he took private art lessons, which led to a place at the Manchester School for Art. In 1915, he began studies at the Salford Royal Technical College, where his particular style of landscape drawing continued to develop.
● Originally, Lowry was inspired when he walked the streets every day working as a rent collector. He was able to watch people go off to work, listen to people chat and enjoy their time off work. Like Bruegel, he included people with disabilities.
● Lowry's paintings are also important historical records of how people lived in the industrial north which, although in the recent past, has changed dramatically.

Week I lesson plans

The first week introduces the main skills the children will use throughout the topic: studying paintings in detail in order to deduce how certain groups of people lived in different historical periods. In the first lesson, the children study the artists' self-portraits to work out who lived long ago and who lived recently. In the second lesson, the children focus on Bruegel by hearing a narrative about his life. They then use two paintings to identify the differences between rich and poor in 16th century Netherlands.

I: Pieter Bruegel the Elder and LS Lowry

Introduction
- Capture the children's interest by showing a range of paintings, both old and modern, and elicit that people who make paintings for a living or as a hobby, are called artists. Tell the children that they will be learning about two famous artists and examining their paintings.
- Display the self-portraits of Lowry and Bruegel and explain that the two paintings show the artists they are going to learn about. Say that they are both portraits, in fact, self-portraits, of the two artists. Elicit that a self-portrait is a picture painted by an artist of him or herself.
- Hold up the name cards and read the artists' names out slowly, with the children repeating them after you. Match them to the portraits.

Whole-class work
- Point to the simple timeline on the board. Show the children as you write long ago on the left-hand end and recent times on the opposite end.
- Explain that one of the artists lived long ago, and one lived in times recent enough that older people today would still remember them.
- Challenge the children to decide when the artists lived so that their name cards can be put in the right places on the timeline. Suggest that they look at each self-portrait for clues.
- Focus on Bruegel's self-portrait first, and ask questions such as: Who can you see? Which one is the artist? How can you tell? Does the portrait look old or new?
- Examine the details. Ask: What clothes is the artist wearing? Do his clothes and hat look like they are from long ago or from recent times?
- Move on to Lowry's self-portrait and follow a similar line of questioning.
- Invite volunteers to place the name cards on the timeline (1887–1976 for Lowry; 1525–1569 for Bruegel).

Independent work
- Ask each child draw their own self-portrait. If needed, they can use mirrors or photographs of themselves. Then ask the children to sign their name underneath.
- Let them decorate card frames and put them around the portraits, which can then be displayed on the wall.

Differentiation
- Support: extra questions may be needed to encourage quieter children to make observations and extend their thoughts.
- Challenge: children could write a few sentences to go with their portrait or write labels to highlight parts of the artists' self-portraits.

Review
- Revisit the timeline and check children's ability to use time words and understand where each artist goes on the timeline.

Lesson objectives
- To develop an awareness of the past, using common words and phrases relating to the passing of time.
- To know where people and events they study fit within a chronological framework.
- To identify similarities and differences between ways of life in different periods.
- To use a wide vocabulary of everyday historical terms.
- To ask and answer questions, choosing and using parts of stories and other sources to show that they know and understand key features of events.
- To understand some of the ways in which we find out about the past.

Expected outcomes
- All children know that one artist lived long ago and one lived in recent times.
- Most children can answer questions about which self-portrait is the older and which the newer.
- Some children can ask and answer their own questions to position the self-portraits on a timeline.

Resources
Bruegel's The Painter and the Buyer and Lowry's Self Portrait, 1925; a range of other paintings; large cards of the artists' names and dates; a timeline in 50-year intervals; paper; card frames to fit the paper; colouring pencils and pens; hand mirrors or photographs of the children

Lesson objectives
● To develop an awareness of the past, using common words and phrases relating to the passing of time.
● To identify similarities and differences between ways of life in different periods.
● To use a wide vocabulary of everyday historical terms.
● To ask and answer questions, choosing and using parts of stories and other sources to show that they know and understand key features of events.
● To understand some of the ways in which we find out about the past.
● To identify different ways in which the past is represented.

Expected outcomes
● All children know that Bruegel the Elder liked to paint peasant life.
● Most children understand the differences between rich and poor in 16th century Netherlands.
● Some children understand why Bruegel wanted to paint peasants.

Resources
Bruegel's *The Painter and the Buyer* and *The Peasant Dance*; a 16th century Dutch painting of a rich person or group (for example, *Family Portrait in a Landscape* by Frans Hals); map of Europe; photocopiable page 'I am Pieter Bruegel' from the CD-ROM; photocopiable page 59 'A rich woman and a peasant in Bruegel's time'; scissors; glue

2: Rich and poor in Bruegel's time

Introduction
● Display the self-portrait of Bruegel and remind the children who it shows and that he lived hundreds of years ago.
● Read photocopiable page 'I am Pieter Bruegel' from the CD-ROM to the children.
● After the account, show the children where Bruegel lived on a map of Europe and relate it to where they live.
● Discuss what Bruegel said about his life in the text, and ask questions such as: *Why was he called 'the Elder'? What did he do so that he could watch the peasants for his paintings?*

Whole-class work and Group work
● Highlight that during Bruegel's time, many people were very poor – *peasants* – while others had a lot of money.
● Show the Dutch painting of a rich family. Explain to the children that when Bruegel first started painting, most artists made paintings like this, of rich people or scenes from the Bible.
● Encourage the children to look at the painting in detail, prompting them to examine clothes, postures, expressions, hair, objects, the background.
● Now display *The Peasant Dance* and tell the children its name. Can the children remember what a peasant is?
● Highlight that Bruegel's paintings capture scenes with great detail. Use prompt questions to encourage the children to examine the painting closely, as they did for the previous picture.
● Pick out one peasant to focus on, and encourage the children to describe their clothing and expression. *What can we say about him (or her)? What is he (or she) doing?*
● Now ask the children why they think Bruegel wanted to paint peasants when other painters were getting well paid to paint rich people. Elicit that he felt it was important to show peasants living, working and playing.
● Say that, unlike the formal, often indoor, paintings of rich people, many of Bruegel's paintings are of scenes outside, and that helps us to find out more about, for example, a place's buildings, landscape, weather, animals and jobs.
● Put the two paintings side by side and ask the children which they prefer and why.
● Explain that both paintings can tell us about what people wore and how they lived in the past. Both paintings are useful because they show us different types of people and ways of life. Ask: *What can we learn about peasants from* The Peasant Dance?

Paired work or Independent work
● Put the children into pairs and give each child a copy of photocopiable page 59 'A rich woman and a peasant in Bruegel's time'.
● Ask the children to cut out the labels and work out where they need to stick them to show the clothing details for a wealthy 16th century woman and a poor 16th century woman.

Differentiation
● Challenge: children could choose a small detail in *The Peasant Dance* and write a few descriptive phrases or sentences to explain what is happening.

Review
● Invite volunteers to share their photocopiable sheets. Take the children through the correct labelling of the pictures.
● Ask: *Why was Bruegel given the nickname 'Peasant Bruegel'?*

Week 2 lesson plans

This week, the children study Bruegel's *Children's Games* to find out what children liked to play over 400 years ago. In the first lesson, they identify similarities and differences between games then and now. In the second lesson, the children create their own photographic version of the painting.

I: Investigating Bruegel's *Children's Games*

Lesson objectives
- To develop an awareness of the past, using common words and phrases relating to the passing of time.
- To identify similarities and differences between ways of life in different periods.
- To use a wide vocabulary of everyday historical terms.
- To ask and answer questions, choosing and using parts of stories and other sources to show that they know and understand key features of events
- To understand some of the ways in which we find out about the past.

Expected outcomes
- All children know that Bruegel's *Children's Games* shows games played long ago.
- Most children can identify similarities and differences between Bruegel's games and modern games.
- Some children can use independent enquiring skills to work out what some of the children are playing.

Resources
Bruegel's *The Painter and the Buyer* and *Children's Games*; paper; drawing pencils

Introduction
- Display Bruegel's self-portrait. Remind the children how he liked to paint people in everyday scenes, and that he painted hundreds of years ago.
- Then show the children his *Children's Games*, but don't give them the title yet. Challenge the children to have a look at the painting to try to work out what it is showing.
- Once the children have given their answers, tell them the title and confirm that it shows 250 children and young people playing over 80 children's games – games played hundreds of years ago.
- Ask the children: *Do you recognise any of the games and activities the children are playing? Which ones do we still play today?*

Whole-class work
- Ask a range of questions to get an overview of the painting. For example: *Why do you think so many children are playing outside? Where are they playing? Are all the children the same age? What are they wearing? Can you see all their faces?*
- Then focus on the games. Explain that in the painting there are lots of different types of game that children liked to play, such as make-believe, various team games, playing with objects, making crafts, performing gymnastics, looking at nature, and activities such as climbing, dancing and even swimming.
- Lead the children to look at examples in different parts of the painting. (Use a zoom tool or 'detail' pictures if possible.)
- Ask specific questions such as: *What can you see by the river? What are the children playing with under the arches? Why are most of the toys made from everyday objects?*
- Develop a wordbank on the board by compiling a list of the different games as the children discover them. Explain some of the less familiar games.

Independent work
- Give each child a sheet of drawing paper and ask them to draw the game they would have liked to have played if they were in the painting.
- Once they have completed their picture, ask the children to write a simple explanatory sentence using the correct game word: *the Bruegel game I would like to play is...* Make sure that the children can use the wordbank and that the painting is displayed as large as possible for reference.

> **Differentiation**
> - Support: the amount of detail in the picture can be overwhelming; gently guide children to certain areas; help children to complete their sentences as necessary.

Review
- Encourage the children to share their pictures and give reasons for their choice of game.
- Invite one or two children to point to a figure or game in the painting and challenge the class to say what is being played and if it can be compared with a similar game played today.

Lesson objectives
● To identify similarities and differences between ways of life in different periods.
● To use a wide vocabulary of everyday historical terms.
● To ask and answer questions, choosing and using parts of stories and other sources to show that they know and understand key features of events.
● To understand some of the ways in which we find out about the past.

Expected outcomes
● All children can discuss and show games that are played today.
● Most children can compare Bruegel's *Children's Games* their modern photographic version.
● Some children can explain why some of the old games are not played today.

Resources
Bruegel's *Children's Games*; games equipment, such as hoops, toys, dressing-up clothes, balls, skipping ropes; digital camera that can take panoramic views; large space (playground or hall); display board for the photograph (for a project like this, it would be useful to have several adults to support the various groups, gathering props and helping with the set-up of the photograph)

2: A photograph of modern children's games

Introduction
● If needed, this lesson can be split over two sessions.
● Display a large image of Bruegel's *Children's Games* and revise that the games shown in the painting were played by children who lived a very long time ago.
● Explain to the children that, as a class, they are going to create a similar image – their own picture showing games that are played by children today.
● Go on to say that, instead of a painting, the picture will be a large photograph of them playing different games and that they will need to 'freeze' their game while the photograph is taken.
● Draw up a table on the board with the types of game shown in Bruegel's painting as headings, such as make-believe, role play, team games, playing with objects/toys, crafts, gymnastics, looking at nature and physical activities such as climbing, swimming, dancing, building and balancing.
● Ask the children what modern-day games they could show for each heading. Add the suggestions to the table on the board, along with notes of any props that might be needed. Disallow any potentially violent or dangerous games.
● Add any new types of game if appropriate, such as multimedia.

Group work or Paired work
● Working with the whole class first, choose the final games and allocate who should do which one. If possible, try to avoid having any child on their own unless they are happy to do it.
● Give the children time and space to practise how they are going to show their game in a freeze-frame.
● Have a practice with a count-down and then call *Freeze!* Check how well it looks, then hold another quick rehearsal incorporating any necessary changes.

Whole-class work
● Once the children are ready, go to the large space, preferably but not essentially outdoors, to put the children into their positions with their games equipment.
● Find an elevated position from which to take the panoramic photograph.
● Give the children a countdown to get themselves in position, 'mid-play', then call *Freeze!* and take the photograph.
● If possible, take further photographs of the individual groups and games to use for display and class work.
● Once the photographs have been taken, let the children have a little time to play their games.

> ### Differentiation
> ● Support: have mixed-ability groups if possible.

Review
● Put the class photograph on display. As an extension, you could use string to link the games to game name labels at the side.
● Display Bruegel's painting alongside, for discussion on the similarities and differences between games played long ago and in present times. Ask comparison questions such as: *Why do you think these games in the old painting are still played today? Why are some of the games not played today? Did you enjoy playing your game for the photograph?*

Week 3 lesson plans

Here the focus is LS Lowry and the industrial Lancashire landscape. In the first lesson, the children find out that many of Lancashire's towns in the past were dominated by cotton mills. They read about the hard conditions in the mills. Then the children identify the main features of a mill building and find the same features in a Lowry painting. The children use Lowry's paintings to find out how people lived and what places were like then compared with today.

1: Working in a 1930s Lancashire cotton mill

Lesson objectives
● To develop an awareness of the past, using common words and phrases relating to the passing of time.
● To know where people and events they study fit within a chronological framework.
● To identify similarities and differences between ways of life in different periods.
● To use a wide vocabulary of everyday historical terms.
● To ask and answer questions, choosing and using parts of stories and other sources to show that they know and understand key features of events.
● To understand some of the ways in which we find out about the past.
● To identify different ways in which the past is represented.

Expected outcomes
● All children know that in the recent past Lancashire had many cotton-mill towns.
● Most children know that cotton-mill workers worked in difficult conditions.
● Some children understand how bad conditions affected mill workers' health.

Resources
Lowry's Piccadilly Circus, London and Self Portrait, 1925; UK map; an old photograph of cotton-mill workers; spools of cotton; cotton cloth; photocopiable pages 'Working in the mill' and 'Rose and the cotton mill' from the CD-ROM; colouring pencils

Introduction
● Introduce LS Lowry by showing his self-portrait, and then show his painting of Piccadilly Circus, London.
● Let the children look closely at the painting. Ask: *Does this painting show London a very long time ago or in recent times?*
● Encourage the children to find details that show it was painted in fairly recent times, such as cars, double-decker buses, advert signs, people's clothes.
● Confirm that Lowry did live in recent times and that many people still remember what life was like when he made his paintings.

Whole-class work
● Explain that, although he painted this scene of London, Lowry lived in Lancashire. Show it on a map and relate it to where the children live and to London.
● Say that in the past, Lancashire had many buildings called mills. They were similar to factories and many people worked there to make cotton and cotton cloth.
● Pass around spools of cotton and cotton sheets so the children can feel the textures.
● Show an old photograph of mill workers and encourage the children to talk about what they can see.
● Display photocopiable page 'Working in the mill' from the CD-ROM and read the account to the children.
● Afterwards, ask questions such as: *What did Rose do in the mill? What did she find hard? Why did her sister have to stop working?*
● Explain that mill workers didn't get much money and that their work often made them overtired and ill.

Paired work
● Put the children into mixed-ability pairs. Give each child a copy of photocopiable page 'Rose and the cotton mill' from the CD-ROM.
● Ask the children to look at the set of true and false pictures and statements about Rose's account of working in the mill. Let them discuss which ones are true and put a tick by them.
● Let the children colour in the 'true' pictures. Then encourage them to read out the accompanying statements.

> #### Differentiation
> ● Challenge: children could write a simple sentence on one thing they would find hard in a cotton mill.

Review
● At the end of the lesson, check that the children understand the working conditions and can empathise with the workers. Ask them what they would find hard if they worked in one of the Lancashire cotton mills – the noise, the heat, the long hours, the dangerous machines, the dust?

2: Lowry's mill paintings

Lesson objectives

● To develop an awareness of the past, using common words and phrases relating to the passing of time.
● To identify similarities and differences between ways of life in different periods.
● To use a wide vocabulary of everyday historical terms.
● To ask and answer questions, choosing and using parts of stories and other sources to show that they know and understand key features of events.
● To understand some of the ways in which we find out about the past.

Expected outcomes

● All children know that in the recent past Lancashire had many mill towns.
● Most children can recognise typical features of a mill.
● Some children understand why Lowry wanted to paint mill towns.

Resources

A Lowry mill painting such as Coming from the Mill or Outside the Mill; photograph; a Lancashire cotton mill; photograph of a converted mill as it is today; blank cards (or similar on whiteboard); photocopiable page 60, 'Checklist for a Lowry mill painting'; writing and drawing pencils; ICT access (optional)

Introduction

● Remind the children that they are studying the artist LS Lowry who lived in Lancashire when many people worked in the cotton mills there.
● Display the photograph of an old cotton mill. Explain that the photograph was taken at the time when Lowry was painting his pictures.
● Encourage the children to describe the different architectural features of the mill, for example: tall chimney, big building, many windows, six levels.
● Starting from the children's suggestions, write label cards for the painting and let the children match them to the features.
● Then show the children one of Lowry's mill paintings, such as Coming from the Mill or Outside the Mill.
● Explain that Lowry lived in a mill town and wanted to paint what the town, the mill and the people looked like in detail, so he walked around with his paper and pencils and sketched what he saw.

Group work or Independent work

● Put the children into small mixed-ability groups and give each child a copy of photocopiable page 60 'Checklist for a Lowry mill painting'. Ask the children to talk about and tick off the picture features on their sheet when they find them in the Lowry painting on display.
● Invite each child to draw a particular part of the painting that catches their eye. This might be, for example, a person, a building or a chimney. If the children can view the painting on their own computer screens, advise them to zoom in or enlarge the image to support this.
● Then encourage them to write a descriptive sentence about their chosen object or person.

Whole-class work

● Bring the children together and let volunteers share their sentences and discuss what they have drawn and why.
● Look at some of the people in the picture and ask the children whether they look tired or lively, and why. (Tired, because they have been working hard.)
● Ask: Why do you think Lowry wanted to paint the mill pictures? (To record what life was like for mill workers as well showing how important mills were to the local life and community.)
● Show a modern photograph of a converted mill and explain that, today, many mills are either museums, flats or offices, or they have been knocked down altogether.

Differentiation
● Support: when working on the photocopiable sheet, ask open questions to help children focus on the painting.
● Challenge: children could write an explanation sentence on why they chose their feature.

Review

● Encourage the children to talk about any former mills they have seen or visited. What are they used for now?
● Highlight how Lowry's paintings, like the photograph, help us to see what life was like in the recent past.
● Check children's deductions and understanding of features in the photographs and painting. Ask, for example: Why do you think Lowry wanted to paint the smoky mills and the working people?

Week 4 lesson plans

This is the start of a two-week project on creating a Lowry-style mural of a 1930s mill landscape or a landscape of their local area. The children use their observation skills to decorate card buildings in a Lowry style. Local buildings can be used instead of a mill landscape, if you prefer a local focus, but should be drawn in a Lowry style. (Show photographs of the local buildings chosen.) For an authentic Lowry look, offer a limited selection of paints in shades of red, brown, grey and blue, as well as black and white. The second lesson this week reinforces the children's knowledge and recognition of how Lowry created his buildings in his mill paintings.

1: Class mural – Lowry-style buildings

Introduction
● Explain to the children that they are going to make a class mural of their own Lowry-style painting.
● Highlight that in this first week of the project, they are going to concentrate on the landscape, particularly the buildings, and that next week they will create the figures.

Whole-class work
● **Lowry landscape option:** look again at Lowry's painting and work with the children to identify the different buildings and their features, for example: the large mills, tall chimneys and many windows, the small homes with two curtained windows and a door, the shop fronts, a church spire.
● **Local option:** show a set of photographs of a variety of local buildings and identify their features: flats, terraced houses, modern houses, a shop, factory, old shop, school, church, mosque and so on.
● Show the children the prepared blank cut-out shapes for the Lowry-style buildings.

Group work
● Put the children into small groups and give each group a section to work on. The tasks could include:
    ● adding pre-cut window shapes or making and cutting out window shapes for buildings
    ● colouring chimneys
    ● painting cotton wool black and grey for smoke
    ● colouring buildings using coloured pencils or paints
    ● drawing and decorating items for the shop windows
    ● drawing a clock face for the church or decorating the dome and tower for a mosque
    ● designing signs.
● Once all the buildings have been coloured and decorated, attach them to the sky-grey backing to create the first part of the class mural. Ask the children what they think of the mural so far. What do they like? Could it be shown in a better way?

> **Differentiation**
> ● Support: groups will need careful organisation, particularly when drawing features and colouring in the buildings and cutting out windows and door shapes.
> ● Challenge: encourage children to draw and write signs for buildings and the road.

Review
● Assess children's progress through their discussion and answering questions at the end of the session as well as their execution in creating the mural. Ask: *In what way does the mural look like a Lowry painting?* Elicit that it makes use of the same muted colours and similar long simple lines and tall shapes.

Lesson objectives
● To use a wide vocabulary of everyday historical terms.
● To ask and answer questions, choosing and using parts of stories and other sources to show that they know and understand key features of events.
● To understand some of the ways in which we find out about the past.

Expected outcomes
● All children can decorate building cut-outs in a Lowry style.
● Most children can identify how Lowry buildings looked.
● Some children can understand how their mural looks like a Lowry painting.

Resources
Lowry's *Our Town* and/or *Industrial Landscape: River Scene*; a large display board or papered section of wall ready for the mural, with light grey backing; a variety of Lowry-style building shape outlines (either for a Lowry mill painting or of local buildings); craft materials; Lowry-coloured paints or colouring pencils and pens; glue; scissors; cotton wool; stapler; (as the children will be creating finger-paint figures for the mural in a future lesson, keep in mind the degree of size and perspective when making the building cut-outs so the figures aren't too big or small)

■SCHOLASTIC
www.scholastic.co.uk

Lesson objectives
● To use a wide vocabulary of everyday historical terms.
● To ask and answer questions, choosing and using parts of stories and other sources to show that they know and understand key features of events.
● To understand some of the ways in which we find out about the past.

Expected outcomes
● All children can identify building types in Lowry paintings.
● Most children can draw missing features on a Lowry building.
● Some children can draw their own buildings in a Lowry style.

Resources
Lowry's *Our Town* and *Industrial Landscape: River Scene*; photocopiable page 61 'LS Lowry buildings'; drawing and colouring pencils; rulers; paper

2: Drawing LS Lowry buildings

Introduction
● Display Lowry's *Our Town* or *Industrial Landscape: River Scene* for the children. Point to the different types of building and encourage the children to say their names, such as *terraced house, church, mill, gatehouse, shop*.
● Remind the children how Lowry uses simple straight lines to create the buildings.

Independent work
● Give each child a copy of photocopiable page 61 'LS Lowry buildings', colouring pencils, paper and rulers.
● Ask the children to match the building-name labels on the sheet to the three buildings shown.
● Note that some of the features are missing from each drawing. Ask the children to identify what these are and then draw in the missing features before colouring the buildings. Encourage them to select muted Lowry colours, as for their mural.
● If possible, display other Lowry mill painting examples for the children's reference.
● Once they have completed their tasks on the photocopiable sheet, encourage the children to draw and colour their own home on a separate piece of paper. Ask them to use the tall shapes and simple straight lines used by Lowry for the houses he painted, using a ruler to create long straight lines.

Differentiation
● Support: some children might need help to read the labels on the photocopiable sheet, with using rulers for drawing straight lines and with using a Lowry-style for their own homes.
● Challenge: children could draw another building of their choice in a Lowry style. Additionally, you could adapt the photocopiable sheet by blanking out the labels for children to write in themselves.

Review
● Bring the children back together at the end of the lesson. Let them share their completed photocopiable sheets and their pictures of their own homes. Encourage the children to discuss why they have chosen the colours for the buildings on the sheet, and to explain some of the features of their own house that they have drawn.
● Go through the features on the photocopiable sheet and the style of drawings to check children's knowledge and understanding of Lowry-type buildings.

Week 5 lesson plans

This week, the children finger-paint Lowry-style figures for their mural. In the first lesson, they first look closely at Lowry's 'matchstick' people and their clothing, postures and actions. (To continue the Lowry look, limit the paint colour selection as before.) Then the children hear a song about Lowry's matchstick people and draw and write about their own matchstick character. Bear in mind relative sizes and the perspective of the building background so that the children's figures are not too small or big for the mural.

1: Finger-painted Lowry figures

Lesson objectives
● To develop an awareness of the past, using common words and phrases relating to the passing of time.
● To identify similarities and differences between ways of life in different periods.
● To use a wide vocabulary of everyday historical terms.
● To ask and answer questions, choosing and using parts of stories and other sources to show that they know and understand key features of events.
● To understand some of the ways in which we find out about the past.

Expected outcomes
● All children will recognise and discuss the figures in a Lowry painting.
● Most children will be able to create Lowry-type figures.
● Some children will be able to paint Lowry figures using appropriate colours, shapes and form.

Resources
Lowry's *Lancashire Fair: Good Friday, Daisy Nook*; finger paints; white A3 card or paper; wet wipes or washing facilities; pre-painted figures, including some without pen details; black pens (for details when figures are dry)

Introduction
● Display *Lancashire Fair: Good Friday, Daisy Nook* and discuss the painting by asking questions such as: *What are the people visiting? How do you know that it is a fair? Have you been to a fair like this one?*

Whole-class work
● Focus on the children in the painting. Discuss their clothes, socks, shoes and hats. Ask: *What are the children doing?* Explain that in the past many people wore hats for much of the time. Ask: *What else is different about what they are wearing from what we might wear to a fair today?*
● Now ask the children what colours they can see. Note reds, browns, greys, blues, black and white – the only colours Lowry usually used.
● Draw attention to the way Lowry paints his characters consistently with long 'stick' legs, long bodies, and dark shoes.
● Remind the children of their Lowry mural and its buildings. Say that, this week, they are going to paint Lowry figures for the mural, using finger paint.
● Show the children some finger-paint characters you have made in advance. Then demonstrate how to create the figures:
  ● Put paint on an index finger and press to make a body shape.
  ● Add a face-colour paint blob to make a smaller shape for the head.
  ● Form a skirt or shorts and then skin colour to make thin lines for legs.
  ● Make straight black or brown lines for trousers.
  ● Add dark-brown or black blobs for shoes.
  ● Make lines of paint for arms and finger-dots for hands.
  ● Add hair or a hat.
  ● Draw in the face and details with a pen after the paint is dry.
● Let the children experiment painting with their figures on white paper. Remind them to clean their fingers between colour changes.
● At the end of the lesson, let the children choose their best figure or two by putting a tick near them.
● Once the figures are dry, cut out the children's chosen ones and let them add pen dots for eyes and buttons and a line for a mouth.
● When placing the figures onto the mural, encourage the children to help you select suitable positions.

Differentiation
● Support: help children with less developed hand and eye control to create their figures.
● Challenge: children could paint a couple of characters with a different stance: hunched or upright.

Review
● Once the mural is complete, ask the children to suggest a title to add above it. Ask: *How does our mural give information about how the people in it live and what the area is like?*

■ SCHOLASTIC
www.scholastic.co.uk

2: My matchstick person

Lesson objectives
- To develop an awareness of the past, using common words and phrases relating to the passing of time.
- To use a wide vocabulary of everyday historical terms.
- To ask and answer questions, choosing and using parts of stories and other sources to show that they know and understand key features of events.
- To understand some of the ways in which we find out about the past.
- To identify different ways in which the past is represented.

Expected outcomes
- All children will recognise and discuss a figure in a Lowry painting.
- Most children will be able to create Lowry-type figures.
- Some children will be able to draw and write about their own Lowry figure.

Resources
Lowry painting with lots of people in the foreground, such as *Coming from the Mill*, *Going to the Match* or *Lancashire Fair, Good Friday: Daisy Nook*; a recording of the song 'Matchstick Men and Matchstick Cats and Dogs' (or the lyrics so you can sing or read it yourself); photocopiable page 'My matchstick person' from the CD-ROM; drawing and colouring pencils

Introduction
- Show one of the Lowry paintings for all the children to see clearly. Draw attention to the figures in the foreground and remind the children of their mural figures they have painted.
- Discuss how the people in the painting and the figures they finger-painted look similar to stick figures that we sometimes draw quickly, with simple lines and circles or blobs.

Whole-class work
- Introduce the song to the children and explain that it is about Lowry's painted figures.
- After listening to the recording or your version, ask the children why the song said that Lowry painted matchstick men and matchstick cats and dogs. Prompt the children to re-examine how Lowry has drawn his figures (not just 'men', but including women and children), with long straight 'matchstick' legs with big blobs for shoes, and long thin bodies.
- Give each child a copy of photocopiable page 'My matchstick person' from the CD-ROM along with drawing and colouring pencils.
- Tell the children that you want them to draw their own matchstick person in the space on the sheet and then complete the short sentences about the figure.
- Read through the sentences, such as *My name is _____. I am _____ years old. My shoes are _____*. Use the wordbank to fill in the blanks in one or two examples.
- Point out the wordbank at the bottom of the page and read through the words with the children. Explain that the words are there to help them if they need some ideas for completing the sentences.
- Display one or two more Lowry paintings for reference, if possible.

Independent work
- Set the children to work individually drawing and writing.
- Once the children have completed their sheets, let them share their work with another child or a small group to talk about their choices.

> ### Differentiation
> - Support: use details in the Lowry paintings to help children who are not confident in drawing Lowry-style figures; direct children to the wordbank to support their sentence-writing.
> - Challenge: children could write independent sentences about their matchstick person or a short story about them.

Review
- Display the children's work on the wall, near the mural, so all the children can see the different matchstick figures. Check how well the children have been able to understand and reproduce Lowry's style.
- Ask the children why Lowry's figures were called 'matchstick men' in the song.

Week 6 lesson plans

In the first lesson, you could focus on either Bruegel or Lowry. The children use their investigative skills and historical language to discuss a celebration painting. They put themselves in the painting and recount their day. In the last lesson, the two artists are brought together, allowing comparison of two of their paintings. Understanding how paintings can help us to find out about the past, the children draw pictures of their school for children of the future.

1: Character recounts

Bruegel focus: Introduction
● Display *Peasant Wedding*. Elicit that it was painted hundreds of years ago. Ask: *How can we tell it was from long ago?*
● Remind the children of their studies on Bruegel and what the word *peasant* means.

Whole-class work
● Ask: *Which part of the wedding does the painting show?* (The reception, a feast.) Make comparisons with present-day wedding receptions.
● Guide the children through the details of the painting, such as the decorations, food and drink and music.
● Then focus on the characters. Ask: *What are they doing? Who might they be?*

Paired work or Whole-class work
● Working in mixed-ability pairs, let the children imagine that they are a pair of guests, musicians or servants at the wedding feast. Ask them to chat to each other about their experiences. What did they enjoy? Was there anything they didn't enjoy?
● After some time, bring the pairs together and let them point to who they are in the painting and talk about their day. Write key words on the board as the children talk, such as: First, Then, Next, After that, Finally. Make the point that the pairs of characters all had different experiences of the same celebration.
● Now ask all the pairs to imagine they had been guests at the wedding and to write a thank-you letter to the bride and groom. If needed, write out a letter framework for the children to refer to.

Lowry focus: Introduction
● Display *VE Day*. Explain that it shows a street party celebrating the end of the Second World War in Europe. Elicit that this is within living memory.
● Let the children share their experiences of street parties or communal celebrations and make comparisons with the painting.
● Focus on the different activities, decorations, characters and groups within the painting.

Paired work or Whole-class work
● Working in mixed-ability pairs, ask the children to imagine that they are a pair of characters at the street party and to give an oral recount of what they did. Write key words on the board as the children talk. Model an example first, such as: *Our names are Flo and Stan. We went to the VE Day party in our town. First we helped put up the flags in the street...*

Review
● When the children are ready, bring the class together and let them give their oral recounts. Point out that the pairs of characters all had different experiences of the same celebration.
● If time, let the children draw comic-strip versions of their recounts with brief sentences underneath the pictures.

Lesson objectives
● To develop an awareness of the past, using common words and phrases relating to the passing of time.
● To know where people and events they study fit within a chronological framework.
● To identify similarities and differences between ways of life in different periods.
● To use a wide vocabulary of everyday historical terms.
● To ask and answer questions, choosing and using parts of stories and other sources to show that they know and understand key features of events.
● To understand some of the ways in which we find out about the past.
● To identify different ways in which the past is represented.

Expected outcomes
● All children will be able to answer questions about a painting and say simple recounts.
● Most children can use some elements from a painting to include in recounts.
● Some children can use details in a painting and use historical vocabulary in their recounts.

Resources
Bruegel's *Peasant Wedding* or Lowry's *VE Day*; paper; drawing pencils

■SCHOLASTIC
www.scholastic.co.uk

Lesson objectives
- To know where people and events they study fit within a chronological framework.
- To identify similarities and differences between ways of life in different periods.
- To use a wide vocabulary of everyday historical terms.
- To ask and answer questions, choosing and using parts of stories and other sources to show that they know and understand key features of events.
- To understand some of the ways in which we find out about the past.
- To identify different ways in which the past is represented.

Expected outcomes
- All children can see the main similarities and differences between Lowry and Bruegel paintings.
- Most children can make more detailed comparisons between the paintings.
- Some children will understand that paintings can help us to find out about the past.

Resources
Bruegel's self-portrait *The Painter and the Buyer* and Lowry's *Self Portrait, 1925*; two comparable Bruegel and Lowry paintings, such as Bruegel's *Children's Games* and Lowry's *Britain at Play*; paper and colouring materials and/or tape

2: Comparing Bruegel and Lowry

Introduction
- Display the self-portraits of Bruegel and Lowry with an example of their paintings.
- Recall with the children who the artists are, and ask them which one lived long ago and which one lived in recent times.

Whole-class work
- Taking each artist in turn, focus on the painting that's not the self-portrait.
- Tell the children the title of the painting and briefly discuss what it shows.
- After looking at both paintings, explain that they both paintings show some similar things and things that are different.
- Draw a table on the board with the headings *Similarities* and *Differences* and begin to list the examples suggested by the children.
- If necessary, use prompting questions to look for similarities, such as the colours, scenes of people playing, lots of figures, not rich clothes.
- Do the same with the differences, such as the clothes, buildings and people's actions and the greater detail in the figures by Bruegel. Suggest that Lowry's focus for detail is more on the landscape and what is in it.
- Discuss how paintings like Bruegel's and Lowry's help us to understand how some people might have lived, and what places could have looked like in the past.

Independent work
- Tell the children to imagine that, many years in the future, a group of children want to find out what their school looked like in the past. Suggest that they could draw a picture to help the children of the future.
- Discuss possible background situations for the picture, such as their classroom, playground or the school hall.
- Ask the children who they are going to include in their pictures: *Lots of children, or just two or three children? Any teachers?*
- Remind them to show details of what the figures are wearing, such as a school uniform or PE kit.
- Give out drawing paper and colouring materials for the children to draw their pictures.

Differentiation
- Support: some children may need to be encouraged to talk about the similarities and differences between the two paintings; some children may need help visualising their ideas for a school drawing.
- Challenge: children could carry out an independent comparison investigation of two more Bruegel and Lowry paintings.

Review
- At the end of the lesson, bring the children back together and encourage them to show and talk about their pictures. What notable differences are there? How do they think children from the future might interpret their pictures?
- Bring the lesson and topic to an end by discussing the work they have covered on Bruegel and Lowry. Ask the children which paintings they have enjoyed looking at and why. Ask: *What have they taught us about life in the distant and recent past?*

Lesson objectives
● To know where the people and events they study fit within a chronological frame.
● To understand some of the ways in which we find out about the past.

Resources
Self-portraits of Bruegel the Elder and LS Lowry and an assortment of works by both painters; access to the Bruegel's painting *Children's games* and LS Lowry's painting *Coming from the mill*

Pieter Bruegel the Elder and LS Lowry

Revise
● Show the self-portraits of Bruegel the Elder and LS Lowry to the class. Ask the children which one is Pieter Bruegel the Elder and which one is LS Lowry.
● Ask the children to explain which painter is from long ago and which painter lived within living memory. Encourage them to give their reasons for their answer.
● Revise what the children know about each painter, putting the information into fact files.
● Now show the class a mixed-up selection of some of the paintings of both Bruegel the Elder and LS Lowry.
● For each painting, ask the children who painted it and what clues tell us if the scene shown is from long ago or in recent times.

Assess
● Let the children work in pairs to produce simple oral quizzes for 'What's in the painting?'
● Split the pairs into two class groups, with one group preparing a quiz about Bruegel the Elder's painting *Children's games* and the other group preparing a quiz about one of LS Lowry's painting *Coming from the Mill.*
● Give each pair of children access to IT or book sources of their painting. Give them time to study the painting in detail to help them choose their five best questions for their quiz.
● Once the quizzes are created, match a 'Bruegel the Elder' pair of children with a 'LS Lowry' pair of children.
● Let each pair take it in turns to test each other with their painting quiz.
● Bring the class together and let the children share some of their quiz questions.
● Ask the children what each painting is about and what it tells us about the past.

Further practice
● Let the children look at other, less-familiar, paintings by Bruegel and Lowry that have linked scenes or themes such as winter or houses.
● They could also focus on comparisons of the people or places in the different periods of history shown, such as the characters' clothing, or details in the landscape.

Lesson objectives
● To answer questions, choosing and using parts of stories and other sources to show that they know and understand key features of events.

Resources
Interactive activity 'Y1 Spring 1 quiz' on the CD-ROM

Y1 Spring 1 quiz

Revise
● Ask each child to take the role of Pieter Bruegel or LS Lowry and to talk about their work and why they chose their particular subject matter.

Assess
● Ask the children to complete interactive activity 'Y1 Spring 1 quiz' on the CD-ROM. There are ten multiple choice questions that test what the children will have learned throughout the topic. They will need to read each question carefully before choosing the correct answer.
● Give children a set length of time (such as 15 minutes) to answer the questions. This can be used as part of a formal assessment or as a fun challenge activity, giving children the opportunity to show what they have learned about the topic.

Further practice
● Review any common misconceptions from the quiz.
● Ask children to talk about what they like or dislike about the two artists' work.

A rich woman and a peasant in Bruegel's time

■ Cut out the labels and stick them in the right places to show what rich women and peasant women wore in Bruegel's time.

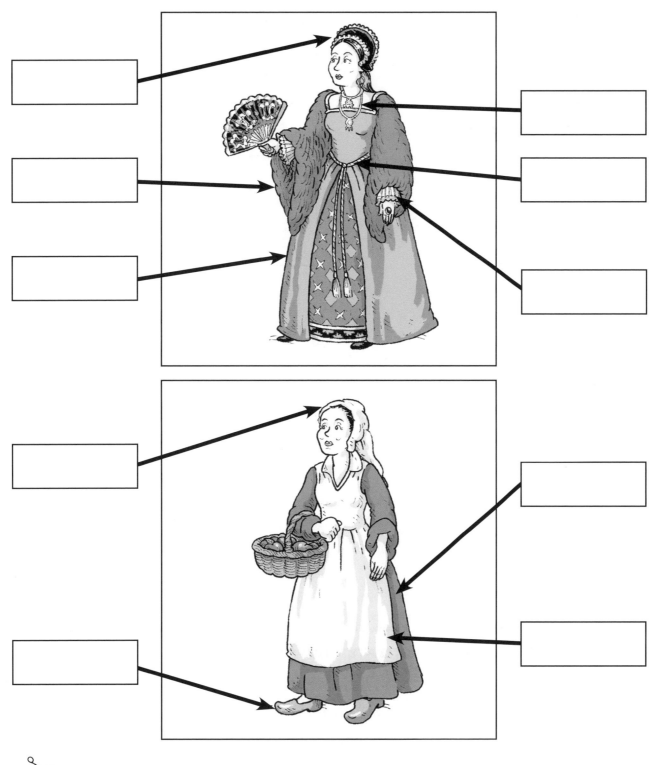

apron	velvet dress	fur	necklace	belt
headdress	head scarf	clogs	simple dress	lace

Checklist for a Lowry mill painting

■ Tick each feature you find in the Lowry painting.

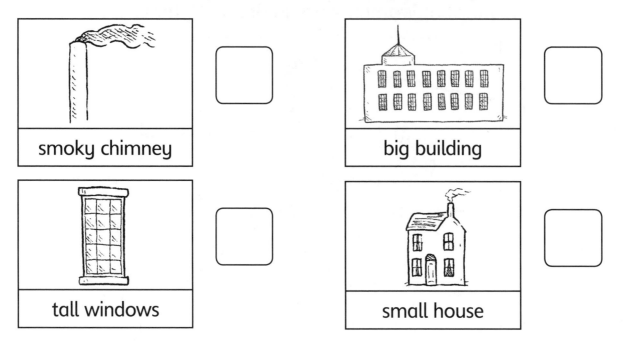

■ In the box below, draw something from the picture that you like.

■ Explain what you have drawn, and why.

This is a _____

_____

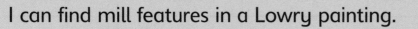
I can find mill features in a Lowry painting.

How did you do?
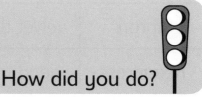

PHOTOCOPIABLE   **SCHOLASTIC**
www.scholastic.co.uk

LS Lowry buildings

■ Match each label to the correct building.
■ Some parts of the buildings are missing. Finish the drawings and colour them in.

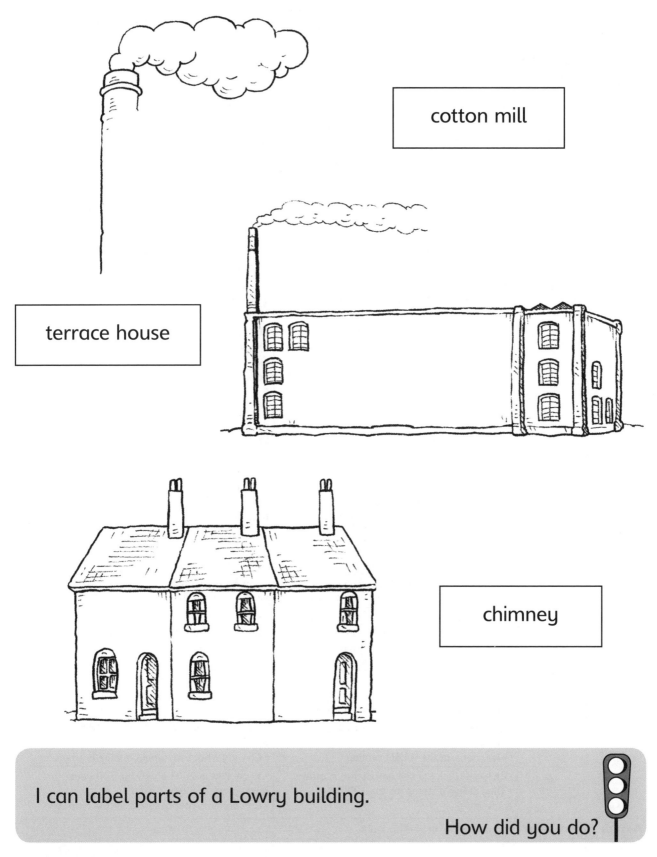

cotton mill

terrace house

chimney

I can label parts of a Lowry building.

How did you do?

Events beyond living memory: the first aeroplane flight

This chapter looks at the first aeroplane and the inventors, Orville and Wilbur Wright. The topic starts by sorting types of aeroplane and sequencing their 100-year development onto a timeline. The children use a wide range of sources to find out more about the Wrights and their gliders and planes. They also investigate their experiments by making and flying kites and designing model gliders, as well as use an inventor's den to appreciate the Wright brothers' passion for inventing. The chapter ends with the children 'asking' the Wright brothers about their achievements, and designing an anniversary postage stamp.

Chapter at a glance

Curriculum objective

• Events beyond living memory that are significant nationally or globally (the first aeroplane flight).

Week	Lesson	Summary of activities	Expected outcomes
1	1	• Children discuss what an aeroplane is. • They sequence aeroplanes onto a timeline and sort aeroplanes into groups.	• Can put aeroplanes in chronological order.
	2	• Children listen to the myth of Daedalus and Icarus. • They look at examples of flying machines by pre-Wright inventors. • They design their own flying machines.	• Know what flying machines from the past looked like. • Know who invented flying machines. • Can understand why some flying machines were unsuccessful.
2	1	• Children use a map and photographs to see when and where the Wright brothers lived. • They hear about the Wrights' early days. • They add words to a diary extract.	• Know who Orville and Wilbur Wright were and where and when they lived. • Can suggest what made the brothers want to invent a flying machine.
	2	• Children listen to more of the Wright brothers' story and add dates to the timeline. • They compare a high-wheel bicycle with the Wrights' safety bicycle. • They create an advert for a futuristic bicycle.	• Know that the Wrights designed and built bicycles. • Can compare bicycle designs.
3	1	• Children look at different types of kite. • They learn that the Wright brothers used box kites and then create box kites.	• Can understand how box kites helped the Wright brothers.
	2	• Children hear how wing warping helped the Wrights to control their gliders. • They fly kites to test steering. • They draw wing warping on a box kite.	• Can fly kites to investigate how they can be controlled. • Can understand how kites helped the Wright brothers.
4	1	• Children discuss why the geographical features of Kitty Hawk made it good for flight tests. • They compare and label gliders.	• Learn how the Wrights experimented with gliders. • Can label a Wright aircraft.
	2	• Pairs design, make and improve a simple glider, recording test notes on a design sheet.	• Can make and test gliders to discover how the Wright brothers improved their designs.
5	1	• Children listen to an account of events on 17 December 1903 and discuss the importance of the photographs recording the moment. • They create a notebook of events.	• Know what happened on 17 December 1903. • Can recount the day chronologically.
	2	• Children watch a film clip of the Wright brothers flying in 1908. • They write an acrostic poem about flying.	• Can write a poem about what it would be like on one of the earliest flights.
6	1	• Children compare the planes of 1905 and 1908 with the 1903 *Flyer*. • They hot-seat the Wright brothers.	• Know what the Wright brothers did from 1903 to 1911. • Can say what they would ask the brothers.
	2	• Children recall the first aeroplanes in order. • They design a stamp for the 100th anniversary.	• Know that in 2003 it was the 100-year anniversary of the first flight. • Can design a special stamp for the occasion.
Assess and review		• To review the half-term's work.	

■SCHOLASTIC
www.scholastic.co.uk

Expected prior learning
- Children can sequence specific events on a timeline and use common time words and phrases.
- Children can use a range of sources to find out about the past.
- Children can ask and answer questions and choose sources to understand key features of events.

Overview of progression
- During this chapter, children describe differences between old and new aeroplanes to put them on a timeline, and study photographs to work out that the Wright brothers lived 'long ago'. They develop a timeline about the Wright brothers.
- Children explore aeroplanes since 1903 and how life has changed with their invention. They also compare old bicycles with newer ones and their own futuristic designs. They use photographs and film clips to compare the changes in the Wright brothers' gliders and aeroplanes.
- The children use their enquiring skills to find out what inspired the Wrights to be inventors, how making bicycles helped them, why they used kites and gliders in their flight tests and how they felt on that first aeroplane flight.
- By the end of the chapter, the children should be able to explain why the photographs taken of the first flight are so important. They also understand the use of eyewitness accounts, diaries and inventors' notebooks.
- Children see that the past can be represented in different ways by hot-seating the Wright brothers and creating a commemorative stamp.

Creative context
- This chapter works well with topics on transport and flight. Cross-curricular links include:
    - writing labels, captions, reports and letters; taking notes; creating a poem; as well as taking part in discussions and a hot-seat session;
    - drawing designs for a flying machine and a bicycle for the future; making a model glider and a box kite and designing their own inventions in an inventor's den;
    - working scientifically through investigations by asking simple questions, observing closely, performing tests and using observations;
    - recognising shapes, taking simple measurements, using positional language;
    - locating Dayton on a world map and looking at the geographical features of Kitty Hawk;
    - drawing and designing an anniversary postage stamp.

Background knowledge
- **Wright brothers timeline:** 1867 – Wilbur Wright born. 1871 – Orville Wright born. 1878 – Milton Wright gives the brothers a rubber-band-powered helicopter toy. 1886 – Orville and Wilbur run a printing press and newspaper. 1892 – Wright Cycle company opens. 1895 – Wright brothers make two new safety bicycles. 1896 – Otto Lilienthal dies in glider crash; the brothers start designing ideas for a safe flying machine. 1899 – Wilbur Wright discovers wing warping; the brothers use box kite gliders. 1900 – Wrights fly the first manned glider at Kitty Hawk. 1901 – Wrights try a full-sized glider. 1902 – Wrights use wind tunnels to test new glider. 1903 – Wrights add an engine to the glider. 1903 – 17 December, first aeroplane flight. 1904 – Wrights make a stronger *Flyer*. 1905 – First proper aeroplane flies 24½ miles in 39 minutes. 1908 – Wrights show their two-seater aeroplanes in Europe. 1909 – The Wright Company manufactures aeroplanes and trains pilots. 1912 – Wilbur Wright dies. 1948 – Orville Wright dies.

Week 1 lesson plans

This week introduces the topic of the first aeroplane flight. In the first lesson, the children discuss what an aeroplane is and share their experiences. They then put aeroplane photographs into a timeline. They use comparison skills to note the changes of aeroplanes over the years. In the second lesson, the children find out about pre-Wright flying machines, how they worked and why they weren't successful.

1: Sequencing and sorting aeroplanes

Introduction

- Display photographs of different types of modern aeroplane, such as a jumbo jet, small private plane, cargo plane, fighter jet and seaplane. Ask the children: *What is an aeroplane?* (A transport machine that flies.)
- Discuss what each of the aeroplanes might be used for. For example, the cargo plane is for transporting goods.
- Note features that all of the aeroplanes have, such as the wings, engines, cockpits and so on.
- Let the children share their own experiences of going on an aeroplane or seeing one.

Whole-class work

- Display interactive activity 'Timeline of aeroplanes' on the CD-ROM. Point to the date of 1900 at the beginning of the timeline and 1950 at the end.
- Drag the Wright brothers' 1903 plane into position and explain that this year was when the first flying machine ever to be driven by an engine and controlled by a person was flown.
- Use the timeline to highlight that 1903 was over 100 years ago, and discuss that aeroplanes have changed a lot since then.
- Ask the children to help you put the aeroplane pictures in the right order on the timeline. Prompt the children to use time words and phrases when talking about and deciding where the aeroplanes go. Encourage the children to look at the aeroplanes' features for clues, such as: overall shape; wing shape, size and number; and material the plane is made from.
- Once the aeroplanes are in the right chronological order, ask: *What parts of aeroplanes have changed? What are still the same?*

Group work

- Put the children into small mixed-ability groups and give each group pictures of different types of aeroplane, a large sheet of paper and glue.
- Ask the children to work together to sort out the aeroplanes into different sets. Discuss possible sets, such as ones related to size, use, appearance or age.
- Once the children have decided, let them stick the aeroplanes in their sets on the paper and write titles for the sets.

> ### Differentiation
> - Support: children may need guided questions to help them with their observations and decisions in both the sequencing and sorting activities.
> - Challenge: children could research different types of aeroplane.

Review

- Bring the groups together, and let them show and discuss their sets. Check how well they use time words and phrases.
- Briefly compare the different sets and different aeroplanes.

Lesson objectives

- To know where people and events they study fit within a chronological framework.
- To identify similarities and differences between ways of life in different periods.
- To use a wide vocabulary of everyday historical terms.
- To ask and answer questions, choosing and using parts of stories and other sources to show that they know and understand key features of events.

Expected outcomes

- All children know that aeroplanes have changed over the past 100 years.
- Most children can use the time words *oldest* and *newest* correctly.
- Some children can identify differences between older and more modern aeroplanes.

Resources

Interactive activity 'Timeline of aeroplanes' on the CD-ROM; photographs of modern aeroplanes; cut-out pictures of various types of old and new aeroplane; A2 or A3 paper; glue; pencils

■SCHOLASTIC
www.scholastic.co.uk

Lesson objectives

- To develop an awareness of the past, using common words and phrases relating to the passing of time.
- To know where people and events they study fit within a chronological framework.
- To use a wide vocabulary of everyday historical terms.
- To ask and answer questions, choosing and using parts of stories and other sources to show that they know and understand key features of events.
- To understand some of the ways in which we find out about the past.

Expected outcomes

- All children know what an inventor is and that some wanted to invent a flying machine.
- Most children will understand what a heavier-than-air flying machine is.
- Some children will understand why early flying machines were unsuccessful.

Resources

A range of illustrations and photographs of pre-Wright flying machines, including those by Alexander Goupil and Otto Lilienthal; photograph of the 1903 Flyer; a text of the myth of Daedalus and Icarus; small ball; bottle of blowing bubbles

2: Heavier-than-air flying machines

Introduction

- Before starting, create a corner to become an inventor's den. Have drawing tables with a supply of blank and squared paper, rulers and pencils. Display images of flying machines and other odd inventions, such as those by Heath Robinson and Rowland Emmett (source online).
- Talk to the children about how significant aeroplanes are in everyday life in the world. Discuss what we use aeroplanes for, such as carrying people or cargo to faraway places. Encourage children to share their experiences of aeroplanes and what we would do if aeroplanes didn't exist.
- Explain that for thousands of years people have wanted to fly and some have tried to find ways of doing so.
- Tell the children the ancient Greek myth of Daedalus and Icarus. Discuss where the men got their idea on how to fly and how they made the wings. Why didn't it work?

Whole-class work

- Blow some bubbles into the air and let the children watch them float up and then down. Then throw a ball in the air and catch it.
- Ask: Why do the bubbles stay in the air? (They are nearly as light as air and can float on it for a short time). Why can't the ball stay in the air? (It is much heavier than air.)
- Highlight that, in the past, some inventors tried to make flying machines that could fly people long distances. But the problem was that any machine would be heavier than air. Check that the children understand the terms inventor and invention.
- Display a picture of an early attempt at a flying machine, such as Goupil's Flying Machine. Discuss why the machine was unsuccessful.
- Show pictures of Otto Lilienthal's gliders. Highlight that, although the gliders had no engines, he could control them for a short time. Help the children to talk about his ideas.

Independent work

- Display a selection of images of pre-Wright flying machines and challenge the children to design their own flying machine.
- As the children work, walk around the class and listen to them talk about their ideas.
- Ask them to write simple descriptive captions underneath the drawing and give the machine a name.

Whole-class work

- At the end of the lesson, ask volunteers to discuss how their flying machines would work.
- Explain that many ideas of past inventors of flying machines helped the Wright brothers, who went on to make successful flying machines.
- Introduce the class inventor's den and tell the children that they can use it to design and plan inventions of their own throughout the topic.

Differentiation

- Support: support children in putting their ideas on paper and writing out captions; if needed, write out their oral sentences for them to copy.
- Challenge: children could write more detailed labels or captions to show how their machine works.

Review

- Share the children's work and note similarities. Can the children suggest why Lilienthal's gliders were better fliers than the other machines? Which of the inventors' ideas might have helped the Wright brothers in their invention of the aeroplane?

Week 2 lesson plans

This week introduces the Wright brothers and begins a Wright brothers timeline. In the first lesson, the children locate where the family lived and use photographs to establish that they lived long ago. They listen to an account of the brothers' early years and look at a letter about a toy helicopter to suggest why the brothers were interested in inventions and flight. Then the children learn about the brothers' bicycle shop and compare an old bicycle design with the brothers' new safety bicycles. They connect the brothers' bicycle inventions with the start of their flight inventions.

1: Who were the Wright brothers?

Lesson objectives

● To develop an awareness of the past, using common words and phrases relating to the passing of time.
● To know where people and events they study fit within a chronological framework.
● To identify similarities and differences between ways of life in different periods.
● To use a wide vocabulary of everyday historical terms.
● To ask and answer questions, choosing and using parts of stories and other sources to show that they know and understand key features of events.
● To understand some of the ways in which we find out about the past.

Expected outcomes

● All children should know that the Wright brothers lived long ago in the USA.
● Most children will understand that the Wright brothers liked to invent things.
● Some children will understand why a toy helicopter made them want to invent a flying machine.

Resources

Photocopiable page 77 'The toy helicopter'; world map; photographs of the Wright brothers as boys, and their family members; photograph of the Wrights with the *Flyer*; photocopiable page 'The Wright brothers story (1)' from the CD-ROM; Wright brothers timeline (see Introduction) and timeline date cards with Orville's and Wilbur's birth dates and the date of the toy helicopter present (see Background information)

Introduction

● Before the lesson, set up an eye-catching timeline from 1860 to 1950. It could be on a display board within the shape of an aeroplane wing or on a washing line with dates going across the air.
● Display a photograph of the Wright brothers with their 1903 aeroplane, the *Wright Flyer* and introduce the Wright brothers. Explain that they were the inventors of the first successful heavier-than-air aeroplane.
● Tell the children that they are going to find out about the brothers and investigate why they became inventors.

Whole-class work

● Explain that the Wright brothers grew up in Dayton in Ohio in the USA. Use a world map to connect the location of the school to Dayton.
● Show a photograph of the Wright brothers as children and encourage the children to study the photographs for clues that show they lived long ago.
● Look at the dates of the boys' births and highlight that they were born over 140 years ago, so, beyond living memory.
● Use the dates to begin the Wright brothers timeline. Tell the children that more dates will be added as they find out more about the brothers.
● Display family photographs of the Wright family and read part 1 of photocopiable page 'The Wright brothers story (1)' from the CD-ROM.
● After the story, discuss what might have encouraged the brothers to invent things, such as their personalities and their upbringing (the encouragements and interests of their parents).

Paired work or Independent work

● Give out photocopiable page 77 'The toy helicopter' to each child, and, with the children, read out Orville Wright's diary extract.
● Set the children to work in pairs or individually to write in the correct missing words from the extract, using the wordbank for support.
● Then ask them to label a diagram of the toy helicopter.

Differentiation
● Support: provide support for children with the reading and writing on the photocopiable sheet.
● Challenge: children could suggest instructions on how to play with the toy helicopter.

Review

● At the end of the lesson, re-read the diary extract with the correct words in place. If possible, show the helicopter diagram on the whiteboard, and ask volunteers to write in the labels.
● Then ask the class: *Why would a toy helicopter make Orville and Wilbur Wright interested in flight?* (They were fascinated by flying and wanted to know how it worked and if they could make their own flying machine.)
● Tell the children that the brothers made bigger models of the helicopter to see what they would do.

2: The Wright brothers, bicycle makers

Lesson objectives
● To develop an awareness of the past, using common words and phrases relating to the passing of time.
● To know where people and events they study fit within a chronological framework.
● To identify similarities and differences between ways of life in different periods.
● To use a wide vocabulary of everyday historical terms.
● To ask and answer questions, choosing and using parts of stories and other sources to show that they know and understand key features of events.
● To understand some of the ways in which we find out about the past.

Expected outcomes
● All children know that the Wright brothers repaired and made bicycles.
● Most children can compare a high-wheel bicycle with a Wrights safety bicycle.
● Some children understand how the Wrights' bicycle inventions helped them with their aeroplane inventions.

Resources
Photocopiable page 'The Wright brothers story (1)'; media resource 'Advert for a Wright safety bicycle' on the CD-ROM; Wright brothers timeline; date cards for the timeline for their printing press, opening of bicycle shop, bicycle inventions (see Background information); photographs of the Wright brothers' bicycle shop and bicycles; picture of a high-wheel bicycle; photocopiable page 78 'Comparing bicycles'

Introduction
● Remind the children of the first part of the story of the Wright brothers' lives. Then read the second part of the story from the photocopiable page 'The Wright brothers story (1)' on the CD-ROM.
● Ask volunteers to add the date cards from this part of their lives to the Wright brothers timeline set up in the classroom.

Whole-class work
● Display photographs of the Wrights' bicycle shop and tell the children that the brothers were quite young – Wilbur was 25 and Orville 21 – when they opened up their bicycle business.
● Ask the children questions about the account they have just heard, such as: *Why did the brothers set up a bicycle repair shop? What else did the brothers do at the shop?*
● Show a picture of a high-wheel bicycle (also known as a penny-farthing) and compare it with Wright safety bicycle on the media resource 'Advert for a Wright safety bicycle' on the CD-ROM. Encourage the children to tell you what they notice straight away (the relative sizes of the wheels) and then to look in more detail for any other differences.
● Read the advert with the children and discuss how the new Wright bicycle was safer and better to ride than the high-wheel bicycle.

Paired work or Independent work
● Give a copy of photocopiable page 78 'Comparing bicycles', to each child and ask the children to draw in the pictures in the two advertisements: one for a high-wheel bicycle, and the other for the Wright brothers' safety bicycle.
● Then, on a separate piece of paper, encourage them to draw and write a simple advert for a bicycle of the future.
● Encourage the children to compare the first two bicycles and then their bicycles. What have they added to their future-bicycle invention and why?

Differentiation
● Support: help less skilled artists with positioning and scale when drawing; help children to read the labels and write their own adverts.
● Challenge: encourage children to write labels for their drawings; for their own adverts, they could also write a catchy slogan.

Review
● At the end of the lesson, check how well the children have been able to see the changes made between the bicycles.
● Encourage the children to show and talk about their bicycles for the future. What are their unusual features?
● Ask the children: *Why did the Wright brothers want their own bicycle shop?* Highlight that the bicycle shop helped the Wright brothers try out different ideas for machines, including ones that might be able to fly. It also gave them the money to try out their flying experiments.

Week 3 lesson plans

During this week, the children investigate how the Wright brothers used large box kites to help them work out how to control a flying machine. In the first lesson, the children find out about the invention of the box kite and why it was used by the Wrights for their kite gliders. They then make their own simple box kite to investigate its shape and flying abilities. In the second lesson, they hear about Wilbur Wright's discovery of wing warping. The children have a kite-flying session to investigate how to 'steer' a kite.

1: Box kites

Lesson objectives
● To develop an awareness of the past, using common words and phrases relating to the passing of time.
● To use a wide vocabulary of everyday historical terms.
● To understand some of the ways in which we find out about the past.

Expected outcomes
● All children know that the Wright brothers used box kites.
● Most children can use photographic sources to discuss how the box kites were used.
● Some children understand why box kites were used by the Wright brothers.

Resources
Film clip of modern-day kite flying, including a box kite, if possible; photographs of Lawrence Hargrave and his box kites; photographs of the Wright brothers flying their kites; a model box kite; photocopiable page 'Box kite instructions' from the CD-ROM; kite-making resources: dowel sticks or straws; strong tape; string; 'wing' material such as thin plastic, plastic bags, brown paper or newspaper

Introduction
● You might want to send a letter home in advance to ask if the children could bring in a kite if they have one at home. Aim to gather a collection of kites so there is at least one kite per three children.
● Show the children a kite and ask them what it is. Share experiences of flying kites. Ask the children if they know how to launch and fly a kite: go through the steps together.
● Watch a video of kite flying. Look at the different shapes and features of kites. Pause the film to point out box kite (if shown).

Whole-class work
● Explain that the box kite was invented by an Australian called Lawrence Hargrave in 1893. Show the photograph of the box kites. Look at how large they are, and explain that they were considered stronger and better-lifting kites than any other kite at that time.
● Examine why box kites are strong. Focus on the square or oblong cells. Note the middle of the cells are open with a framework holding the kite together. Discuss how strong a frame of square and oblong shapes can be when pressure is put on it. Highlight how the wind rushes through the middle to make it lift quickly.
● Remind the children of Wilbur and Orville Wright's interest in flying and inventions, and go on to say that they loved to make and fly kites as part of their experiments in flying. When they got a new box kite, they knew that it was the shape for their aeroplane.
● Show a photograph of the Wright brothers with their box kites. Ask: *How did they use the box kites? Why do you think they wanted to use box kites?* (They were light but strong, stable and balanced).
● Ask: *Why are the kites so big? Why do you think flying kites was a good way of working towards inventing an aeroplane?*

Paired work
● Put the children into mixed-ability pairs and explain that they are going to make simple box kites.
● Display photocopiable page 'Box kite instructions' from the CD-ROM on the whiteboard. Show an example of a pre-made box kite and then and go through the instructions with the children so that they understand what to do.
● Move around the classroom, offering help and advice.

Differentiation
● Support: extra adult support would be useful to help with following the shape and sticking and putting the plastic or paper together.
● Challenge: children could create another box kite and put the two together to create a double box kite.

Review
● Find space to have a kite-flying session.
● Ask the children how well their box kites flew. Did they fly differently from simple flat kites?

■SCHOLASTIC
www.scholastic.co.uk

2: Birds and wing warping

Lesson objectives
● To know where people and events they study fit within a chronological framework.
● To use a wide vocabulary of everyday historical terms.
● To ask and answer questions, choosing and using parts of stories and other sources to show that they know and understand key features of events.
● To understand some of the ways in which we find out about the past.

Expected outcomes
● All children understand that kites can be controlled by a pulling system.
● Most children know how wing warping was discovered and what it is.
● Some children understand how the Wright brothers used wing warping.

Resources
Photocopiable page 'The Wright brothers' story (2)' and media resource 'Wing warping on kites' from the CD-ROM, and a selection of images to illustrate the story (optional); Wright brothers timeline; date card for the timeline: wing-warping discovery (1899); several long cardboard tubes; a range of easy-to-fly box kites; outside space in which to fly the kites, and additional adult support

Introduction
● Remind the children about the box kite designs they created in the previous lesson and how the Wright brothers used them for their experiments in flying. Read the part three of photocopiable page 'The Wright brothers' story (2)' from the CD-ROM to the children and invite a volunteer to add the date card to the timeline.

Whole-class work
● Ask the children questions about the text they have just listened to, such as *Why did the brothers write notes about how birds flew? What could happen if it wasn't possible to control a plane to change direction, lift, dive or land?*
● Suggest to the children that they have a class experiment of flying kites to investigate how they can make the kites move in different directions.
● With additional adult support, take the children outside and have a kite-flying session, ideally with one box kite between three children. Remind the children that they are trying to keep their kite under control and use the strings to see if they can change its direction and height. Advise the others in each group to look carefully at the 'wings' of the kite as it flies.
● After the kite-flying session, go back into the classroom and discuss with the children how they were able to make their kites move in different directions. Draw diagrams for clarification if needed.
● Now, or in another session, remind the children about the wing-warping discovery in the story.
● Use cardboard tubes to demonstrate the effect of wing warping. Pass them around for to the children to investigate. Did anyone notice a similar effect on their kites?
● Highlight that wing warping would help to keep a kite, glider or aeroplane from rolling about and to move smoothly.
● Display media resource 'Wing warping on kites' on the CD-ROM on the whiteboard. Explain that the Wright brothers decided to use the effect of wing warping to help them to control a large box kite in the shape of an aeroplane.
● Note the strings and discuss how it is controlled. Note the four lines on the top and bottom of the wings which are attached to two sticks held by the kite flyer.
● Highlight that the kite flyer twists the sticks in opposite directions in order to twist the wings and make the kite move left or right.

Independent work
● Encourage the children to use the image on the whiteboard to draw their own picture of the kite with the wing-warping strings.
● As an extension, let the children make paper planes and experiment with adjusting the wing tips to see how this affects how the planes move.

Review
● Remind the children of the text they read earlier about the Wright brothers. Ask: *Why did they study the flights of birds? What did they find out about their wings? How did they use that discovery in their flying experiments?*

Week 4 lesson plans

This week, the children find out how the Wright brothers progressed from kite gliders to full-size gliders and eventually the first aeroplane. In the first lesson, the children use photographs to understand why the Wrights chose Kitty Hawk as a test ground, and compare the gliders and 1903 *Flyer* to see the changes. They then label the 1903 aeroplane. In the second lesson, the children work like the Wrights by creating notes and diagrams as they design and make a glider.

1: The Wright brothers' gliders

Introduction

● Remind the children how the Wright brothers used kites to work out how to control an aeroplane. Recap that they used large box kites, which had the strength and balance to carry loads as well as being able to lift up into the air well.
● Use the children's diagrams from the last lesson or media resource 'Wing warping on kites' to recall how wing warping could control the roll and direction of kite planes.
● Explain that, in 1900, the Wright brothers moved to Kitty Hawk, North Carolina, to try out large kite gliders and then full-sized gliders. Ask the children what a glider is. (An aircraft that flies without an engine and which, therefore, needs to be 'pulled' into the sky.) Say that other inventors had also tried gliders, but many crashed.

Whole-class work

● Show photographs of Kitty Hawk. Explain that it was near the ocean and had quite strong winds, soft sandy ground, a few sandy dunes and a wide-open space with no houses or trees. Ask: *Why do you think Wilbur and Orville chose Kitty Hawk to fly their gliders?*
● Suggest the children look closely at photographs of the gliders to work out why they made so many versions.
● Then show photographs of a 1901 Wright glider and a 1902 version side by side. Ask: *How did they launch a glider? Can you see wing warping? Where is the pilot? What has been added to the 1902 glider?*

Paired work

● In pairs, let the children study a photograph of the 1903 *Flyer* aeroplane to find differences between it and the 1902 glider, such as the two propellers, and an engine. Explain that aeroplanes with two wide wings are called biplanes.

Whole-class work

● Open interactive activity 'The Wrights' 1903 *Flyer*' on the CD-ROM and invite the children to drag the captions to the right positions. Discuss each section with questions such as: *Where did the Wright brothers get the idea of using bicycle chains to move the propellers? Why is it a 'proper' aeroplane and not just a glider? Why did it use linen?*
● Highlight that, after many years of experimenting with kites and gliders, the Wright brothers had finally created the first powered heavier-than-air aeroplane.

Differentiation
● Support: use prompt questions to encourage less confident learners to contribute.
● Challenge: children could draw and label the 1903 *Flyer*.

Review

● Hold up the date cards and ask volunteers to add them to the Wright brothers timeline. Ask the class what differences they can remember between those four aircraft. What was so different about the 1903 *Flyer*?

Lesson objectives
● To develop an awareness of the past, using common words and phrases relating to the passing of time.
● To know where people and events they study fit within a chronological framework.
● To use a wide vocabulary of everyday historical terms.
● To know where people and events they study fit within a chronological framework.
● To ask and answer questions, choosing and using parts of stories and other sources to show that they know and understand key features of events.
● To understand some of the ways in which we find out about the past.

Expected outcomes
● All children will be able to use photographs to recognise differences between the Wright gliders and the *Flyer*.
● Most children can explain differences between the gliders and the *Flyer*.
● Some children understand the different parts of the 1903 *Flyer*.

Resources
Interactive activity 'The Wrights' 1903 *Flyer*' and media resource 'Wing warping on kites' on the CD-ROM; photographs of Kitty Hawk in the 1900s; photographs of the 1901 and 1902 Wrights' gliders; Wright brothers timeline; date cards for the timeline: 1900 first glider, 1901 glider, 1902 glider, 1903 *Flyer*

Lesson objectives
● To use a wide vocabulary of everyday historical terms.
● To ask and answer questions, choosing and using parts of stories and other sources to show that they know and understand key features of events.
● To understand some of the ways in which we find out about the past.

Expected outcomes
● All children can design and make gliders and discuss improvements.
● Most children understand why the Wright brothers made notes of their flight tests.
● Some children understand why the Wright brothers made many gliders before they developed the *Flyer*.

Resources
Photographs of the Wrights' gliders; photocopiable pages 'How to make folded-paper gliders' and 'Our model glider notes' from the CD-ROM; Wright brothers timeline; thick paper; writing and drawing pencils; space to test the gliders

2: Making paper gliders

Introduction
● Display a series of photographs of the Wright brothers' gliders for all the children to see. Remind the children that the Wright brothers made many models of their gliders, with the aim of each one improving on and flying better than the previous one.
● Tell the children that the brothers would draw diagrams and make notes about their gliders and the flight tests. Ask the children: *Why would they take notes and draw diagrams?* (To help with their investigations; to see what, if anything, went wrong and what could be made better in the next model.)

Whole-class work
● Explain to the children that they are going to make and investigate their own folded-paper glider to work out how to make it fly well.
● Display photocopiable page 'How to make folded-paper gliders' from the CD-ROM on the whiteboard and look at the different examples. Note that they are made just from folded paper with no other items stuck on.
● Choose one of the folded-paper glider examples and demonstrate how to make it. Tell the children that they can choose one or more of the examples shown or try out their own design.

Paired work
● Organise the children into mixed-ability pairs and hand out photocopiable page 'Our model glider notes' from the CD-ROM and several sheets of thick paper to each child.
● Once they have made their first glider, let them test it in a designated space for flight tests, then come back to their work area to write up their notes and work on improvements.
● Prompt improvement ideas: *Would it need longer or shorter wings? Could it need some small weight (perhaps by folding the paper) on the wings? Is the length right?*
● As the children work on their gliders, walk around the room and check their understanding and questioning of how to improve their gliders.

Whole-class work
● Once the children have completed their final gliders, ask pairs to show them and discuss how they made it and what they did to improve the way it flew.
● Use the timeline to show the children that the Wright brothers took years to invent and experiment with models, kites and gliders before developing the first aeroplane.
● Once all the gliders have been completed, they can be attached to horizontal hoops and hung from the ceiling in the classroom.
● Display the children's design notes from the photocopiable sheet on a board or wall near the gliders.

Differentiation
● Support: children may need support with completing their notes; an adult or writing partner could act as scribe for the children's ideas and observations.

Review
● Before the gliders and design notes are displayed, encourage the children to show their gliders and explain its good and bad features. What would they change further if they made another model?

Week 5 lesson plans

This week looks at the famous events of the first aeroplane flight, which took place on 17 December 1903 near Kitty Hawk. In the first lesson, the children listen to an eyewitness account of what happened that day and then re-order and retell the event through pictures and captions put into a Wright-style notebook. The children also study photographs taken on the day and discuss how they help us to know what it was like to experience. In the second lesson, the children use empathy skills to create an acrostic poem about flying in an aeroplane for the first time.

1: The first flight, 1903

Introduction

- Show photographs of the Wrights' *Flyer* and remind the children that it was the first aeroplane to fly with an engine which was controlled by the pilot. Tell them that its first successful flight happened on 17 December 1903, just over 100 years ago.
- Tell the story of what happened on the day by reading part 4 of 'The Wright brothers story (2)' from the CD-ROM.
- After the story, show photographs of the flight. Explain that it was very unusual to have photographs from such a long time ago, but the Wrights and their friends knew, if the flight test was successful, it was going to be a very important event worth recording with the latest technology.
- Ask the children: *How do the photographs help us to know what happened that day?*

Paired work

- Give a copy of photocopiable page 79 'The first aeroplane flight' to each child. Working in pairs, ask the children to cut out the pictures and captions so that they can match them together and put them in the correct sequence.
- Encourage the children to retell the events to each other before they stick the pictures and captions into a mini-book that acts as a Wright brothers notebook.
- Once the mini-books are finished, let the children copy the title of the photocopiable sheet onto the front cover and draw a cover picture.
- Let the children share their books with other children and talk about what they chose to put on the cover and why.

Differentiation
- Support: children might need adult support for cutting and ordering the events.
- Challenge: children could write the captions themselves and add an extra sentence for each page.

Review

- Bring the class together and encourage volunteers to read out their notebooks. Then, with notebooks shut, challenge the children to retell the events of the day in order.
- Discuss how the Wright brothers might have felt on that day. Ask: *What do you think the local people who helped them felt as they saw the plane fly? What can we tell from the photographs taken that day?*

Lesson objectives
- To develop an awareness of the past, using common words and phrases relating to the passing of time.
- To know where people and events they study fit within a chronological framework.
- To use a wide vocabulary of everyday historical terms.
- To ask and answer questions, choosing and using parts of stories and other sources to show that they know and understand key features of events.
- To understand some of the ways in which we find out about the past.

Expected outcomes
- All children can retell the events of 17 December 1903.
- Most children understand how the photographs can show us what happened.
- Some children understand the importance of that date for aviation history.

Resources
Photocopiable page 'The Wright brothers story (2)' from the CD-ROM; photographs of the *Flyer* and the 1903 launch; photocopiable page 79 'The first aeroplane flight'; eight-page notebooks with a blank front cover; writing and colouring pencils; scissors; glue

■SCHOLASTIC
www.scholastic.co.uk

Lesson objectives
- To use a wide vocabulary of everyday historical terms.
- To ask and answer questions, choosing and using parts of stories and other sources to show that they know and understand key features of events.
- To understand some of the ways in which we find out about the past.

Expected outcomes
- All children can create a simple acrostic poem about flying.
- Most children are able to imagine flying in the air for the first time.
- Some children can imagine what the first flights might have felt like for the Wright brothers.

Resources
Film footage of the brothers' 1908 flight in France (for example, from British Pathé News); writing and colouring pencils; ICT word-processing access (optional)

2: Flying: an acrostic poem

Introduction
- Show a film clip of Orville and Wilbur Wright flying in their biplane in 1908.
- Explain that it was filmed in 1908 and that they are in a newer and better aeroplane than the 1903 version.
- Compare the differences between the newer biplane and the original *Flyer*. Ask: *What has changed? What can this aeroplane now do?*
- Discuss what it might have felt like, flying in the air in one of those first flights. Would they feel nervous, excited, free as a bird, amazed, proud?

Whole-class work
- With the children's help, begin a list on the board of words and phrases relating to the five senses. Ask questions to prompt ideas, for example: *What can you see? What can you hear? What can you smell? What can you taste? What can you touch?*
- Then begin lists of suitable movement words such as *twist, turn, glide* and *dive*, and position words such as *high, low, above, under*.
- Suggest to the children that they could create an acrostic poem about flying in the air for the first time.
- Remind the children that an acrostic poem uses the first letter of a word for the first word of each line. Write the word *flying* vertically down the board.
- Work with the class to create a shared-writing acrostic poem.

Independent work
- Set the children to start writing their own acrostic poem using the word *flying*.
- Advise them to use the wordbank on the board if they like, and encourage them to draft, read through and redraft their work.
- Once they have written their poem, let the children draw around the text with pictures to do with aeroplanes and biplanes. The poems could also be presented in a shape format, such as in a cloud above a picture of a biplane. (ICT would be useful here.)

> ### Differentiation
> - Support: children could work in small groups with adult support to use shared writing for their poem. ICT might also help children in setting down their ideas.
> - Challenge: children could write slightly longer lines to their poems or use imaginative layouts.

Review
- Invite volunteers to show and read out their poems. Note their use of appropriate 'flying' words and their empathy skills in imagining what the Wright brothers might have felt when they took these early flights.

Week 6 lesson plans

In the final week of the topic, the children review what they have learned about the Wright brothers and the first aeroplane flight. In the first lesson, they see how the first aeroplanes rapidly improved in design. In a hot-seat session, the children ask the Wright brothers about their life and flying invention. In the final lesson, the Wright brothers timeline is completed and the children design a 100th-anniversary stamp with an image they think is important or stood out for them during the topic.

1: Character recounts

Lesson objectives
- To develop an awareness of the past, using common words and phrases relating to the passing of time.
- To know where people and events they study fit within a chronological framework.
- To identify similarities and differences between ways of life in different periods.
- To use a wide vocabulary of everyday historical terms.
- To understand some of the ways in which we find out about the past.

Expected outcomes
- All children know that the Flyers improved and were redesigned as proper aeroplanes.
- Most children can ask and answer questions about the Wright brothers' lives and flight inventions.
- Some children can ask and answer in-depth questions.

Resources
Photographs of the 1903 Flyer and 1905 Flyer; film clip of the 1908 flight in France; Wright brothers timeline; date cards for the timeline: 1905 – first 'proper' aeroplane flight, 1908 – two-seater displays in Europe, 1909 – Wright Company begins manufacturing; space for hot-seat session

Introduction
- Show a photograph of the 1903 Wright brothers' Flyer. Explain that although the biplane could fly safely, it still needed development to make it a useful aeroplane that could fly a long way.
- Show the photograph of the 1905 Wright aeroplane and explain that, in October 1905, the Wright brothers managed to fly it for 25 miles. Compare this mileage with local places to help the children to understand the distance.
- Go on to say that in 1908, five years after the first flight, the Wright brothers took their aeroplane to France to show people there what it could do.
- Let volunteers put the date cards of these two events on the class timeline.

Whole-class work
- Show the film clip of the Wright brothers in France. Ask: *How has the design changed since the early aeroplanes?*
- Note the people watching in wonder and ask the children what they would feel if they saw someone flying in a machine for the first time.

Group work
- Ask the children to imagine that they are at the 1908 air display and have the chance to meet Orville and Wilbur Wright.
- Working in mixed-ability groups, ask the children to decide on a question each that they would like to ask the brothers about their life or their aeroplanes.
- Once the groups have decided on their questions, bring all the groups together.
- Pair up two groups and hold a hot-seat session with one group asking their questions to two volunteers from another group, and vice versa.
- Let the other groups listen quietly to the session before swapping the groups for another hot-seat session.

Whole-class work
- Tell the children that, at first, many people did not believe the Wright brothers' claim that they had invented a real aeroplane, but after the French trip, they became world famous.
- Note that, in 1909, the Wright brothers set up a company to build aeroplanes and train pilots. Hand over this last date card to a volunteer for putting in position on the timeline

Differentiation
- Support: adult support might be needed to help children to record their questions on paper. Or, let each child record their question orally.

Review
- Use the timeline and the photographs to encourage the children to describe the differences and similarities between the Wrights' later aeroplanes.
- Ask the children what they found out during the hot-seat sessions.

2: 100th anniversary of the first flight

Lesson objectives
● To develop an awareness of the past, using common words and phrases relating to the passing of time.
● To know where people and events they study fit within a chronological framework.
● To use a wide vocabulary of everyday historical terms.
● To choose and use parts of stories and other sources to show that they know and understand key features of events.
● To understand some of the ways in which we find out about the past.
● To identify different ways in which the past is represented.

Expected outcomes
● All children know that it is over 100 years since the first aeroplane flight.
● Most children understand why we celebrate the first aeroplane flight.
● Some children understand the importance of the achievements of Orville and Wilbur Wright.

Resources
Wright brothers timeline; date cards for the timeline: Wilbur's and Orville's deaths (1912; 1948); 100th-anniversary Wright brothers postage stamps; A4 card or thick paper; writing and colouring pencils or pens; word-processing access

Introduction
● Draw attention to the Wright brothers timeline and recount the main events with the children.
● Tell the children the dates when the Wright brothers died, and state that Orville's at least was within living memory. Invite volunteers to add the final dates to complete the timeline.
● Ask questions to judge what the children remember about the Wright brothers, such as their early days and the toy helicopter influence, the bicycles, kite designs and box kites, the gliders and their experiments at Kitty Hawk and the later biplane models.

Whole-class work
● Invite a child to find 1903 on the timeline, and ask why it is such an important date: the first flight of a heavier-than-air aeroplane.
● Elicit or explain that in 2003, it was 100 years since the *Flyer* was flown for the first time.
● Use a time reference that the children can relate to, to highlight that 2003 was just over ten years ago.
● Tell the children that many people wanted to celebrate this anniversary of the invention of the aeroplane, as it was such a significant, world-changing event and a magnificent achievement.
● Discuss how the Wrights' invention has made such a difference to the world and our lives. Ask: *What do you think life would be like without aeroplanes?*
● Suggest to the children that you would like them to design and decorate large images that could have been made into stamps for the 100th anniversary.
● Show some pictures of the 100th-anniversary Wright brothers stamps and examine how the designs are laid out.
● Go through ideas for designs with the children, such as a picture of the two brothers, the toy helicopter, a kite glider, Kitty Hawk or the *Flyer*.

Paired work or Independent work
● Organise the children to work in pairs or individually and give out drawing paper for the designs and then thick A4 paper or thin card for the final stamp pictures.
● Let the children use the computer for text, using their choice of fonts to be printed out and added to the image designs.

Whole-class work
● Once the stamps have been created, let the pairs hold up their stamp designs and explain why they chose the image and text and their importance in what the Wright brothers achieved.

Differentiation
● Support: ask prompt questions to help children with design ideas.

Review
● Invite the children to take turns choosing a date from the timeline for the rest of the class to explain the significance of the event.
● Bring the topic to an end by having a brief discussion about what the children think aircraft will be like in the distant future when they are old.

Lesson objectives
● To know where the people and events they study fit within a chronological framework.

Resources
Wright brothers information and photographs from which to create a multiple-choice quiz; interactive activity 'Ordering events of the first flight' on the CD-ROM

The first aeroplane flight

Revise
● Create a short multiple-choice quiz for the children on the Wright brothers and the first aeroplane flight using information that they have learned from their work on the topic. Include photographs as well as text-based questions.
● Organise the children into teams and ask each team a question in turn. Allow them to confer as a team to discuss their answer with each other before giving their final answer to you.
● After the quiz, discuss with the children what kind of resource they found the most useful in the topic and why; these could be photographs, diary accounts, notebooks, contemporary film footage.

Assess
● Set the children to work individually, at a computer, tablet or laptop, on interactive activity 'Ordering events of the first flight' on the CD-ROM.
● Demonstrate the interactive activity first on the whiteboard, showing the children that they need to put the events of how the Wright brothers invented the first aeroplane into chronological order.
● Demonstrate that they do this by dragging the pictures into the right places below the sentences.
● Once they have completed the task, ask the children to create their own comic-strip version of the key events leading up to and including the first flight.

Further practice
● Ask the children to create a biographical poster of the Wright brothers using pictures, mini factfiles and diagrams.
● Encourage the children to find out how the aeroplanes have developed since the Wright brothers, from 1911 to the present day, or focus on one area, such as: the biplanes of the First World War; stunt flyers of the 1920s and 1930s; or how helicopters or jet planes were invented.

Lesson objectives
● To answer questions, choosing and using parts of stories and other sources to show that they know and understand key features of events.

Resources
Interactive activity 'Y1 Spring 2 quiz' on the CD-ROM

Y1 Spring 2 quiz

Revise
● Ask children to compare the Wright Flyer with planes we have today. What has changed and what remains the same.

Assess
● Ask the children to complete interactive activity 'Y1 Spring 2 quiz' on the CD-ROM. There are ten multiple-choice questions that test what the children have learned throughout the topic. They will need to read each question carefully before choosing the correct answer.
● Give the children a set length of time (such as 15 minutes) to answer the questions. This can be used as part of a formal assessment or as a fun challenge activity, giving children the opportunity to show what they have learned about the topic.
● Less confident readers may need adult support to read the questions aloud.

Further practice
● Review any common misconceptions from the quiz. Ask the children why they consider the Wright brothers' to be important and to talk about their achievements.

■SCHOLASTIC
www.scholastic.co.uk

The toy helicopter

- Read Orville Wrights' extract.
- Write in the missing words from the wordbank.

6th June 1878

Dear Diary,

Wilbur and I have had a great day. Our _____ came back from a long trip.

He gave us a little _____ helicopter.

It has three long sticks with a rubber band on the middle one.

It has two big wings at the bottom and two small wings on the top.

To make it fly, you twist the rubber band and then let it go.

Wilbur and I are going to make a bigger _____ in our den.

Here is a picture of it.

two small w _____

two big w _____

rubber b _____

| toy | father | wings | bands | helicopter |

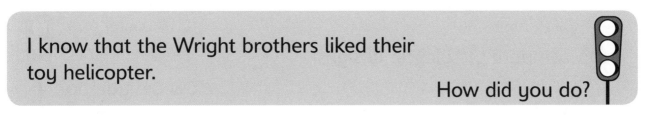

I know that the Wright brothers liked their toy helicopter.

How did you do?

SCHOLASTIC
www.scholastic.co.uk   PHOTOCOPIABLE

Comparing bicycles

■ Draw pictures of the missing bicycles in the advertisements.

A Gaskin High-wheel Bicycle

The best bicycle of 1885

Wright Cycle Company 1895 introduces a 'Van Cleve' Safety Bicycle

Have fun and be safe.

I can compare old bicycle designs.

How did you do?

PHOTOCOPIABLE   SCHOLASTIC   www.scholastic.co.uk

The first aeroplane flight

■ Cut out the pictures and captions.

■ Match them up and put them in the right order.

■ Stick them into your first-flight notebook.

The *Flyer* landed safely on the sand.	Orville got onto the *Flyer*.	Orville and Wilbur put the *Flyer* in position.
The *Flyer* flew!	The *Flyer* took off.	The photographer set up the camera.

Victorian children at play

This chapter looks at rich and poor Victorian children at play. It covers three aspects: toys and games; music; and parks and pleasure gardens. Throughout the topic, the children compare rich and poor Victorian children and their own experiences of toys, games, music and parks. Through artefacts, role play, drama, and studying visual sources of the Victorian period, the children build up a picture of how children played in the distant past and what has changed or stayed the same since. If possible, visit a local museum to see toys and games from the past and, at a Victorian park, encourage the children to draw features such as a bandstand. Check local historical societies, books, museums and newspapers for resources on local parks.

Chapter at a glance

Curriculum objectives

• Changes within living memory. Where appropriate these should be used to reveal aspects of change in national life.
• The lives of significant individuals in the past who have contributed to national and international achievements.

Week	Lesson	Summary of activities	Expected outcomes
1	1	• Children use images to find out who Queen Victoria was and when she lived. • Pairs create Victoria's family tree.	• Know who Queen Victoria was and that she lived a long time ago. • Can make Queen Victoria's family tree.
	2	• Children compare photographs of rich and poor Victorian children. • Groups link items to either a rich or poor Victorian child.	• Understand differences between rich and poor in Victorian times.
2	1	• Children investigate popular Victorian games by playing them. • They compare the games with today's games.	• Have learned how rich and poor Victorian children played by trying out some of their games.
	2	• Children find out that poor children had toys made from everyday objects and rich children had bought toys. • They make a peg doll or a jack-in-the-box.	• Can make simple Victorian toys.
3	1	• Children learn that poor children heard music all round them, including on the street. • They listen and sing along to folk songs.	• Know the sort of music poor Victorian children might have listened to and how they heard it. • Can sing some Victorian songs.
	2	• Children learn that rich families liked to sing parlour songs. • They perform the 'Grace Darling Song'.	• Know the sort of music rich Victorian children might have listened to, and how. • Can sing a popular Victorian song.
4	1	• Children use photographs to compare a Victorian park and a modern one. • They put pictures of parks in chronological order.	• Know why going to parks was popular in Victorian times. • Can compare parks from Victorian times to the present and put them in chronological order.
	2	• Children label modern and old playground equipment. • They design a new piece of playground equipment for the future.	• Can compare Victorian and present-day playgrounds.
5	1	• Children compare today's theme parks with Victorian pleasure parks. • They identify features of a pleasure park and use them to plan a new park.	• Can recognise features of a Victorian pleasure garden. • Can compare a pleasure garden with a theme park.
	2	• Groups create different features for a class model of a Victorian pleasure garden.	• Can work together to create a model of a Victorian pleasure garden.
6	1	• Children look at the features of a steam train and how cheap travel helped day trips. • They design train posters to encourage visitors to their class pleasure garden.	• Can understand that cheap train fares allowed less wealthy children to visit pleasure gardens for a treat. • Can draw a train poster to advertise a pleasure garden.
	2	• Children listen to recounts of a day trip by rich and poor Victorian children. • They create a storyboard of a day trip.	• Can listen to oral accounts of day trips to a pleasure garden. • Can create a storyboard about an outing to a pleasure garden.
Assess and review		• To review the half-term's work.	

SCHOLASTIC
www.scholastic.co.uk

Expected prior learning

● Children can see differences and similarities between life in the distant past and today.
● Children can use a range of sources to find out about the past.
● Children can ask and answer questions, choosing sources to understand similarities and differences between two elements of the same time period.

Overview of progression

● The children find out when Queen Victoria was queen and that her reign was known as the Victorian period. They create her family tree and compare and discuss artefacts and sources. They also place changes in parks since the Victorian period in a chronological framework.
● The children investigate the lives of rich and poor Victorian children by finding out about the games they played and the music they listened to. The children compare their own experiences of playgrounds and parks with those of a Victorian child.
● In this chapter, children find out more about the Victorian period by studying a wide range of photographs, plans, artefacts, music and oral accounts. In the last lessons, they are able to picture a visit to a pleasure park through the eyes of either a rich or poor Victorian child.

Creative context

● Cross-curricular links include:
  ● writing labels, captions, diary recounts, poster text, storyboards; asking and answering questions and listening to answers; giving descriptions and explanations;
  ● using mime and movement to re-create the Grace Darling story;
  ● building models for a pleasure garden and a toy with moving parts;
  ● drawing a plan of a Victorian pleasure garden and designing and making a model pleasure garden and simple old-fashioned toys; creating a poster and designing futuristic playground equipment;
  ● taking part in team games, and practising movement, balance and co-ordination;
  ● singing songs and rhymes, listening to different styles of music.

Background knowledge

● Queen Victoria came to the throne when she was 18 years old on 20 June 1837. She reigned for 63 years until her death in 1901, when she was 81. She married her cousin, Albert of Saxe-Coburg and Gotha, in 1840 and went on to have nine children – five girls and four boys. During this long period, Britain grew wealthy, thanks to the industrial revolution, and became the most powerful country in the world, with a large empire.
● **Toys and games:** poorer children often played in the streets due to cramped living conditions. Many of their toys and games were made from everyday or reused materials. Wealthy children could play in their nursery or gardens. Toys and games were specially bought or created for them. Many children at that time used role play and imaginative games.
● **Music:** poorer children would have regularly heard folk music, street chants, and music hall songs played in the streets, in bars, or within or near their homes. Most of the music would have been played on instruments such as fiddles, bagpipes, barrel organs and pipes. Wealthy children would often play or sing along to the family piano in their parlour and listen to ballads.
● **Park and pleasure gardens:** in the 1840s, in response to the terrible living conditions in the London slums, the first public park was created. This led to the creation of parks in towns and cities across the UK for all social classes. It was believed that everyone should have the opportunity to spend time in a place where they could breathe fresh air and play or walk in pleasant surroundings. In late Victorian times, pleasure gardens grew in popularity. Similar in concept to today's theme parks, they offered a range of attractions such as boating lakes, grottos, bandstands, outdoor theatre and fairground rides. People could use cheap train fares to travel to the gardens.

Week 1 lesson plans

This first week establishes when the Victorian period was and looks at differences between the lives of rich and poor Victorian children. In the first lesson, the children use their chronological skills and time vocabulary to create Victoria's family tree. In the second lesson, the children sort images that relate to either a rich or poor child and then note the differences.

1: Queen Victoria and her family

Lesson objectives
● To develop an awareness of the past, using common words and phrases relating to the passing of time.
● To know where people and events they study fit within a chronological framework.
● To use a wide vocabulary of everyday historical terms.
● To answer and ask questions, choosing stories and other sources to show that they know and understand key features of events.
● To understand some of the ways in which we find out about the past.

Expected outcomes
● All children know that Queen Victoria lived long ago.
● Most children know that Victoria's reign was called the 'Victorian period'.
● Some children can use Victoria's family tree to find out information.

Resources
Queen Victoria's coronation portrait and a photograph of her as an old woman; photograph of Victoria and her family; photocopiable page 95 'Queen Victoria's family'; interactive activity 'Create your family tree' from the CD-ROM; glue; scissors; photocopiable page 'Queen Victoria's family tree' from the CD-ROM; interactive activity 'Timeline maker' on the CD-ROM (optional)

Introduction
● For chronological support use interactive activity 'Timeline maker' on the CD-ROM to set up a simple timeline that shows major events from the Victorian period to today.
● Show a coronation portrait of Queen Victoria. Ask: *What sort of portrait is this? What is the person wearing and holding? Is she young or old? How do we know she lived long ago?* Direct the children to the old-fashioned styling of the picture and the queen's hair, for example.
● Explain that this is Queen Victoria when she was crowned queen in 1838. Highlight that she was only 18 years old at the time.
● Compare the portrait with a photograph of Victoria as an old woman. Note that she died when she was 81 years old.
● Work out together that this means Victoria was queen for 63 years. Compare that time with the ages of the children's older relatives.
● Explain that this block of time was called the Victorian period.

Whole-class work
● Show a photograph of Queen Victoria with her family. Point out Prince Albert and explain that he and Victoria married when she was 21 years old, when she was already queen.
● Encourage the class to use the picture to investigate the queen's children. Ask: *How many children are there? Which are boys and which are girls? How can we tell they lived long ago?*
● Explain that one of the best ways of seeing who is who in a family is to create a family tree. Display the interactive activity 'Create your family tree' on the CD-ROM and demonstrate its layout by inputting details of an imaginary child's family.
● Tell the children that you would like them to work in pairs to create a family tree for Queen Victoria.

Paired work
● Organise mixed-ability pairs and give each pair the cut-up pictures from photocopiable page 95 'Queen Victoria's family' (or let the children cut them out themselves) and a large printout of photocopiable page 'Queen Victoria's family tree' from the CD-ROM. Explain to the children that they need to lay out Queen Victoria's family tree.
● Walk around the class to listen to the children's discussions as they decide who goes where. Ask them about their choices. Check their work before they stick down the names on their family tree.
● Tell the children that our current monarch, Queen Elizabeth II, is the great-great-granddaughter of Queen Victoria.

Review
● Check the children's family trees and ask questions such as: *Who was eldest? Who was the youngest? Why do you think the first daughter was called Victoria?*
● Ask the children if they can remember for how long Victoria was queen, and check their understanding of the term 'Victorian period'.

2: Rich and poor Victorian children

Lesson objectives
● To develop an awareness of the past, using common words and phrases relating to the passing of time.
● To identify similarities and differences between ways of life in different periods.
● To use a wide vocabulary of everyday historical terms.
● To understand some of the ways in which we find out about the past.

Expected outcomes
● All children can identify differences between rich and poor Victorian children.
● Most children can sort different aspects of life for rich and poor Victorian children.
● Some children can recognise the large gap between the lives of rich and poor Victorian children.

Resources
Photographs of Victoria and her family; photographs of poor Victorian children; images relating to rich and poor Victorian children; photocopiable page 'Victorian childhood images' from the CD-ROM cut into individual pictures; A4 or A3 paper headed *Poor children* and *Rich children*; scissors; glue

Introduction
● Display a photograph of Queen Victoria with her children. Recap with the children who it shows and that she was queen for 63 years.
● Ask the children what we call the block of time when she was queen: the Victorian period.

Whole-class work
● Highlight that life was very different for rich children and poor children during the Victorian period, and display a photograph of poor Victorian children alongside the picture of the royal children.
● Encourage the children to examine the photographs to notice the differences between the two types of Victorian child, such as the clothing, background setting, the 'condition' of the children (health, cleanliness and grooming), and so on.

Group work
● Organise the class into mixed-ability groups of three to four children.
● Give each group the cut-out pictures from photocopiable page 'Victorian childhood images' from the CD-ROM together with additional photographs of your own choice, as well as two sheets of paper with the headings *Poor children* and *Rich children*.
● Explain to the children that you want them to work together to sort out the Victorian photographs into pictures linked to the lives of either a wealthy Victorian child or a poor Victorian child.
● Once they have agreed, ask the groups to stick the chosen pictures onto the appropriately headed sheet of paper.
● As the groups work, walk around the class and listen to the children's discussions. Ask them to explain their choices to each other and to you.

Independent work
● As an assessment activity, let the children use their sorting sheets to help them to draw pictures of a poor Victorian child and a rich Victorian child and write a simple sentence or two describing each picture.

Differentiation
● Support: use simple questioning that will encourage less-confident learners to answer more fully and help children to identify items in the photographs.
● Challenge: children could write a set of sentences about the different aspects of the lives of Victorian children.

Review
● Bring the groups together and check their sorting work. Invite the children to take turns to talk about certain items from their sheets. Encourage the rest of the class to make comparisons between similar items on different sheets.
● Give the children a little extra information about the images introducing themes such as on education and child labour, and encourage a brief class discussion about some of these areas.

Week 2 lesson plans

This week investigates the games and toys of rich and poor Victorian children. In the first lesson, the children study pictures of different children playing games and see where they were played, such as the street or garden. They then have the chance to try some Victorian games. In the second lesson, the children investigate how toys were made. They then make a peg doll or a jack-in-the-box.

I: Victorian children's games

Introduction

- Take the children to the play space and settle them down where they can see the games stations set around.
- Choose one of the old-fashioned games or toys to demonstrate, such as a spinning top or pick-up sticks, and explain that it is a toy or game that Victorian children might have played with.
- Hold up a picture of poor Victorian children playing games in the street. Encourage the class to discuss what games are being played.
- Point to the street location and ask: *Why do you think they are they playing in the street? Why would it be difficult to do that today?*
- Suggest that wealthy children would also play some of these games, but they would play in their gardens, at school or in a park.

Whole-class work

- Divide the class into groups of four children. Explain that the groups are going to try out some games played by Victorian children. At each game station, go through the game and how to use any equipment. Games and activities could include: skipping games and rhymes; hoop rolling; Noah's ark, top spinning; hopscotch; pick-up sticks; skittles; marbles; make-believe or role play with props; and games where no equipment is needed, such as 'What's the Time Mr Wolf?' or 'Oranges and Lemons'.

Group work

- Allocate a game station to each group and give them a chance to practise and play the games.
- The groups could either move from station to station or stay with one game so that they become proficient at it.

Differentiation

- Support: extra adult help will be needed to supervise some game stations such as marbles.

Review

- At the end of the lesson, ask the children to talk about their experiences and what they enjoyed about the games.
- Ask them how trying out the Victorian games helps us to understand more about how children played in the Victorian period.
- Encourage the children to compare the games they tried in the lesson with the ones they usually play today. Discuss why some of the popular Victorian games, such as rolling a hoop with a stick, have gone, but many others, such as hopscotch, rope-skipping and rhyme-based games, are still enjoyed today.
- As an extension, encourage the children to ask their older family members about games they used to play.

Lesson objectives
- To develop an awareness of the past, using common words and phrases relating to the passing of time.
- To identify similarities and differences between ways of life in different periods.
- To use a wide vocabulary of everyday historical terms.
- To understand some of the ways in which we find out about the past.

Expected outcomes
- All children can experience games played by Victorian children.
- Most children know how children played games in the Victorian period.
- Some children can identify why some games have survived and some have disappeared over the years.

Resources
Six or more games stations set up in the hall or playground with equipment such as marbles, skipping ropes, wooden skittles with ball, hoops and sticks, Noah's ark, spinning tops, pick-up sticks, hopscotch layout, a make-believe box with clothes, dolls, boxes to sit in, old bric-a-brac and toy models; two large pictures, of rich and poor Victorian children playing

■SCHOLASTIC
www.scholastic.co.uk

Lesson objectives
- To develop an awareness of the past, using common words and phrases relating to the passing of time.
- To identify similarities and differences between ways of life in different periods.
- To use a wide vocabulary of everyday historical terms.
- To ask and answer questions, choosing stories and other sources to show that they know and understand key features of events.
- To understand some of the ways in which we find out about the past.

Expected outcomes
- All children can compare the toys of rich and poor Victorian children.
- Most children understand why toys for poor children were made from everyday materials.
- Some children understand that investigating toys helps us to understand how children lived in the Victorian period.

Resources
A selection of images and replicas of Victorian toys such as such as a peg doll, kite made from sticks and paper, a clay marble, a length of rope, wool pom-pom, paper boat, football made from rags; a skipping rope with wooden handles, leather football, doll, tin soldier, jack-in-the-box, wooden yacht or train, toy theatre; materials for peg dolls: wooden pegs, bits and pieces of material, wool or embroidery thread for hair, pipe cleaners for arms (optional), felt markers, glue and scissors; materials for jack-in-the-boxes: small boxes, long paper strips for springs, card or paper for the body or face to add to spring, colouring pens

2: Making simple Victorian toys

Introduction
- Pass around examples (as replicas or in pictures) of poor Victorian children's toys, such as a peg doll, a paper kite, a clay marble, a length of rope for skipping, woollen pom-pom, paper boat, rag football. Investigate how they look and what they are made of. Explain that many of the toys were made from everyday items and cheap materials. Ask the children why this was.
- Then pass around examples of rich Victorian children's toys to investigate, such as a skipping rope with wooden handles, leather football, doll, tin soldier, jack-in the-box, wooden model yacht or train, toy theatre. Say that these were bought in shops or made especially for the children by craftspeople. Again ask why.
- Emphasise that, although the *quality* of the toys and equipment was different for rich and poor children, they still played the same games, for example, with dolls, footballs and skipping ropes.

Whole-class work
- Explain to the class that they are going to make a simple Victorian toy – a peg doll or a jack-in-the-box.
- Show the children the resources they could use to make peg dolls and how to make one. Demonstrate how they can use scraps of material and wool to make hair, hats, shoes and bags as well as clothes for a male or female figure.
- Now demonstrate how to make a simple jack-in-the box. Fold the paper strip to make a spring. Draw a face or body on the card and glue it to one end of the spring and fix the spring into the box. Remind the children that rich children often had more complex decorated wood and metal ones.

Group work
- Organise the children into the two groups to make one or the other of the toys. Make available pictures or replicas of peg dolls and jack-in the-boxes for design and construction ideas.

Whole-class work
- Bring the class together and have a show-and-tell session on how they made their toy and the ways it could be used.
- Ask: *How does finding out about Victorian toys help us to know how Victorian children lived?*
- Emphasise that children didn't have television, computers or films then, and used their imagination to play games. Discuss with the children what toys they use today to play make-believe.

Differentiation
- Challenge: children could write a display label for their toy or add extra features; they could think about how to improve their toys, such as by making a Queen Victoria peg doll with accessories or a jack-in-the-box with a turning handle.

Review
- Bring the children together. Invite volunteers to select one of the toy replicas or pictures and challenge the rest of the class to say whether it was for a rich child or a poor child. How can they tell? Ask: *Why were toys for poor children made from everyday and reused materials? How were the toys for rich children made?*

Week 3 lesson plans

This week lets the children use music and drama to find out about music that Victorian children might have listened to. The first lesson focuses on music enjoyed by poor children, including street rhymes, simple folk music and street-seller songs. The children also get a chance to role play street sellers. In the second lesson, the children act as rich Victorian children by performing a Victorian parlour song.

1: Victorian music for poor children

Lesson objectives
- To develop an awareness of the past, using common words and phrases relating to the passing of time.
- To identify similarities and differences between ways of life in different periods.
- To use a wide vocabulary of everyday historical terms.
- To ask and answer questions, choosing stories and other sources to show that they know and understand key features of events.
- To understand some of the ways in which we find out about the past.
- To identify different ways in which the past is represented.

Expected outcomes
- All children know that poor Victorian children had opportunities to listen to music.
- Most children know about some of the instruments and types of music poor Victorian children would listen to.
- Some children understand why music might have been important to poor Victorian children.

Resources
Large space for music and movement; audio player; large picture of a Victorian organ grinder; pictures of real Victorian instruments, plus audio clips (optional); selection of percussion instruments; music or recording of a folk song; media resource 'Barrel organ' and photocopiable page 'Street-sellers' calls' from the CD-ROM

Introduction
- Show the children a picture of a Victorian organ grinder along with media resource 'Barrel organ' on the CD-ROM being played for the children to listen to. Encourage the children to share their reactions.
- Explain that in the Victorian period, poor children could listen to music played in the streets, in or near their homes, or at local fairs, parks and dances.
- Show pictures or examples of real instruments that Victorian children might have heard, such as a penny whistle, bagpipes, a fiddle (violin), drum, accordion.
- If possible, let the children listen to some being played.

Whole-class work
- Have a music session to investigate different types of music that poor Victorian children might have come across.
- Warm up by singing a Victorian rhyme such as 'Here we go round the mulberry bush' or 'A sailor went to sea, sea, sea'. Ask: *Where might poor Victorian children have sung rhyme songs like these?*
- Explain that poorer families often enjoyed listening to and singing along to folk music at home or with their extended family or friends. Listen to a UK or local folk song or tune such as 'Dance to your daddy' or 'Aiken Drum'. Teach the children some or all of the lyrics so that they can sing along with it. Let them follow the beat with percussion instruments.

Group work
- Towards the end of the lesson, or in a shorter session during the week, introduce Victorian street-sellers' calls.
- Explain that in the Victorian period, children would have heard street sellers singing short songs to tell possible customers about their goods.
- Put the children into four groups and, using photocopiable page 'Street-sellers' calls' from the CD-ROM and ask each group to create a street seller song.
- Then ask all the groups to imagine they are selling their goods in Victorian times and to walk around the room singing the four songs at the same time.

Differentiation
- Support: give children more simple musical parts that they would feel happier to follow or learn.
- Challenge: children could be given more lyrics or rhymes to learn or more complex music to follow.

Review
- At the end of the lesson, ask the children how playing along with or hearing the folk songs made them feel. Discuss why music might have been important to poor children. Encourage the children to compare it with why, how and where they listen to and sing music today.

■SCHOLASTIC
www.scholastic.co.uk

2: Victorian music for rich children

Lesson objectives
● To develop an awareness of the past, using common words and phrases relating to the passing of time.
● To identify similarities and differences between ways of life in different periods.
● To use a wide vocabulary of everyday historical terms.
● To answer and ask questions, choosing stories and other sources to show that they know and understand key features of events.
● To understand some of the ways in which we find out about the past.
● To identify different ways in which the past is represented.

Expected outcomes
● All children know that rich Victorian children would listen to music in their homes.
● Most children understand that some families liked to play and sing popular songs.
● Some children know that rich Victorian children put on small performances for family and friends.

Resources
Space for music and movement; audio player; large picture of a wealthy Victorian family singing around the piano; picture of Grace Darling and story or animation of her rescue (source online from the RNLI website); audio clip and music/lyrics of 'Grace Darling Song' by Felix McGlennon; percussion instruments for sound effects (optional)

Introduction
● Remind the children of the songs they heard in the previous lesson. Explain that now they are going to find out what sort of music rich Victorian children listened and sang along to.
● Show a picture of a wealthy Victorian family singing around the piano. Ask: *What is happening? What musical instrument is being played?* Confirm that rich families often had a piano for singing and playing songs that were popular at the time.

Whole-class work
● Look at the room in the picture and explain that it was called a parlour – a room in a large house for games and entertainment. Note that the Victorians would often sing songs called parlour songs based on poems or true stories.
● Explain to the children that they are going to listen to a well-known parlour song about Grace Darling. Ask the children if they know who Grace Darling was. Show a picture and tell or show them the story of what she did.
● Let the children listen to the song and join in with the chorus of *Help! Help!*
● Now tell the children that rich Victorian children often also put on small plays at home in the parlour. Suggest that the class could create a mime performance to go with the song about Grace Darling.
● First, ask the children to find a space and imagine that they are sailing on a ship on a calm sea. Build up the sea conditions into a storm. Let the children show this in their body and facial movements. Ask them to imagine they are shipwrecked, holding onto wreckage or slippery rocks. Now ask the children to imagine they are Grace Darling and her father in a small boat rowing out against large waves.

Group work
● Move on to organising the performance. Suggestions include:
  ● Two or three groups of children performing as the song is played. Each group would consist of Grace, her father, nine people to be saved and eyewitnesses.
  ● One group acting out the mime while other children create sound effects or join in with the music and song.

Whole-class work
● After the performance, bring all the children together and remind them that a little play like this was a popular pastime in wealthy families.
● Encourage the children to compare the different musical experiences of rich and poor Victorian children.

> **Differentiation**
> ● Support: extra adult support might be needed to help children to focus on their roles in the mime or accompaniment activities; allocate mixed-ability groups where possible.

Review
● Encourage the children to compare the differences from how we experience music that is popular today, such as listening to the radio, mp3 players, iPods or smartphones or watching videos on television or computer.
● Highlight the similarities too, such as performing songs and dances to their families or friends, singing along to recorded and live music and learning to play a musical instrument.

Lesson objectives
● To develop an awareness of the past, using common words and phrases relating to the passing of time.
● To know where people and events they study fit within a chronological framework.
● To identify similarities and differences between ways of life in different periods.
● To use a wide vocabulary of everyday historical terms.
● To understand some of the ways in which we find out about the past.

Expected outcomes
● All children know that rich and poor Victorian children played in parks.
● Most children can see the differences between a Victorian park and a present-day park.
● Some children can put pictures of parks into chronological order and explain their reasons.

Resources
A picture of a Victorian park with children playing; a recent photograph of a local park; photocopiable page 96, 'Parks over time'; scissors; glue; timeline from Victorian era to today

Week 4 lesson plans

In this week, the children start their study on Victorian parks. In the first lesson, the children use their sequencing skills by placing photographs of parks in the right chronological order. In the second lesson, the children investigate visual sources to learn and use vocabulary describing old playground equipment. They are encouraged to talk to older family members about their memories of playground equipment. (Local historical societies, museums or newspapers may have a photograph archive which shows the changes of a local park. Look particularly for ones that show old heavy playground equipment.)

I: Parks over time

Introduction
● Display a large picture of a Victorian park with children playing in it. Explain to the class that, in the Victorian period, many public parks were created where both rich and poor children could play and have fun.
● Draw out details from the photograph by asking questions such as: *What are the children wearing? What are they doing? Can you see any toys or games? How do we know that the children lived long ago?*

Whole-class work
● Now show the children a recent photograph of a local park that they might know. Allow them to talk about their experience of it, and then compare it with the Victorian park in the other photograph.
● Identify any similar features, such as flower beds, paths and green grass, a pond and a play area.
● Discuss the features that are significantly different, such as the children's clothes, newer (and possibly more) playground equipment, tennis courts, skate-park area, and so on.
● Note that both parks provide space and equipment that children wouldn't have at home, so allowing them to have exercise, fresh air and different kinds of play in a relatively safe environment.

Paired work
● Put the children into pairs and give each child photocopiable page 96 'Parks over time'.
● Working in their pairs, encourage the children to identify and talk about the features of each park to show whether they are older or newer.
● Let the children cut out the pictures of the parks and put them into chronological order.
● Check the children's understanding as they work and ask them to explain why they have arranged the park pictures in that chronological order.
● Let the children stick their pictures onto paper or in their workbooks in the correct sequence.

> **Differentiation**
> ● Support: extra adult support might be needed for scissor use; help children to compare the parks by prompting them with open questions.
> ● Challenge: children might be able to write dates and captions under the pictures.

Review
● At the end of the lesson, bring the class together and ask the children to help you place the park pictures on your timeline (Victorian, 1960s, today). Encourage the children to volunteer the reasons.

SCHOLASTIC
www.scholastic.co.uk

Lesson objectives
● To develop an awareness of the past, using common words and phrases relating to the passing of time.
● To identify similarities and differences between ways of life in different periods.
● To use a wide vocabulary of everyday historical terms.
● To ask and answer questions, choosing and using parts of stories and other sources to show that they know and understand key features of events.
● To understand some of the ways in which we find out about the past.

Expected outcomes
● All children know that Victorian children played on play equipment in parks.
● Most children can compare old and modern playground equipment.
● Some children understand why some Victorian playground equipment is no longer used.

Resources
Photograph of a local playground; cards for labels (or whiteboard ICT); labels for the poster (on whiteboard or cards); photocopiable page 'My favourite playground equipment' from the CD-ROM; drawing and writing pencils

2: Playground equipment then and now

Introduction
● Display on the board a modern photograph of a local park showing the playground equipment. Ask the children to help you label the equipment with, for example, *slide, swings, roundabout, see-saw, climbing frame, monkey bars, sandpit, trampoline, balance beam, tunnel, football goal, basketball hoop, zip wire*.
● Point to one piece of the playground equipment, such as the slide, and ask the children what it is and how they would play on it or with it.
● Write a label and let a child come out to put the label by the piece of equipment.
● Continue with all the playground equipment you can see.

Whole-class work
● Show pictures of a Victorian playground (in a park): showing as much different play equipment as possible, for example, slide, swing, merry-go-round, maypole, roundabout, rocking horse, see-saw, climbing frame. Ask the children to help you attach labels to the equipment in the picture.
● Encourage the children to discuss how each piece of equipment is being used in the picture. Ask: *Which one would you like to play on or in? Why?*
● Ask the children to compare the playground equipment with today's equipment, such as steep metal steps to the slides compared with rubberised steps with hand ropes or a slide built into a mound of earth; wobbly wooden see-saws versus plastic solid see-saws; unprotected ground compared with soft surfaces. Ask: *Why do you think they have changed?* (Note, for example, how metal could heat up on slides or can have sharp edges.)
● Ask: *What items of playground equipment are not in parks any more. Why?*
● Emphasise that playground equipment has been improved so that it is safer to play on.

Independent work
● Hand out a copy of photocopiable page 'My favourite playground equipment' from the CD-ROM to each child. Make sure the labelled displays of the old and new playgrounds can still be seen by all the children.
● Invite the children to draw their favourite piece of playground equipment from the Victorian and modern playgrounds and write simple sentences about why they like them.
● They can then draw a picture of a piece of playground equipment for the future and write a brief description of what it is.

Whole-class work
● At the end of the lesson, ask the children to share their choices and their futuristic piece of playground equipment.
● As an extension, encourage the children to ask older family members about their memories of playgrounds when they were young and let them report back to the class.

Differentiation
● Support: children might need writing support with their simple sentences; if necessary, act as a scribe, either straight onto the photocopiable sheet or to be copied by the children.
● Challenge: children could add more detailed labels or captions to show how their futuristic play equipment would be used.

Review
● Select one or two comparable examples of Victorian and modern play equipment, such as a climbing frame, and invite the children to compare the two. Note those who use appropriate historical vocabulary here and in their captions and sentences on the photocopiable sheet.

Week 5 lesson plans

This week looks at the popularity of pleasure gardens, which all classes of Victorian children were able to enjoy. The lessons make comparisons with today's theme parks. In the first lesson, the children investigate features and attractions of a typical pleasure garden and use this to create a plan of their own pleasure garden. Then, they create a class model of a Victorian pleasure garden. For a local focus, find out where your nearest Victorian pleasure park or garden is or used to be (many became housing or industrial estates) and try to find resources that show it in its heyday.

1: Features of a Victorian pleasure garden

Lesson objectives
● To develop an awareness of the past, using common words and phrases relating to the passing of time.
● To identify similarities and differences between ways of life in different periods.
● To use a wide vocabulary of everyday historical terms.
● To ask and answer questions, choosing and using parts of stories and other sources to show that they know and understand key features of events.
● To understand some of the ways in which we find out about the past.

Expected outcomes
● All children know that Victorian pleasure gardens were popular for rich and poor families.
● Most children recognise the main features of a Victorian pleasure garden.
● Some children can identify why certain features were popular.

Resources
Photograph of a Victorian pleasure garden; modern photograph of a UK theme park; individual photographs of pleasure park features or enlarged copies of the features from photocopiable page 97 'A plan of a Victorian pleasure garden', plus a copy of the sheet per pair of children; scissors; glue; colouring pencils

Introduction
● Show a recent photograph of a modern-day UK theme park and establish what it is. Encourage the children to talk about their own experiences of theme parks.
● Explain that, in the Victorian period, pleasure gardens were just as popular as theme parks today, with both rich and poor families. Display a photograph of a Victorian pleasure garden. Elicit what the word *pleasure* means.
● Encourage the children to investigate the photograph to find out what the people are doing, where they might be and how we can tell the picture was taken a long time ago. If the photograph is of a local pleasure park, say where it is or where it once was.

Whole-class work
● Explain to the children that they are going to investigate the different features of and activities that people could do in a Victorian pleasure garden.
● Show the children a range of photographs to investigate the different features, such as a bandstand, boating lake, ornate gardens with a fountain, maze, grotto, stage, tea and cake shop, and ask questions to help the children decide what they were and why Victorian children and their families would enjoy them. Would they be fun to walk in or run around? Would people be able to do different things from life at home?

Paired work
● Put the children into mixed-ability pairs and hand out a copy of photocopiable page 97 'A plan of a Victorian pleasure garden', to each pair.
● Ask the children to imagine that they lived in the Victorian period and have been asked to design a plan for a new pleasure garden for their town or city (or nearest town).
● Explain that they need to decide which features they want to include in the park and where to put them.
● Check the children's understanding as they work and ask them to explain why they have placed the different features in their chosen places.

Differentiation
● Support: mixed-ability pairs should provide support for the photocopiable activity, although adult help might be needed with cutting.
● Challenge: ask children to think of another feature for the garden, such as a miniature castle or tower or a magic wood.

Review
● Encourage the children to share their plans with the class and to explain their choices of attractions and sites.
● Ask: *Do you think the pleasure parks from long ago were like the ones we have today? Why? What can we tell about Victorian pastimes from the photographs we have looked at?*

■SCHOLASTIC
www.scholastic.co.uk

Lesson objectives
● To develop an awareness of the past, using common words and phrases relating to the passing of time.
● To use a wide vocabulary of everyday historical terms.
● To ask and answer questions, choosing and using parts of stories and other sources to show that they know and understand key features of events.
● To understand some of the ways in which we find out about the past.

Expected outcomes
● All children can create and name a main feature from a Victorian pleasure garden.
● Most children know why their Victorian pleasure garden feature was popular.
● Some children can use their knowledge to create and discuss a class Victorian pleasure garden.

Resources
The children's garden plans; a variety of pictures of Victorian pleasure gardens and their features; a large base board for the model; modelling materials, such as paints, pens, green net and moss, air-drying clay, shells, pebbles, shiny blue paper, fabric, tissue paper, crêpe paper, straws, round tins or card boxes (such as cheese triangle boxes), pipe cleaners, wooden sticks and strips, card; scissors; glue; adhesive tape

2: A Victorian pleasure garden model

Introduction
● Explain to the children that they are going to make a class model of a Victorian pleasure garden.
● Display a selection of photographs and the children's plans from the last lesson to revise the different features that could be included on the model. Discuss what these features might be: for example, a bandstand, boating lake, a miniature hedge maze, a tea shop, grotto, animal and/or dinosaur models, flower beds, a fountain, rockery, statue, outdoor stage, a playground area with a slide, swings and other play equipment. Agree on choices appropriate to the number of groups in the class.
● Show the children the base for the model and explain that they will be working in groups to make the different features to go on the base.

Group work
● Organise the children into small mixed-ability groups and give them a feature to work on. Make sure pictorial references are available for all the groups.
● Either as a whole class or in individual groups, show the children ways of creating their feature and the materials they could use to create it. Ideas could include:
  ● base – painting it green and making the fence and special gates;
  ● bandstand – made from a round tin or card base, round card floor, sticks or straws for pillars, round top, cone roof;
  ● hedge maze – Draw and put glue on the shape and fill it in with green net, moss or clay;
  ● grotto – clay shape cave decorated with items such as small shells and sparkling stones;
  ● boating lake – shiny blue paper with small boats made from clay or card.
  ● animal or dinosaur models – made from clay;
  ● formal garden – green fabric, paint, crêpe or tissue paper for the flower bed; small shrubs made from wool or moss;
  ● playground equipment – made from strips of wood, string, straws, wooden sticks, card;
  ● tea shop – small open-sided box with a crenelated or sloping roof.

Whole-class work
● When the features have been created, encourage the children to refer to their garden plans and work as a class to decide where they should be placed on the base.
● Then help them to decide what their pleasure garden should be called. Tell them that many gardens like this were called Victoria Park or Victoria Gardens. Ask the children why they think that was.
● In other sessions, let volunteers add models of Victorian children and adults and use the model for comparison skills and imaginative play.

Differentiation
● Support: extra adult support would be helpful as groups create their models and need assistance with cutting, sticking and choosing materials and putting different aspects of the features together.
● Challenge: some children could be given more complicated or more imaginative tasks to do in the model making.

Review
● Review and talk about the finished model. Note in the discussion the use of the correct vocabulary of Victorian pleasure garden features. Assess the children's awareness that the model is of a pleasure garden from the past, not a modern-day theme park.

Week 6 lesson plans

In the final week of the topic, the children learn how Victorian families were able to visit pleasure gardens far from their homes. The children use their knowledge and empathy skills to imagine they are a Victorian child visiting a garden. In the first lesson, they learn about railways in order to understand how trains allowed rich and poor families to visit the gardens. In the last lesson, the children use oral and visual sources to help them to create a simple recount of a day trip to a pleasure garden.

1: Pleasure gardens and the railway

Introduction
● Ask the children how they have travelled when they have visited parks and theme parks. Show a picture of a car and agree that most people travel to theme parks by car.
● Ask the children to think about how Victorian children travelled to the pleasure gardens before we had cars. Show a picture of a Victorian train to confirm understanding.

Whole-class work
● Look at photographs or footage of trains in the 1900s. Discuss what the trains look like. Help the children to explain in simple terms how the steam engine works. Clarify the use of coal, which is burned to heat water and to make steam (reference to how a kettle works might be useful).
● Tell the children how the building of railways across the country allowed many people, both rich and poor, to go on day trips to places such as the seaside and the pleasure gardens. Explain that groups such as clubs, Sunday school groups and extended families would get together and enjoy themselves for the day.
● Discuss that most people did not have much money to spend on leisure activities and were not paid if they took time off work to go on holiday, but a train journey for an outing was relatively cheap.
● Show the children examples of old-fashioned train posters advertising day trips.
● Look at the features, such as the bright colours, large lettering and the picture of the destination.

Group work
● Ask the children to design their own train poster to encourage people to come to their class Victorian pleasure garden.
● With the children, decide on the text for the poster and write it on the board for spelling support.
● Give out paper for design ideas and then the poster paper for the final drawing. Children can write out the poster text in their own hand or use the computer.

> **Differentiation**
> ● Support: help children to formulate and put down their ideas for their posters; use open questions to help children to clarify their thoughts.
> ● Challenge: children might be able to create a logo to go on the poster.

Review
● Ask some children to show their posters to the rest of the class and to explain why they have chosen to use particular images or text.

Lesson objectives
● To develop an awareness of the past, using common words and phrases relating to the passing of time.
● To identify similarities and differences between ways of life in different periods.
● To use a wide vocabulary of everyday historical terms.
● To ask and answer questions, choosing and using parts of stories and other sources to show that they know and understand key features of events.
● To understand some of the ways in which we find out about the past.
● To identify different ways in which the past is represented.

Expected outcomes
● All children understand how train travel let Victorian families visit pleasure gardens.
● Most children understand how steam trains worked.
● Some children understand how Victorian train companies encouraged visitors to visit pleasure gardens.

Resources
Photographs and film clips of old steam trains; photograph of a (modern) car; old railway advertising posters; poster paper; sketch paper; drawing and colouring pens and pencils; ICT access; the class model of a pleasure garden

■SCHOLASTIC
www.scholastic.co.uk

2: A day trip to a pleasure garden

Introduction

- Show one or two photographs of Victorian children enjoying themselves at a pleasure garden from the past.
- Explain to the children that you are going to read to them diary recounts of a day trip to a pleasure garden experienced by a poor child and a rich child who lived in the Victorian period.

Whole-class work

- Show the photocopiable pages 'Day trips to a pleasure garden' from the CD-ROM and read the first diary recount from the poor Victorian child. Discuss it with the class. Ask questions such as: *Why did Annie go to the pleasure garden? How did she get there? What did she do when she got there? What did she enjoy the most? Did she like her day trip?*
- Read the second recount, from the wealthy Victorian child, and discuss it with the class, asking similar questions.
- Compare the two recounts. What was different about them? What was similar?
- Now ask the children to imagine that they are either a poor or rich Victorian child visiting a pleasure garden.
- Tell them that you would like them to write a simple storyboard recount.
- Draw their attention back to the recounts from the photocopiable sheet, and use sentence and time-word starters to model orally and then in writing your own recount, for example: *Today, First, Then, Next, After that, In the end, It was fun to... because...*

Paired work or Independent work

- Organise the children into pairs and let them work together to create an oral recount of their day.
- Then give each child some paper to make an eight-section storyboard of their day trip. Support the children as they write simple sentences using the recount framework under each storyboard picture.

Whole-class work

- At the end of the lesson, let volunteers show their storyboards and use them to recount their day trip. Note those who make good use of historical vocabulary and create a believable story of the day. Invite the rest of the class to say whether each recount is from a poor child or a rich child. How can they tell?
- Continue this to compare recounts by poor children and rich children.

Differentiation
- Support: children might need help in putting their ideas of the events into chronological order and to draw their images or write their sentences.
- Challenge: encourage some children to write more sentences for each storyboard cell.

Review

- Discuss the topic and ask the children what they have learned about how poor and rich Victorian children played.
- Encourage the children to discuss how they play today. Ask them: *What has changed and what is similar to the way children played long ago?*

Lesson objectives
- To develop an awareness of the past, using common words and phrases relating to the passing of time.
- To identify similarities and differences between ways of life in different periods.
- To use a wide vocabulary of everyday historical terms.
- To ask and answer questions, choosing and using parts of stories and other sources to show that they know and understand key features of events.
- To understand some of the ways in which we find out about the past.

Expected outcomes
- All children can give simple recounts of a day trip to a Victorian pleasure garden.
- Most children can draw and write a recount of a day trip to Victorian pleasure garden.
- Some children can use their knowledge and learned vocabulary to create a recount as a Victorian child.

Resources
Photographs of Victorian children at or travelling to a pleasure park; photocopiable pages 'Day trips to a pleasure garden' from the CD-ROM; paper; drawing pencils

Lesson objectives
● To identify similarities and differences between ways of life in different periods.

Resources
Photograph of Queen Victoria; variety of resources relating to the three main areas of the topic – toys, music, parks and pleasure gardens; photocopiable page 'Comparing Victorian play and present-day play' from the CD-ROM; note-paper; drawing pencils

Victorian children at play

Revise

● Show the children the photograph of Queen Victoria and ask the children who she is and what we call the block of time when she was queen: the Victorian period.
● Organise the children into six groups and give them one aspect of the three areas of the topic that they have studied to focus on: toys for rich children, toys for poor children, music for poor children, music for rich children, parks and pleasure gardens (two groups).
● Give them resources such as pictures, artefacts, photographs, books and their own work to prompt discussion within their groups on what they have learned about that particular subject. Encourage the groups to nominate a scribe to take notes during their discussion.
● Ask the groups to report back to the rest of the class about what they have remembered and learned. Encourage them to use their resources as visual aids during their report.
● Encourage all of the children to discuss what they enjoyed most about the topic of Victorian children at play, and why.

Assess

● Hand out a copy of photocopiable page 'Comparing Victorian play and present-day play' from the CD-ROM to each child.
● Let the children draw an example of what they have learned from each of the three main topic areas in one section.
● Next, they can draw their present-day experience of the same type of play.
● They could, for example, show children at play or be more specific and draw items such as a Victorian toy or a piece of Victorian park equipment.
● They can then complete the simple captions underneath their pictures.
● Afterwards, encourage the children to discuss their examples and explain why they chose them.

Further practice

● Encourage the children to focus on one of the areas covered in the topic and go into it in more depth using craft, role play, non-fiction accounts and storytelling.
● The children could also listen to oral accounts of play in the recent past and invite members of the older generation to discuss their memories of toys, music and parks.

Lesson objectives
● To answer questions, choosing and using parts of stories and other sources to show that they know and understand key features of events.

Resources
Interactive activity 'Y1 Summer 1 quiz' on the CD-ROM

Y1 Summer 1 quiz

Revise

● Ask children if they can remember the features of a Victorian pleasure garden. List on the board.

Assess

● Ask the children to complete interactive activity 'Y1 Summer 1 quiz' on the CD-ROM. There are ten multiple-choice questions that test what the children have learned throughout the topic. They will need to read each question carefully before choosing the correct answer.
● Give the children a set length of time to answer the questions. This can be used as part of a formal assessment or as a fun challenge activity.

Further practice

● Review any common misconceptions from the quiz. Establish that children understand some of the differences between the lives of poor and rich children living in the Victorian era.

■SCHOLASTIC
www.scholastic.co.uk

Queen Victoria's family

■ Cut out the picture cards and add them to the sheet 'Queen Victoria's family tree'.

Queen Victoria, born 1819	Prince Albert, born 1819

Princess Victoria born 1840	Prince Albert born 1841	Princess Alice, born 1843
Prince Alfred, born 1844	Princess Helena, born 1846	Princess Louisa, born 1848
Prince Arthur, born 1850	Prince Leopold, born 1853	Princess Beatrice, born 1857

Name: _____   Date: _____

Parks over time

■ Cut out the pictures of the parks and put them in order, with the oldest first and the newest last.

I can put parks into chronological order.

How did you do?

PHOTOCOPIABLE

SCHOLASTIC
www.scholastic.co.uk

A plan of a Victorian pleasure garden

■ Cut out the Victorian pleasure garden features at the bottom of the page.

■ Add all or some of them to your plan.

Maze	Bandstand	Boating lake	Playground
Grotto	Flowerbed	Tea shop	Fountain

Our heritage: folk stories and castles

This chapter gives the children the chance to explore their national and local heritage through a range of folk stories and castles. The children listen to folk stories about the emblems of the four UK countries. The children then move on to national folk stories based on real people from the past, followed by a folk story with a local link. The chapter then focuses on castles. Once the children are aware of the many castles in the UK, they learn about their uses as a defence and home, and put examples in chronological order. Through labelling and making model castles they learn about the defensive features, and use drama and role play to investigate the lives of castle inhabitants. (To enhance the topic, try to arrange a visit by a storyteller and a trip to a nearby castle.)

Chapter at a glance

Curriculum objectives
• Events beyond living memory that are significant nationally and globally. • Significant historical events, people and places in their own locality.

Week	Lesson	Summary of activities	Expected outcomes
1	1	• Children locate the four UK countries and their school on a map. • They find out what an emblem means and hear about the emblems of the UK.	• Can understand the term 'United Kingdom' and can locate the four countries on a map. • Know the four historic symbols of the UK. • Recognise the origins of the emblems.
	2	• Children choose a local feature to create their own emblem flag design.	• Can create an emblem to represent an important aspect of their local area.
2	1	• Children learn about the oral tradition. • They demonstrate how stories are passed down over hundreds of years. • They learn about Robert the Bruce.	• Learn about the tradition of oral storytelling. • Understand that although some folk tales are about real people, they might not be true.
	2	• Children learn that folk stories had messages. • They write a story message and make a spiderweb plate to display it.	• Understand that in the past many folk tales gave listeners important messages for their lives.
3	1	• Children listen to the story about King Alfred and the burned cakes. • They put pictures of the story in order, choosing an ending. • The class creates an oral story.	• Can listen to a story about a real person from long ago. • Understand that old stories change over the years and that it is hard to know the real truth.
	2	• Children listen to a local folk tale then make it into a class performance.	• Can perform a local folk story.
4	1	• Children look at different UK castles. • They play a memory game with castle cards.	• Know that there are many castles in the UK. • Know that castles in the past were often used for defence and as a family home.
	2	• Children sort pictures of castles into chronological order of when they were built.	• Can put castles from different historical periods into chronological order.
5	1	• Children learn and use the vocabulary castle features. • They add the words to a large picture of a castle.	• Can learn the words for features of a castle and identify what the features' functions.
	2	• Groups make model castles and discuss defensive features.	• Can use their knowledge to make labelled models of castles.
6	1	• Children learn about the different people living in a castle.	• Learn about the different people who worked in a castle long ago.
	2	• Children learn about the Great Hall in a castle and role play an event in a Great Hall.	• Can show their understanding of life in a castle long ago. • Learn about the Great Hall of a castle.
Assess and review		• To review the half-term's work.	

■SCHOLASTIC
www.scholastic.co.uk

Expected prior learning
● Children can ask and answer questions about the past using a range of sources.
● Children can use stories or sources to find out more about past events.
● Children should know that the past can be represented in different ways.

Overview of progression
● The children should be able to understand that the folk stories and castles studied here are from long ago in the distant past, not in living memory. During the folk story focus, the children explain how folk stories are passed down through generations. Then they order castles from different periods.
● The children find out that folk tales were an important entertainment in the past and compare them with their own entertainment. They discuss differences between the use of castles in the past and today. Through discussion and drama they compare the lives of lords and ladies of a castle with the lives of the people who worked there.
● While listening to folk tales, the children deduce why people did things, and see certain things – such as plants or places – in special ways. They learn to extract parts of stories to work out if they are true or not, what messages they send out, how people lived in the past and to gauge the importance of events or historic figures. They use detective skills in studying pictures and models to find out the main uses of a medieval castle.
● The children will already have an understanding of how the past can be represented in different ways. They will learn that, although folk tales can teach us a lot about the past, they might not be totally true.

Creative context
● Cross-curricular links include:
  ● using comprehension skills, writing simple sentences, labels and captions and using a wider vocabulary; speaking and listening and role playing;
  ● naming, locating and identifying the countries of the UK;
  ● drawing emblem designs to represent their local area, making castle parts for a model, drawing castles, illustrating a folk-tale scene and making props for a folk-tale re-enactment;
  ● being aware of the local community and the differences and similarities between each other.

Background knowledge
● **Robert the Bruce (1274–1329):** in 1306, Robert the Bruce was crowned King of Scotland. However, Edward I of England saw this as an uprising. The English army marched to Scotland and all of Robert the Bruce's family were imprisoned or killed. Bruce escaped and hid in the west-coast islands and Ireland. It is during this time that the tale about the spider in a cave is believed to have taken place. Later, Bruce returned and continued the fight against the English until the Battle of Bannockburn in 1314, when he and his supporters finally defeated the English army. The story of the spider was first written down by Sir Walter Scott in *Tales of a Grandfather* in 1828. There is no proof that the story is true, but it has been passed on for centuries.
● **Alfred the Great (849–899):** Alfred was the Anglo-Saxon King of Wessex. In 878, Vikings led a surprise and violent attack on Wessex. Alfred escaped into the Somerset tidal marshes where he planned his successful defeat of the Vikings. The story of the burned cakes is believed to have come from then. The 'moral' was that Alfred realised he had to concentrate on the job in hand. The story was first written down in the early 12th century.
● **Castles:** early Norman motte-and-bailey castles were built mainly for defence and were surrounded by a ditch or a moat. The tall keep was built on top of a small mound. In the late Middle Ages, castles continued to be important for defence, but were also homes. Later, Tudor castles were built more as grand houses with larger windows, bigger living quarters and ornate gardens. The Great Hall would have been used for banquets. It was the focal point of the castle and was often elaborately decorated.

Week 1 lesson plans

In this first week, the children learn which four countries make up the United Kingdom and which of these countries they live in. In this first lesson, they are introduced to the idea that each of the countries has its own identity through traditions, famous places and people and emblems. The children investigate why the emblem for their own country was chosen, after listening to a story about its possible origins. They understand that these stories are from very long ago and have changed over the years, so they might not be true. They show their understanding of what an emblem stands for by drawing one to represent their school or local area.

Lesson objectives
● To develop an awareness of the past, using common words and phrases relating to the passing of time.
● To use a wide vocabulary of everyday historical terms.
● To ask and answer questions, choosing and using parts of stories and other sources to show they know and understand key feature of events.
● To understand some of the ways in which we find out about the past.

Expected outcomes
● All children know that the four UK countries have their own special emblems.
● Most children understand that the UK emblems have a meaning linked to a past event.
● Some children understand that a story about the origins of an emblem might have changed over time.

Resources
UK map; card labels for each country and the location of the school; large pictures of the plant emblems – leek, rose, thistle, shamrock; the actual plants (optional); photocopiable page 113 'Our UK emblems'; photocopiable page 'Stories of the four emblems' from the CD-ROM; scissors; glue; writing and colouring pencils

1: Four UK emblems

Introduction
● Display the map and elicit that it shows the country in which they live.
● Point to the four countries on the map and read out each name label. Explain that the four small countries together become the United Kingdom.
● Help the children to work out where the school is on the map, and add the label. Ask: *Is our school in England, Scotland, Wales or Northern Ireland?*
● Let the children share their experiences of visiting parts of the UK.

Whole-class work
● Show a large image or the actual object of your specific country's emblem and introduce it as a special emblem.
● Explain what *emblem* means. Discuss with the children where and when they may have seen their emblem, such as on a sport shirt, a flag or a coin.
● Say that some emblems are linked to an event that might have happened long ago.
● Ask the children to listen to a short story to help them to work out why their object was chosen as an emblem. Use photocopiable page 'Stories of the four emblems' from the CD-ROM to read out the specific story linked to your emblem.
● Ask: *Do you think the story is true?* Highlight that the story might not have been quite true in the first place and has been retold over hundreds of years so it is hard to know exactly what happened.
● Ask: *Why do you think this emblem has been chosen?*
● Show the other UK emblems and briefly discuss their features, such as their colours and design. Note that they are all natural living items.

Independent work
● Give each child a copy of photocopiable page 113 'Our UK emblems'. Ask the children to cut out the four UK country names and stick them under the right emblem.
● They should then complete a short sentence to say which is the emblem for their country.
● Encourage the children to colour the emblems in the right colours – red rose, green and white leek, purple thistle and green shamrock.
● Bring the children together and read about the other UK emblems.

Differentiation
● Support: children might need support with cutting out and with writing the short sentence.
● Challenge: children could write an extra sentence to suggest why the emblem was chosen for the country.

Review
● Go through the photocopiable sheet to check the children's knowledge of the four UK emblems and why they have been adopted.

2: A local emblem flag

Introduction

● Show the children the display of UK emblems, such as plants and flowers, dragons and animals. As well as the national symbols, you could include regional ones, such as the white rose for Yorkshire and the three-legged symbol for the Isle of Man.
● Remind the children what an emblem is and discuss the reasons why the emblems might have been chosen for the different UK countries, towns or counties (depending on your display).
● If possible, show a local emblem that is familiar to the children, such as that of their school or a famous sports team's emblem.

Whole-class work

● Challenge the children to design an emblem of a specific local area. This could be your choice or the children's choice, such as the school or town. Explain that it is to be drawn onto flag shapes.
● Point to the display board and show how the emblems are very simple and show only one or two objects and tend to use bright colours, such as blue for sea or green for an oak tree.
● Talk about possible local features the children could draw as their emblem, such as a well-known local building, a natural feature such as the sea or a river, a bird, animal or insect, a plant or flower, an object to represent a person from the past or a past event such as an arrow, hat, pen, fossil, bonfire or an aeroplane.
● Help all the children to decide on the emblems for their own flags.

Independent work

● Give out the flag shapes and pencils to each child. Have as many picture resources of the inspirational places or objects as possible available to help the children with their drawings.
● Allow plenty of time for the children to create their flag designs. Encourage the children to consider if they are happy with their emblem or if they need to make any changes.
● Once they are satisfied with their design, they can colour it in.

> ### Differentiation
> ● Support: assist children with representing their idea as a simple design.
> ● Challenge: children could draft on a design sheet with labels and captions to explain their ideas.

Review

● When all the flags have been completed, attach them to dowel or stick 'flagpoles'. Ask volunteers to show and wave their flags to the class and explain the meaning of their emblem.
● Display the finished flags, with the children's names on the reverse, pushed into a pot or 'hill' of air-drying clay.
● Note how each different emblem shows a certain important aspect of or idea about their local area. Ask the children: *What emblem have you drawn on your flag? Why have you chosen it?*

Lesson objectives
● To develop an awareness of the past, using common words and phrases relating to the passing of time.
● To use a wide vocabulary of everyday historical terms.
● To understand some of the ways in which we find out about the past.

Expected outcomes
● All children can draw an emblem to represent something in their local area.
● Most children understand the importance of their local emblem design.
● Some children know that their emblem would help others to understand the importance of a place, person or event in their locality.

Resources
Display board showing images of UK emblems around a UK map; images and information of UK emblems; example of a local emblem; paper and card flag shapes; colouring pencils and pens; images for emblem ideas such as significant local places, events, people, natural features, animals and plants; flagpole dowels or sticks

Week 2 lesson plans

Here the children learn about the oral traditions of storytelling. First, they discover why listening to folk tales was a popular form of entertainment in the past and how the stories would be passed down. In the first lesson, the children listen to the Scottish folk tale about Robert the Bruce and the spider and they discuss how much of the story could be true. In the second lesson, the children use the same tale to look at folk-story messages. They create spiderweb plates with their favourite messages.

1: Robert the Bruce and the spider

Lesson objectives
● To develop an awareness of the past, using common words and phrases relating to the passing of time.
● To use a wide vocabulary of everyday historical terms.
● To ask and answer questions, choosing and using parts of stories and other sources to show that they know and understand key features of events.
● To understand some of the ways in which we find out about the past.
● To identify different ways in which the past is represented.

Expected outcomes
● All children understand that folk tales have been told for many years.
● Most children understand that folk tales are retold over generations.
● Some children understand that folk tales about real people from the past might not be totally true.

Resources
A storytelling corner; a picture of a storyteller and his or her audience; photocopiable page 'Two UK folk tales (1)' from the CD-ROM; picture of Robert the Bruce (optional); paper; drawing and colouring pencils

Introduction
● Before the lesson, create a story corner. Leave out picture books, put up pictures and record a selection of folk tales for the children to listen to.
● Then introduce the storytelling corner and show the children the picture of a storyteller. Note the people listening attentively. Highlight that the storyteller was very skilled at bringing the stories to life for his audience.
● Explain that, long ago, listening to stories about people, places and events from their country or area was a very popular form of entertainment.
● Ask the children what they do before they go to bed. Do they like listening to bedtime stories too? Highlight that, in the past, there were no televisions; and books were rare, so the storytellers remembered the stories.

Whole-class work
● Organise the children to help demonstrate how many of the old rhymes and stories have come to still be told today. Ask five children to sit in a row from left (long ago) to right (now).
● Explain that this is one family that goes back to Victorian times. From the child on the right, go back through the line, saying who each child is: *This is Joel. This is Joel's mum. This Joel's grandfather...*
● Ask the child who is the great-great-grandparent to stand up. Tell the children that s/he was born many years ago when Queen Victoria became queen. Explain that when he grew up and had a child (point to the next child) he told them a rhyme he had learned from his mother. With the class, say a well-known nursery rhyme.
● Continue along the line in the same way. When a child has grown up, let them stand to show their growth from child to adult.
● At the final child ask: *How can the rhyme keep going into the future?*
● Say that some stories have been told like this for hundreds of years and are powerful stories that have stood the test of time.
● Introduce the story about Robert the Bruce. Explain that it is an important story to the people of Scotland, so has been retold many, many times.
● Read 'Robert the Bruce and the spider' from photocopiable page 'Two UK folk tales (1)' from the CD-ROM.
● Then ask questions such as: *Why was Robert the Bruce hiding in the cave? What was the spider trying to do? How did it help Robert?*

Differentiation
● Support: encourage less confident children to join the discussion by asking questions to help them expand their answers.

Review
● Explain that no one knows if the story of the spider is quite true but, it *is* true that Robert the Bruce hid in caves and came back a stronger person.
● Ask the children what they think about the story and whether or not it might be true. Ask: *Does it matter if it is not completely true?*

■SCHOLASTIC
www.scholastic.co.uk

2: Spiderweb folk-tale messages

Lesson objectives
● To use a wide vocabulary of everyday historical terms.
● To ask and answer questions, choosing and using parts of stories and other sources to show that they know and understand key features of events.
● To understand some of the ways in which we find out about the past.
● To identify different ways in which the past is represented.

Expected outcomes
● All children recognise that some folk stories have messages or warnings in them.
● Most children recognise the different types of message used in folk tales.
● Some children understand why the folk-tale messages were important to people long ago.

Resources
Storytelling corner; a display board covered in a large spiderweb design; photocopiable page 'Two UK folk tales (1)' from the CD-ROM; for each child: a paper plate with grooves cut into the rim every 2–3cm, wool or string, a card strip for the message, adhesive tape, colouring pencils or pens; paints (optional)

Introduction
● Settle the children in the storytelling corner.
● Briefly remind the children how folk tales were a main form of entertainment in the past.
● Retell the story of 'Robert the Bruce and the spider' from photocopiable page 'Two UK folk tales (1)' from the CD-ROM. If possible, aim to learn this and some other folk stories off by heart to give the children an authentic storytelling experience, and encourage them to join in with any rhymes or actions.
● Ask the children about the spider: *What did it keep trying to do in the cave? How many times did it try before it succeeded? What is the message?* (Keep trying. You will succeed in the end.)
● Highlight that many folk tales have a message that gives advice or warnings to the listeners on how to behave or live their lives.
● Encourage the children to share experiences of how they kept trying to do something until they succeeded. Ask: *How did it feel when you were failing? But how did you feel when you did it?*
● Ask the children to think of other messages that could be used in folk tales, such as *Be kind* or *Look where you are going.* List the suggestions on the board.

Whole-class work
● Point to the large spiderweb display and tell the children that they are going to make spiderweb plates with their favourite folk-tale message attached to it.
● Show an example of a spider plate. Ask them to colour their plate and then draw a spider in the middle. The spiders can be made from handprints or drawn freehand.
● Note the grooves around the plate rim and demonstrate how to weave the wool or string across the plate to make a web effect and then tie it off at the back.
● Attach a card strip message to the plate with string and then add it to the large web display.

Independent work
● Give each child their card strips and support them in writing their message.
● Then give out the plates, colouring materials and wool or string to create their webs.
● Once the children have completed their web plates, help them to attach their message cards and ask them where they would like to place their plates on the big web.
● Use the display as a reference when listening to other folk tales in class. Ask: *Which spiderweb message matches the tale?*

Differentiation
● Support: offer assistance with tying up the string and attaching the message; children could copy their message from the board or trace over the letters.
● Challenge: ask children to think of a story that would highlight their message and then to tell it to a partner.

Review
● Look at some of the children's suggestions of a folk-tale message and how well they have constructed their webs.
● Ask questions such as: *Why do you think children from long ago loved to listen to folk tales?*

Week 3 lesson plans

In the first lesson, this week the children hear another folk tale about a famous person from the past and one linked to their local area. On hearing the story of King Alfred burning the cakes, they find out that in the hundreds of years of its telling, there are slightly different versions. They put pictures of the story in sequence and choose their own endings, then use this to tell their version. In the second lesson, the children listen to a local folk story and make historical connections to their area. They then perform the story as a class.

1: King Alfred and the burned cakes

Lesson objectives
● To develop an awareness of the past, using common words and phrases relating to the passing of time.
● To know where people and events they study fit within a chronological framework.
● To use a wide vocabulary of everyday historical terms.
● To ask and answer questions, choosing and using parts of stories and other sources to show that they know and understand key features of events.
● To understand some of the ways in which we find out about the past.

Expected outcomes
● All children know that the story of the burned cakes was based on the real King Alfred who lived long ago.
● Most children understand that the story might not be exactly true.
● Some children understand how the story would have changed over the years.

Resources
Storytelling corner; photocopiable page 'Two UK folk tales (2)' from the CD-ROM; picture of Alfred the Great (optional); photocopiable page 114 'King Alfred and the burned cakes'; scissors; glue; colouring pencils

Introduction
● You might want to take this lesson over two sessions to concentrate on just the storytelling in the first session.
● Settle the children in the storytelling corner and remind them that people used to sit and listen to storytellers retell folk tales.
● Recap that the story about Robert the Bruce and the spider was about a real person and say that you are going to tell another story about a king, who lived in England over 1000 years ago.

Whole-class work
● Retell the story 'King Alfred and the burned cakes' from 'Two UK folk tales (2)' from the CD-ROM.
● Then talk about the story, asking questions such as: *Why was King Alfred in the marsh? What did the woman ask him to watch? Why did he let the cakes burn? Did he say sorry? What did he learn from burning the cakes?'*
● Explain that the king was called Alfred the Great because he did many great things, but most people remember this story about burning cakes. Ask: *Why do you think it is still very popular?*

Paired work
● Give each child a copy of photocopiable page 114 'King Alfred and the burned cakes'. Explain that the story is so old that there are slightly different versions and on the sheet there are three different endings that are sometimes used.
● Working in mixed-ability pairs, ask the children to cut out the pictures of the story and stick them in the right order onto paper.
● Encourage them to talk about and choose one of the different endings of the story. Then let them colour in the pictures.
● Then ask the children to check their order of pictures by retelling the story to another pair.

Differentiation
● Support: children might need help with cutting out the pictures and working out the right order.

Review
● Have a shared storytelling session. Set the scene by saying that King Alfred is now a very important king and wants to invite the old woman to his castle.
● Start the story by saying: *King Alfred the Great once decided to have a big birthday feast...* Then let the children take turns in adding the next part of the story.
● Remind the children that the story is slightly different each time because, over the years, different people would tell the story slightly differently. Ask: *Why is it hard to know now what really happened?*

Lesson objectives
● To use a wide vocabulary of everyday historical terms.
● To ask and answer questions, choosing and using parts of stories and other sources to show that they know and understand key features of events.
● To understand some of the ways in which we find out about the past.

Expected outcomes
● All children know that folk tales can be about local places, people, traditions or events from the past.
● Most children can make links between the folk tale and their local area.
● Some children can understand how folk tales help us understand about the past.

Resources
Storytelling corner; a local folk tale to read out and for the children to perform; props for the performance (optional); simple percussion instruments; camera to film the performance; space to perform

2: A local folk-tale performance

Introduction
● Settle the children in the storytelling corner and remind them of the two stories of Robert the Bruce and Alfred the Great, and highlight that they are about real people who lived long ago in Britain (or the UK).
● Remind the children that each part of the UK has its own set of local folk stories, which might be about places, objects, people, traditions or events. They could be set in the real world but might include fantastical elements as in fairy tales, magic stories and ghost stories.
● Encourage any children who know some local folk stories to share them with the class.

Whole-class work
● Explain to the children that you are going to tell them a local folk tale that is very old. Tell them what the focus of the story is, for example a local place, custom, object, person, or event, and provide any local background information.
● Retell the folk story, creating simple musical sound effects with rainsticks or drums for example.
● Ask questions to encourage discussion, such as: *Is there a message in the story? Why would people need to make up a story about a large stone? Do you think the story was true? What can it tell us about how people lived or what they believed in long ago?*
● Explain to the children that they are going to create a class performance of the folk story.
● List on the board the different parts the children can do, such as making the sound effects, story narrators, the story characters, non-speaking parts that could be mimed such as animals, crowds, swaying trees.
● With the children, decide who is doing what. Try to include everyone.

Group work
● Split the children into the groups, for example, miming, sound effects and music, actors, and so on and try to provide adult support for each group.
● Let each group practise their different parts and roles.
● Once the groups are happy with their parts, bring them together and run through the performance, highlighting good use of voice intonation.
● After a run through, let the children give a real performance, and film it for the children to see at a later date.

Differentiation
● Support: make sure that less confident learners are fully included in the performances.

Review
● Ask the children about their performance and how accurately it followed the original story. How do they think the original story might have come about? Do they think it is true?

Week 4 lesson plans

During this week the heritage topic starts its focus on castles. In the first lesson, the children discover that the UK has many castles of all shapes and sizes. They then use investigation skills to work out the two main reasons why a particular castle was built. In the second lesson, children use their chronological skills and time vocabulary by putting UK castles from different periods into the right time order.

1: History detective – what was a castle?

Lesson objectives
- To develop an awareness of the past, using common words and phrases relating to the passing of time.
- To identify similarities and differences between ways of life in different periods.
- To use a wide vocabulary of everyday historical terms.
- To ask and answer questions, choosing and using parts of stories and other sources to show that they know and understand key features of events.
- To understand some of the ways in which we find out about the past.

Expected outcomes
- All children know that castles could be used for defence and as homes.
- Most children know the reasons why people lived in a castle.
- Some children can recognise different parts of a castle.

Resources
Pictures of a variety of UK castles including a local one; photocopiable page 'Castle uses' from the CD-ROM

Introduction
- Show a variety of castles from the UK and draw particular attention to any that are local to the school. Point out that the UK has many castles of different shapes, sizes and ages.
- Allow the children to share their experiences of castles they have visited.
- Explain that they are going to investigate a castle from long ago to see if they can work out why it was built.

Whole-class work
- Display a picture of a castle (source online). Focus on the first reason for its construction (defence) through prompt questions such as: *Why does the castle have high, thick walls and small windows?*
- Once the children have given their answers, explain that most castles were built to protect people if they came under attack during a battle.
- Look at the second reason by asking: *What else is the castle used for?*
- Focus on the people in the castle. Ask prompt questions such as: *Who can you see in the castle? Where do you think they might live?*
- Confirm that a castle could be used as a home for the lord and his family and servants.
- Reinforce the two uses of the castle by writing them on the board.

Paired work
- Use the cards from photocopiable page 'Castle uses' from the CD-ROM for a reinforcement memory game of pairs on the two main uses of a castle.
- Help the children in pairs to lay out two sets of the mixed-up picture cards, face down on the table.
- Ask the children to take turns to turn one picture up and then turn over another card hoping to find the identical picture to make a pair to collect. (If they don't find a pair, both cards should be turned over in the same position for the next player's turn.)
- Once the pairs have been collected, ask the children to sort the pairs into the two castle use groups – defence and home.
- Ask the children to explain why they have placed the pictures in one or the other group.

> **Differentiation**
> - Support: children could play the memory game in teams of two; use the cards for other games such as 'Snap' to reinforce understanding of castle uses.

Review
- At the end of the lesson, show photographs of castles today such as a ruined castle, a lived-in castle or a castle museum. Briefly discuss that most castles today are not used in the same way as for the reason(s) they were built. Ask: *Why do you think that is?*

2: Putting castles in sequence

Lesson objectives
● To develop an awareness of the past, using common words and phrases relating to the passing of time.
● To identify similarities and differences between ways of life in different periods.
● To use a wide vocabulary of everyday historical terms.
● To understand some of the ways in which we find out about the past.

Expected outcomes
● All children know that castles changed in size and use over time.
● Most children can place castles in chronological order.
● Some children can identify features that indicate the order castles were built in.

Resources
A variety of pictures showing forts and castles from two or three different eras (for example, Norman and Tudor); photocopiable page 115 'Castles of the past'; strips of paper made from A3 paper halved vertically; scissors; glue; large blank timeline

Introduction
● Show the children pictures of a variety of castles that were built at different times. Discuss the key features of each one, such as its size, main building material, the shapes of the windows, and so on.
● Talk about the significant differences between the castles. Ask prompt questions such as: *Which castle was built first? How can we tell? What does it look like it was used for? Which is the newest?*

Paired work or Independent work
● Working in pairs or independently, give each child a copy of photocopiable page 115 'Castles of the past', scissors, glue and strips of A3 paper.
● Discuss the pictures briefly and identify together the features that indicate whether they show older or newer castles (see Background information on page 99).
● Ask the children to sequence the pictures chronologically.
● Check the children's understanding as they work and ask them to explain why they have placed the pictures in a particular order.
● Once they are confident that they have the correct order, ask the children to stick their pictures in the correct sequence along their strip of paper.

Differentiation
● Support: children might need adult direction for picking out features to help them identify the relative ages of the castles.
● Challenge: children might be able to write captions or labels for each picture to note how they knew its relative age.

Review
● Ask for volunteers to place enlarged copies of the pictures in the right order on a simple timeline and give reasons for the order they decided on. Note their use of appropriate time vocabulary.
● Discuss that castles were built at different times in the past, using the appropriate names for the periods, such as *Norman* and *Tudor*.

Week 5 lesson plans

During this week, the children go into more depth about the defensive purposes of a medieval castle and have the opportunity to learn and use the historic words given to the different features of a castle. In the first lesson, the children focus on the defensive nature of a castle and match word labels to specific features. They reinforce this knowledge by labelling their own castle drawing. In the second lesson, the children work in groups to create model castles, allowing them to become more familiar with each feature and its purpose.

Lesson objectives
● To use a wide vocabulary of everyday historical terms.
● To ask and answer questions, choosing and using parts of stories and other sources to show that they know and understand key features of events.
● To understand some of the ways in which we find out about the past.

Expected outcomes
● All children know that castles had different defensive features.
● Most children can match the vocabulary to the castle features.
● Some children understand what each feature is called and what its function was.

Resources
Exterior photographs of a castle (this might be a local castle you have visited with the children); pictures of a castle's exterior and defensive features; word cards to label the defensive features of the chosen castle – large set for class use and small set per child; thin A3 card; drawing pencils; glue

1: Features of a castle

Introduction
● Display large pictures of the chosen castle, or (if they are your own photographs) give a set of pictures to each group of children.
● Ask the children to use these pictures to think about how a castle is built to defend itself and its village or a town from attack.
● Prompt the children with questions such as: *Why were castles so big? Why are the windows small and narrow? Why are the walls so thick? Why did some castles have moats? Why weren't the top of the walls built in a straight line?*
● Ask the children if they can think of any other features of the castle that might be used for defence purposes, such as the portcullis and drawbridge, keep and battlements.

Group work or Independent work
● Give the children the sets of word cards containing the key features of the castle you have been examining. These might include: keep, battlements, soldier, portcullis, drawbridge, small window, thick stone wall, moat, ditch, gatehouse, tower, turret, crenulations, arrow slits.
● Working in small groups, invite the children to match the words to the pictures of the castle. First, ask for volunteers to read the words out to the class.
● Display the enlarged picture of the castle on the whiteboard or on a wall.
● Ask the children to place the large word cards in the correct position, so labelling the key defensive features of the castle.
● Provide materials for the children to draw their own castles and then label their drawings with the word cards.

Differentiation
● Support: mixed-ability groups will encourage better readers to help others match the word cards to the pictures.
● Challenge: encourage children to write their own labels instead of gluing the word cards to their pictures.

Review
● Draw attention back to the castle on display. Cover or remove the word cards and challenge the children to quickly identify the different features.
● Encourage discussion about the different features and their uses.

2: Making model castles

Lesson objectives
● To use a wide vocabulary of everyday historical terms.
● To ask and answer questions, choosing and using parts of stories and other sources to show that they know and understand key features of events.
● To understand some of the ways in which we find out about the past.

Expected outcomes
● All children can recognise defensive features of a castle.
● Most children are able to identify and name the castle's defence features.
● Some children can ask and answer questions about how the castle defences would work.

Resources
Large picture of a castle with labelled word cards from the previous lesson; scissors; strong tape; photocopiable pages 'Castle templates and instructions' from the CD-ROM; parts of a model castle ready to be assembled; for each group: castle parts from the templates made from strong card, plus a card base; straws; a small box (as a keep); decorating materials such as silver foil, paints or pens; cards for labels

Introduction
● This lesson can be adapted so that the children can work in groups to make different elements of the castle, thus producing one large castle for the whole class.
● Draw attention to the large labelled picture of the castle from the previous lesson. Point to the labelled features of the castle and encourage the children to say the names and explain what the function was of each feature.
● Explain to the children that they are going to work together in groups to make model medieval castles.

Whole-class work
● Show the children the different sections of the model ready to be put together: the walls, turrets, flags and the keep.
● Then slot the ready-made pieces together. Highlight to the children that your castle is not decorated and that their pieces need to be decorated *before* they are slotted together.

Group work
● Organise the children into mixed-ability groups of around six and give each group the different parts of their castle from photocopiable page 'Castle templates and instructions' from the CD-ROM decorating materials and instructions from the sheet as a reminder.
● Either let the children decide who is doing what in their group or select children for the jobs.
● Once the children have decorated or made the castle parts, and they are dry, help the children to put the pieces together.
● Encourage each group to write or stick labels onto their model and then place the model on a base card.
● Once the models have been made and are secure, the children might like to add other features in other sessions, such as a moat, soldiers, inner buildings, and so on.

Differentiation
● Support: although children will be in mixed-ability groups, extra adult support would be of great benefit to offer assistance in putting the castle model parts together or help with decorating and label writing.
● Challenge: encourage children to read the instructions on the photocopiable sheet if they need reminding how to assemble their castle sections.

Review
● Use the models to encourage enquiring skills by asking the children questions such as: *How do you think the enemy might try to attack? How useful are the crenellations?* Listen to the children's discussions and correct use of vocabulary for the features. Note their asking and answering of questions on how the defences would work.

Lesson objectives
● To develop an awareness of the past, using common words and phrases relating to the passing of time.
● To identify similarities and differences between ways of life in different periods.
● To use a wide vocabulary of everyday historical terms.
● To understand some of the ways in which we find out about the past.

Expected outcomes
● All children know that many different people lived and worked in castles long ago.
● Most children know the names of some castle workers and their roles.
● Some children understand what people did in a castle and why.

Resources
Photocopiable page 'Who am I?' from the CD-ROM made into one set of enlarged cards and one set for the class; space for mime performances

Week 6 lesson plans

This week, the children go into more depth about who lived and worked in a medieval castle. They find out that many people worked in a castle to look after the lord and his family and to defend the castle when necessary. The children mime the actions of each job and encouraging the children to use relevant vocabulary to describe what each person is doing. In the final lesson of the whole topic, part of the classroom is turned into a Great Hall. This allows the children to act out their ideas and strengthen their understanding of what life was like in a castle. Play medieval music and hold a storytelling session in the Great Hall to make the experience even more enriching.

1: Who lived and worked in a castle?

Introduction
● Show the picture cards of six people who lived and worked in a medieval castle from photocopiable page 'Who am I?' from the CD-ROM. Highlight that lots of people lived and worked in a castle: to keep it safe and strong, to defend it should an attack come, and to look after the lord and his family.
● Read out the names and the short captions of what each person did.
● Talk about the different jobs the six people had in more depth and answer any of the children's questions about them.
● Discuss how these sorts of jobs might be done in a castle or other home today. Highlight that in stately homes, wealthy people, including, for example, the Queen and members of the royal family, still have servants to do jobs such as cook, garden, clean and sort out day-to-day life.

Group work
● Put the children into six mixed-ability groups. Give each group one of the picture cards.
● Ask the children to work together to work out how to mime the person's job to the rest of the class.
● Explain that they can either all mime the person doing the same action or they could mime different tasks that one person would have as part of their job or they could choose one of them to mime the job while the others mime other roles to give extra clues, for example a page serving at a feast.
● Give the children time and space to practise their mimes. Remind the children that miming means performing the actions in silence.

Whole-class work
● Bring all the groups together. Remind the children that while one group is miming, they have to concentrate on the actions to work out what they are doing and who they might be.
● Before the mimes start, point to the picture name cards on display and briefly recap the names and what they do.
● After each group has performed their mime, ask the rest of the class who it is and how they could tell. Ask the miming group to confirm the answer and explain what their mimes were showing.
● Once all the children have completed their mimes, let them draw the person they would have liked to be in the castle doing their job.

Differentiation
● Support: adult support and suggestions might be needed as the children decide what they are going to show in their mimes.
● Challenge: children could write sentences to go with their drawings explaining their choice and that person's role.

Review
● Ask the children if they can remember who would live and work in a castle and what their tasks were.

2: Creating a Great Hall

Lesson objectives
● To develop an awareness of the past, using common words and phrases relating to the passing of time.
● To identify similarities and differences between ways of life in different periods.
● To use a wide vocabulary of everyday historical terms.
● To understand some of the ways in which we find out about the past.

Expected outcomes
● All children can imagine what it was like to live or work in a Great Hall.
● Most children can take on different roles in a Great Hall.
● Some children understand that the Great Hall was the centre for castle events.

Resources
Picture of a Great Hall; cardboard castle wall (nearly the same height as the children) with battlements and a cut-out archway for an entrance; craft materials (including paints, felt-tipped pens, crayons, paper, scissors and glue); suitable items for role play, such as dressing-up clothes, tables, chairs, tablecloth, items for mealtimes (such as plates, blunt knives and goblets); medieval music and stories

Introduction
● Display and talk about a picture of a Great Hall and tell the children that they will be making a castle wall with battlements and, within these walls, a small version of a Great Hall.
● Set up the wall and paint outlines of stones in the wall. Add pictures, in the style of tapestries, and flags on the battlements. Make any other items you require, for example, shields for the soldiers. The children could help with this in an earlier session, if possible.
● Arrange tables to form a long banqueting table and put chairs on one side of the table only ('servants' could then serve the food more easily). A chair can be placed at the head of the table for the 'lord' or 'lady'. Cover the table with a long cloth.

Whole-class work
● Remind the children of the previous lesson and discuss the roles of the lord and lady of a castle.
● Talk about special events that might have happened, such as grand processions when important visitors arrived, banquets, storytelling and celebration feasts after a battle or perhaps for a wedding or birthday.
● Discuss the roles of different people when there were visitors to such events, such as cooks and servants and the soldiers who kept a look out for attackers while standing at the battlements.
● Organise the children into small groups and provide each group with a variety of objects, such as dressing-up clothes, cups and plates.
● While the rest of the class is occupied with other activities, such as making more decorations for the hall, allow one group at a time to re-enact life in the Great Hall, taking the roles of lords, ladies, servants, cooks and soldiers.
● Extend the role play by having a medieval feast, dancing to medieval music and listening to a storyteller.

Differentiation
● Support: mixed-ability groups will be useful during the role play, so that less confident learners can be encouraged by ideas and talk by the more confident.

Review
● Encourage the children to talk about their role play and the parts they took. What did they learn about castles and castle life? Elicit that the Great Hall was the centre of life in the castle, and the most important room.
● Take note of those children who are independently asking historical questions that arise from the role play and those who work out the answers to their own queries.

Lesson objectives
● To identify different ways in which the past is represented.
● To use a wide vocabulary of everyday historical terms.

Resources
UK map; stories of Robert the Bruce and the spider and King Alfred and the burned cakes from photocopiable page 'Two UK folk tales (1) and (2)' from the CD-ROM; a local folk tale

Folk stories

Revise
● Use a map of the UK to revise the four UK regions and their emblems.
● Then revise what folk tales and traditions are, using local examples.
● Recap that the origins of many folk tales are from very long ago and that they have been passed down over the years by storytellers and within families.
● Let the children work in pairs to retell one of the stories learned during the topic, such as King Alfred and the burned cakes, Robert the Bruce and the spider, or a local tale.

Assess
● Ask the children to work individually to draw a storyboard with succinct sentences for their chosen story. Check that they have the events of the story in the correct order.
● Once the storyboards have been finished, ask the children how they think the stories might have changed over the years and what their messages are.

Further practice
● Ask the children to find out about other UK folk stories that have a link with a person, place or object from the past and which give a message to their listeners.

Lesson objectives
● To identify different ways in which the past is represented.
● To use a wide vocabulary of everyday historical terms.

Resources
Labelled castle from Week 5, Lesson 1; photocopiable page 'Who am I?' for each child from the CD-ROM; writing and drawing pencils; interactive activity 'Y1 Summer 2 quiz' on the CD-ROM

Castles

Revise
● Display the castle picture with the labelled word cards. Discuss each feature and its uses. Ask the children to say the word for the feature before and after the discussion on what it is.
● Ask the children to summarise what castles could be used for: a place of defence and a home for the lord, his family and servants.
● Use the cards from photocopiable page 'Who am I? to quiz the children on the people who lived in a castle. Read the description and ask the children what their title is. If needed, give them an option of three names to choose from. Alternatively, read out a title and ask the children what they do.
● Discuss with the children what they liked about the castle topic and why. What fact do they remember most of all and why?

Assess
● Leave the labelled castle on display and give a copy of photocopiable page 'Who am I?' to each child, with writing paper and pencils.
● Ask the children to imagine that they are one of the people who lived in a castle and to create a comic-strip short story about them. Encourage them to include some of the new castle words in their text. Make sure they write one or two sentences with each comic-strip cell.
● Let the children share their work with others. What castle words have they used in their stories?

Further practice
● Let the children look at castles around the UK and even those built around the world. Encourage them to identify similar features, note the differences and try to discover why they are different.
● Ask the children to complete interactive activity 'Y1 Summer 2 quiz' on the CD-ROM, which allows children to answer questions on the whole topic.

Name: _____   Date: _____

Our UK emblems

- Cut out each country name and stick it under the right emblem.
- Then complete the sentence about your country.

We live in a country that has the _____ emblem.

✂ --

Scotland	England
Wales	Northern Ireland

King Alfred and the burned cakes

■ Cut out the pictures showing the story of King Alfred and the burned cakes.

■ Put them in the right order.

■ Choose and cut out one of these endings for the story.

PHOTOCOPIABLE

SCHOLASTIC
www.scholastic.co.uk

Name: _____   Date: _____

Castles of the past

Medieval castle

Tudor castle

Norman castle

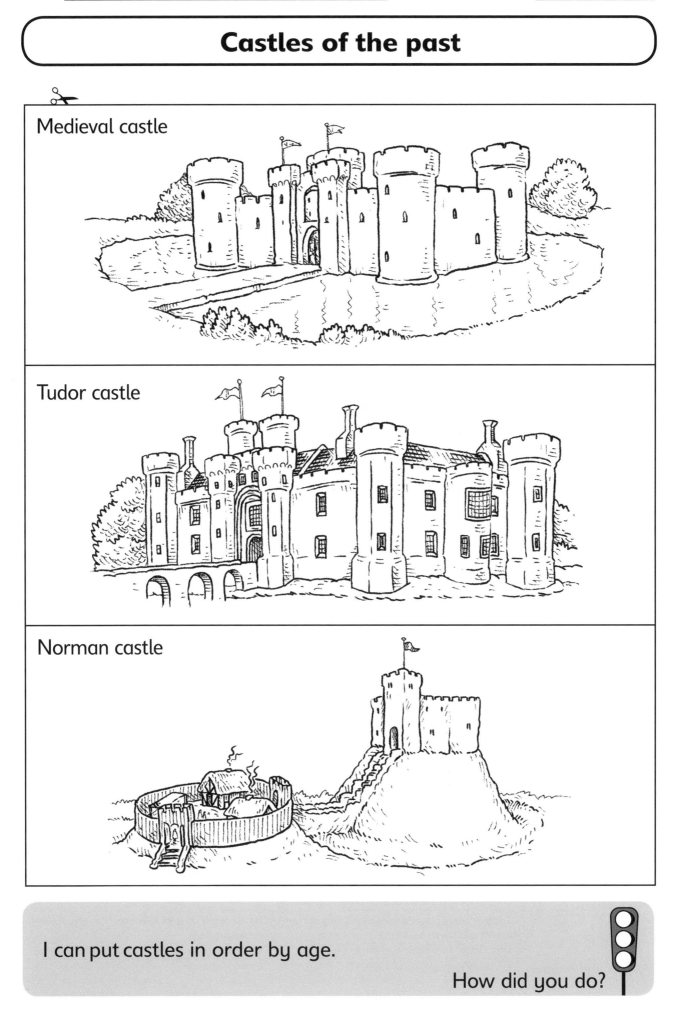

I can put castles in order by age.

How did you do?

Changes within living memory: telephones

This chapter looks at the invention of the telephone and how its use and design have changed within living memory. With the continual changes in technology, this topic should be very relevant to the children's understanding of how things can change within a short period of time. The topic starts with pre-telephone communication and then explores what telephones have looked like over the years. This is followed by studies of Alexander Graham Bell, telephone exchanges and telephone boxes, and ends with a look at uses and designs of telephones over time.

Chapter at a glance

Curriculum objectives

- Changes within living memory. Where appropriate, these should be used to reveal aspects of change in national life.
- Events beyond living memory that are significant nationally or globally.
- The lives of significant individuals in the past who have contributed to national and international achievements.

Week	Lesson	Summary of activities	Expected outcomes
1	1	• Children discuss the uses of telephones. • They investigate different forms of pre-telephone communication. • They find out about message sticks and create their own.	• Know about forms of communication in the past.
	2	• Children put telephones into the correct order on a timeline.	• Can sort telephone designs into chronological order.
2	1	• Children hear and then discuss a story of Bell's life and invention of the telephone. • They complete a text about Bell's invention of the telephone and draw a portrait of him.	• Know who Alexander Graham Bell was and when he lived. • Know about how and why he invented the telephone.
	2	• Children discuss ways to make sound. • They carry out a vibration test with cup telephones and link their findings with Bell's work.	• Can experiment with sound vibrations to understand how Bell invented the telephone.
3	1	• Children study, draw label and compare old and modern telephones.	• Can investigate an old telephone and describe it. • Can make comparisons with a modern telephone.
	2	• Children study two pictures of manual telephone exchanges. • They read oral accounts of operators.	• Can use photographs and oral accounts to find out about telephone exchanges and how they worked.
4	1	• Children study a picture of an old telephone exchange. • They role play what an operator did and said. • They create a simple exchange board.	• Can make simple telephone switchboards and practise dialogue between the operator and callers.
	2	• Children role play in a class exchange. • They write transcripts of their conversations.	• Can use their knowledge and models to role play in an old-fashioned telephone exchange.
5	1	• Children discuss the use of a telephone box. • They create information posters about telephone box designs.	• Can research telephone boxes. • Can suggest why telephone boxes are not used much today.
	2	• Children discuss how ways to use a telephone box have changed. • They write a nonsense instruction poem.	• Can find out how people used telephone boxes. • Can write payphone instructions in the form of a poem.
6	1	• Children look at how telephones can help us get help in an emergency. • They present a drama of an emergency call.	• Know that emergency services are available by telephone.
	2	• Children study unusual telephone designs from the past and present. • They design a telephone of the future.	• Can compare unusual telephone designs of the past and present. • Can design a telephone of the future.
Assess and review		• To review the half-term's work.	

■ SCHOLASTIC
www.scholastic.co.uk

Expected prior learning

● Children are confident in using common words and phrases relating to the passing of time.
● Children can use comparison skills in identifying similarities and differences between different periods.
● Children are confident in using a range of sources to ask and answer questions.

Overview of progression

● Throughout the chapter, the children use time vocabulary to describe differences between telephones, exchanges and phone boxes over one hundred years. The children put telephones in chronological order and place events such as the invention of the telephone onto a timeline. By the end of the chapter, they can date telephone boxes and unusual telephones.
● The children identify similarities and differences between telephones from the 1900s to the present. These include changes in feature, use and design. They also use their comparison skills when investigating telephone exchanges and telephone boxes. Role play, discussion, model making and observational drawings reinforce the learning.
● As the topic progresses, the children build up a historical vocabulary about telecommunication. They investigate a message stick and carry out sound vibration tests. They role play in a class telephone exchange to find out how one was used.
● The children consolidate their skills in using resources such as photographs, artefacts and oral accounts. They also reinforce earlier learning that carrying out tests and making models to see how things work are good methods of learning about the past.

Creative context

● This chapter works well with science, especially sound, and design and technology in relation to telephone and phone box designs. Cross-curricular links include:
   ● reading and writing lists, reports, poems, dialogue and instructions; listening, explaining and discussing; taking part in role play;
   ● testing sound and vibrations;
   ● designing telephones, making a model switchboard, making observational drawings and studying telephone designs.

Background knowledge

● 1876 – Telephone invented by Alexander Graham Bell. 1878 – First long-distance calls in UK. 1879 – Telephone exchanges opened across UK. 1884 – First upright multiple telephone switchboard in England. 1891 – First international service: London to Paris. 1921 – First standard telephone kiosk used. 1924 – Telephone with dial introduced. 1926 – First red telephone box (in London). 1928 – Telephones used in most wealthy homes and offices; first automatic exchange in London. 1932 – First directory enquiries service opened. 1936 – Speaking clock introduced; K6 red telephone box used all over UK. 1937 – 999 emergency service introduced. 1955 – First cordless switchboard. 1958 – First answering machine used in UK. 1959 – lightweight (Bakelite®) telephones; new dialling codes; car radiophone introduced. 1965 – First internet used in USA. 1968 – New telephone box design. 1970 – New telephones made from coloured plastic. 1972 – First email line used in USA. 1976 – World's largest international telephone exchange opened in Edgware, London. 1990 – New dialling codes to cope with amount of telephones. 1992 – 100,000th BT payphone installed. 1994 – Internet use starts to develop. 1996 – New-look telephone boxes.

Week 1 lesson plans

The first week introduces the children to the topic of the history of the telephone and how it has changed in recent memory. In the first lesson, the children discuss what they think a telephone is and its uses in present times. They look at different ways people used to communicate before telephones, including creating an Aboriginal message stick. In the second lesson, the children use their observation skills to place examples of telephones over the ages into the correct chronological sequence.

1: Before telephones

Lesson objectives
● To develop an awareness of the past, using common words and phrases relating to the passing of time.
● To identify similarities and differences between ways of life in different periods.
● To use a wide vocabulary of everyday historical terms.
● To understand some of the ways in which we find out about the past.

Expected outcomes
● All children know that people communicated in different ways before telephones.
● Most children know that communication took a lot longer before telephones.
● Some children know that telephones were invented in the recent past.

Resources
A (landline) telephone; pre-telephone artefacts or pictorial resources such as a letter, postcard, semaphore flag, telegram, mirrors, a picture of a hill-top beacon; a pile of sticks with dry hay; photographs or a real example of an Aboriginal message stick; drawing and writing pens; narrow cardboard tubes

Introduction
● Show the children the telephone and ask them what it is.
● Encourage the children to think of different ways we use a telephone like this one, for example chatting to family and friends, calling for help in an emergency, passing on messages.
● Explain that although telephones are very important and taken for granted in our everyday lives today, they were only invented in the recent past.

Whole-class work
● Show the children your collection of pre-telephone artefacts or pictorial sources, such as the postcard and telegram, and use them to explain that before telephones, people communicated with each other when far away in many different ways.
● Looking at each item, encourage the children to talk to their neighbour about how it might have been used as a form of communication.
● Then share ideas as a class before you tell the children more about the object.
● Highlight that communication tended to take a lot longer in the past. For example, compare writing and sending a letter before the advent of postal vans with typing and sending an email today.
● Now show all the children a picture or real example of an Aboriginal message stick and tell them its name, where it came from and who used it.
● Ask: *How do you think a stick was used to pass on messages?*
● After the children have shared their ideas, confirm that the images on the stick were prompts to help the messenger remember the message correctly.

Paired work
● Put the children into pairs and give each child a sheet of paper and a card tube to make a message stick.
● Ask the children to write down a simple message that can be spoken to their partner as their messenger. Then let the children draw prompt marks and images related to their message onto their card tube message stick.
● Let the pairs tell each other their messages and pass over their message sticks.
● Ask each pair to join with another pair and take turns to deliver the messages.
● At the end of the lesson, ask: *Did the messengers pass on the exact message? Were the marks on the stick clear and useful prompts?*

> #### Differentiation
> ● Support: mixed-ability pairs could work together to create one message with one child acting as scribe; they can take it in turns to pass on the message.

Review
● Ask the children: *Were telephones invented recently or long ago? How did people send messages before telephones?*

Lesson objectives
- To develop an awareness of the past, using common words and phrases relating to the passing of time.
- To show where people and events they study fit within a chronological framework.
- To identify similarities and differences between ways of life in different periods.
- To use a wide vocabulary of everyday historical terms.
- To understand some of the ways in which we find out about the past.

Expected outcomes
- All children can use time words and phrases to explain the differences in age of a new and old telephone.
- Most children can put a range of telephones from the past 120 years into chronological order.
- Some children can use their timeline to explain how telephones have changed over the years.

Resources
A modern telephone and a very old telephone, or photographs of them; interactive activity 'A timeline of telephones' on the CD-ROM; timeline strips with decade dates from 1900 to 2000; photocopiable page 'Telephones past and present' from the CD-ROM; scissors; glue

2: Chronology of telephones

Introduction
- Remind the children that they have just started to learn about telephones, and explain that now they are going to look at how telephones have changed over time.
- Display photographs or real examples of a modern telephone and a much older telephone.
- Briefly discuss the features of each telephone and encourage the children to notice any particular similarities or differences between the two telephones, such as the lack of dial or keypad on the oldest telephone.
- Ask: *Which one do you think is the newer telephone? Which is the older telephone?* Encourage the children to discuss their choices, giving reasons.

Paired work
- Put the children into pairs and give them a long timeline strip and a copy of photocopiable page 'Telephones past and present' from the CD-ROM.
- Choose one pair to work on interactive activity 'A timeline of telephones' on the CD-ROM, at the same time.
- In their pairs, ask the children to cut out the pictures of the telephones on the sheet and discuss which order the telephones should be in, from the oldest to the newest.
- Walk around the groups and observe their actions and discussion. Ask them to explain their choices so far.
- Then ask the children to cut out the dates on the photocopiable sheet and match them to the pictures.
- When they think they have matched them correctly, let the children stick them onto their timeline strips.

Whole-class work
- Bring the pairs back together and encourage them to show their timelines. Use the interactive whiteboard to show the work done by the pair of children who worked on the interactive activity. Let the children discuss the changes in the telephones as time has gone on.
- Point to the dates underneath the telephones and make the point that the 1920s is still within living memory for some people. Suggest to the children that they might like to talk to older relatives about their memories of the telephones they used when they were young.
- As an extension, encourage the children to investigate how mobile phones have changed in the recent past. Children could use printed materials and the internet to look at examples of mobile phones and then use the information to put them into the correct chronological sequence.

Differentiation
- Challenge: give children a larger selection of telephone pictures to represent other decades or encourage children to find examples of other telephone designs from different ages on the internet or in books; let them add the examples to the right places on their timelines.

Review
- Display the timelines in the classroom and invite volunteers to explain why each telephone has been put where it has. What design points or telephone features and facilities gave them clues? What features have gone from the oldest phones and what features have been added to the newest ones?
- Encourage the children to add to the timelines as the topic progresses.

Week 2 lesson plans

This week focuses on the inventor of the telephone – Alexander Graham Bell. In the first lesson, the children listen to a biographical account about Bell's life and use it to ask and answer questions about when and where he lived, his time as a teacher for deaf people and his invention of the telephone. Then the children carry out simple sound tests as a way to understand how Bell used sound vibrations to help him invent the telephone. You could extend this week by looking in more depth at Bell's work. There are many interesting facts about Bell and his life which the children could investigate.

1: Alexander Graham Bell

Lesson objectives
● To develop an awareness of the past, using common words and phrases relating to the passing of time.
● To show where people and events they study fit within a chronological framework.
● To use a wide vocabulary of everyday historical terms.
● To ask and answer questions, choosing and using parts of stories and other sources to show that they know and understand key features of events.
● To understand some of the ways in which we find out about the past.

Expected outcomes
● All children know that Alexander Graham Bell invented the telephone.
● Most children can ask and answer questions about Bell's life.
● Some children can use a biography of Bell to understand why he invented the telephone.

Resources
World map; photocopiable page 'Alexander Graham Bell' from the CD-ROM; label cards for the children's timelines from the previous lesson; photocopiable page 132 'The invention of the telephone'; drawing pencils

Introduction
● Explain to the children that they are going to learn about a famous inventor from long ago called Alexander Graham Bell. Show on the whiteboard a picture of Bell on the photocopiable page 'Alexander Graham Bell' from the CD-ROM and ask the children how they can tell it was taken a long time ago: by the picture quality, his dress and hair, for example.

Whole-class work
● Explain to the children that they are going to listen to a short biography about Alexander Graham Bell. Display the photocopiable sheet as you read it out.
● Ask the children: *What did Alexander Graham Bell invent?* Continue to ask general questions to reinforce the children's understanding of the account. Help the children to understand terms such as *harmonic telegraph* and *transmit*.
● Then ask more specific questions, such as: *How did teaching at the deaf school help him with his telephone invention?*
● Use the world map to show where Bell was born, in Scotland, and its distance from Canada and the USA.
● Go back through the text to discuss the events leading up to Bell inventing the first telephone.

Independent work
● Give each child a copy of photocopiable page 132 'The invention of the telephone' and pencils.
● Working independently, the children work on the cloze activity by completing the sentences using key words shown in the wordbank.
● Once they have completed the sentences, encourage the children to draw their own portrait of Bell.
● Ask the children to add a label to their telephone timelines to show the year when the telephone was invented.

Differentiation
● Support: children may need extra reading and writing support for the cloze activity; in the class discussion, prompt children to give examples to reinforce their answers to questions.

Review
● Bring the class together and ask the children what characteristics Bell had that helped him to be a successful inventor. You may want to link these characteristics to other famous inventors such as the Wright brothers. Ask: *Why do you think we still remember him today?*
● Use the photocopiable sheet to check the children's knowledge of Bell and the events leading up to his invention of the telephone.

Lesson objectives
● To develop an awareness of the past, using common words and phrases relating to the passing of time.
● To use a wide vocabulary of everyday historical terms.
● To ask and answer questions, choosing and using parts of stories and other sources to show that they know and understand key features of events.
● To understand some of the ways in which we find out about the past.

Expected outcomes
● All children understand that sound can be felt through vibrations.
● Most children know that Alexander Graham Bell used sound vibrations for his telephone invention.
● Some children understand that by trying out a vibration test we can understand more about what Bell was trying to achieve.

Resources
Cup telephones: two plastic cups with holes in the bottoms connected by different lengths of string (knot or tape the string though the holes); simple observation sheets to record results for loose and tight strings and strings of different length

2: Experimenting with sound vibrations

Introduction
● Recap with the children who Alexander Graham Bell was and remind them that he studied sound and worked with people who had hearing difficulties.
● Ask the children to give examples of things that make sound, such as their voices, musical instruments, work tools, animals.
● Try out some simple sounds, such as clapping or tapping fingers on the table.
● Point out that although you cannot see sound, it can be felt through its vibrations and that these vibrations are what our ears record so we can distinguish sounds.
● Let the children hum onto the back of their hands to feel the vibrations. (Check that the children understand the term *vibration*.)
● Explain that Bell taught his students at the deaf school how to speak by letting them feel different sound vibrations through touch.
● Emphasise that sound can only happen if something is vibrating.
● Go on to explain that Bell was also interested in making sound travel over long distances, along wires.
● Tell the children that they are going to carry out their own small sound vibration experiment, creating a cup telephone to find out how sound could travel along wires.

Paired work
● Give each pair a cup telephone and an observation sheet to record their predictions and results of the test.
● Ask one child to speak fairly quietly into their cup using Bell's famous words: *Mr Watson, come here. I want to see you* while their partner holds their cup to their ear to feel for vibrations and listen for sounds. Suggest they try doing the task with the string loose at first and then tight. Remind them to note results on their observation sheet.
● Then arrange for the pairs to swap their telephones with other pairs so they can test different lengths of string to discover if sound or vibrations could still be heard or felt further away.

Whole-class work
● Bring the class together and discuss the children's results. Ask: *Did you get a clearer message when the string was tight or loose? Why was that? What was vibrating?* (The string.) *What was making it vibrate?* (A voice.)
● Highlight that Alexander Graham Bell used this basic sound idea along with his experiments using electricity to help him invent the first telephone.
● Write the word *telephone* on the board. Explain to the children that the prefix *tele* means 'from a distance' and the word *phone* means a speech sound'.

Differentiation
● Support: extra adult support may be needed to help children to record their results.
● Challenge: children could record their results with diagrams and sentences.

Review
● Note the children's progress through their discussion and feedback throughout the vibration tests.
● Ask the children how Bell's vibration work helped him with his invention of the telephone.

Week 3 lesson plans

This week focuses on learning new vocabulary, enquiring, observing and finding out more about telephones from the past. In the first lesson, the children study old and new telephones and compare their features. In the second lesson, the children are introduced to telephone exchanges. If possible, for a local focus, invite a visitor to the class who has a good knowledge of telephone exchanges or used to work in a telephone exchange.

1: Comparing old and new telephones

Lesson objectives
● To develop an awareness of the past, using common words and phrases relating to the passing of time.
● To show where people and events they study fit within a chronological framework.
● To identify similarities and differences between ways of life in different periods.
● To use a wide vocabulary of everyday historical terms.
● To understand some of the ways in which we find out about the past.

Expected outcomes
● All children can use time words and phrases to indicate the differences in age between telephones.
● Most children can describe similarities and differences between telephones of different periods.
● Some children can explain why some telephone features have changed over time.

Resources
Interactive activity 'Telephones: old and new' on the CD-ROM; a range of old and new telephones (real or pictorial); photocopiable page 133 'Comparing telephones'; drawing pencils

Introduction
● Display interactive activity 'Telephones: old and new' on the whiteboard. Ask the children to look at the images and say which is the older telephone and which is the newer telephone. How can they tell?
● Remind them of their telephone timelines from the first week, and ask the children approximately when they think the older telephone might have been used. Again, encourage the children to support their answer with reasons and to use appropriate time words and phrases in their discussion.

Whole-class work
● Focus on the older telephone and explain that it is called: *a candlestick telephone*. Ask the children why it might have been given that name.
● Then focus on the newer telephone and ask: *Why do you think it is called a cordless touchpad telephone?*
● Now ask the children to help you to drag the right labels showing the different features of the two telephones to the correct places on the photographs.
● Go through the different features of each phone that they can see and compare features, such as shape, weight, size, design, materials, and distinct features such as the circular dial or rectangular keypad.
● Identify and talk about significant differences and similarities, such as the changes in material, method of dialling, ear piece.

Group work or Independent work
● Put the children into small groups and, in the middle of their table, place a photograph of an old telephone and a newer telephone.
● Give a copy of photocopiable page 133 'Comparing telephones', to each child. Ask the children to look closely at the telephones on their table in turn and discuss their features.
● They can then carefully draw the telephones and label them using vocabulary support from the interactive activity.
● Once they have completed the drawings, let the children work individually or in pairs to write on the photocopiable sheet lists of differences and similarities between the two telephones.
● As an extension, encourage the children to create 2D or 3D models of old telephones and modern telephones using card and colouring materials. These could be displayed in the classroom, with captions.

Differentiation
● Support: children might need extra writing support with their labelling and lists and directing to particular features to see comparisons between the telephones.
● Challenge: encourage children to use their lists to write sentences to explain the differences between the telephones.

Review
● Bring the class back together and encourage the children to share their findings on the photocopiable sheet. *Are there any features that all of the telephones have?*

2: Telephone exchanges of the past

Introduction

Lesson objectives
● To develop an awareness of the past, using common words and phrases relating to the passing of time.
● To identify similarities and differences between ways of life in different periods.
● To use a wide vocabulary of everyday historical terms.
● To ask and answer questions, choosing and using parts of stories and other sources to show that they know and understand key features of events.
● To understand some of the ways in which we find out about the past.

Expected outcomes
● All children know that telephone calls were once linked through a telephone exchange.
● Most children can find out what a manual telephone exchange was.
● Some children understand how oral accounts can tell us how telephone operators worked.

Resources
Media resource 'Manual telephone exchanges, 1890s and 1950s' and photocopiable pages 'Telephone operators' oral accounts' from the CD-ROM; photograph of the nearest telephone exchange (optional)

● Show the children media resource 'Manual telephone exchanges, 1890s and 1950s' from the CD-ROM.
● Focus first on the picture from the 1890s. Ask the children: *What do you think the people are doing?* Explain that the place was a manual telephone exchange where calls were connected. Elicit that *manual* means 'by hand', and explain that when someone used their telephone, the wires at the exchange were put into different places in the exchange boards to connect the caller with the person they wanted to speak to.
● Point to the women in the picture and explain that they were called telephone operators. Ask: *Why do you think they are all women?*

Whole-class work
● Now focus on the second picture and comment that it is of a similar telephone exchange, but in the 1950s, which is in recent memory. Compare the two pictures, noting the similar vast quantity of wires and that the operators are still all women.
● Suggest that it would be useful to find out how the telephone exchanges worked.
● Display the text from photocopiable pages 'Telephone operators' oral accounts' from the CD-ROM. Explain that these are two transcripts of oral accounts given by women remembering about working in manual telephone exchanges – one from long ago and one in recent times.
● Ask the children why the oral accounts could help them to find out more about the exchanges.
● Read out the first account. Then ask the children to summarise what they have learned about how the exchange worked.
● Now let the children listen to the second oral account of an operator in the 1950s. Ask: *How has it changed since the older exchange? Why is it bigger?*

Group work
● Organise the children into groups of three or four and ask them to list, orally, four things that telephone operators needed to have in order to be good at their job, such as the ability to keep calm, a clear speaking voice, being able to concentrate for a long time, being polite.

Whole-class work
● Let the groups feed back their ideas and reasons. Did most groups think of the same reasons?
● Discuss why some of these are old-fashioned views. What abilities would a telephone operator need today?
● Show a photograph of your nearest modern telephone exchange and ask the children: *What is different about this exchange? How do you think the exchanges work now?* (By computer, not manually.)
● Ask: *When can we still hear a telephone operator?* (Emergency services, directory enquiries.)

Differentiation
● Support: during the class discussions you might need to ask prompt questions to encourage less-confident learners to contribute their ideas and observations; help children to expand their answers with reasons and examples.

Review
● Encourage the children to summarise how telephone exchanges have changed since the 1890s. Are there still manual exchanges today?
● Ask: *Why are oral sources so important in helping us to find out about the past?*

Week 4 lesson plans

This week focuses on consolidating the children's knowledge and vocabulary of old-fashioned manual telephone exchanges through creating a model telephone exchange switchboard and using it for role play within a class telephone exchange and telephone calling area. The children get a chance to write and perform a telephone conversation as a caller, operator and call receiver from the past. Through role play, the children can also investigate the possible reasons why manual exchanges have now developed into automatic operators.

1: Telephone exchange switchboards

Introduction
- Display the media resource 'Manual telephone exchanges, 1890s and 1950s' from the CD-ROM.
- Focus the children's attention on the picture of the exchange from the 1890s. Go through the process of how a call would be taken by an operator, encouraging the children to share their knowledge and vocabulary.
- Remind them what the operator might say and the need for a clear, polite voice. For example:
  - To the caller: 'Number please... Trying to connect you.'
  - To the receiver: 'I have a caller on the line. Will you take the call?'
  - To the caller: 'Putting you through.'

Whole-class work
- Explain to the children that they are going to create an old-fashioned telephone exchange for their classroom. Say that they are going to start in this lesson by working in pairs to make model telephone switchboards.
- Display photocopiable page 131 'How to make a model telephone switchboard' on the whiteboard.
- Show your prepared example of the switchboard model and, with reference to the instructions on the photocopiable page, demonstrate how it was created so the children can understand what they need to do.
- Point to the numbers 1 to 9 and the three names shown on the switchboard. Explain that this switchboard was for a small community in the past where there were only 12 telephones.
- Ask the children: Why are Doctor, Fire and Police shown as names or words, not numbers?

Paired work
- Organise the children into pairs and give out the craft materials and printouts of the photocopiable sheet.
- Let the children stick a bendy straw on the top of the vertical switchboard for the mouthpiece.
- Help the children to make a headset to go with the switchboard by attaching a length of card strip to two card circles for headphones.
- Once they have completed their models, encourage the children to take turns practising their operator voices and using their switchboards.

Review
- Note how the children use the switchboards once they have completed them and the dialogue they use in the telephone conversations.
- Encourage the pairs to show and describe their switchboard models, using historical vocabulary.
- Ask the children to think of what they would say as an operator if the called number is busy (already on another call) or unable to take a call, or if they wanted to talk urgently to the doctor, fire station or police.

Lesson objectives
- To develop an awareness of the past, using common words and phrases relating to the passing of time.
- To use a wide vocabulary of everyday historical terms.
- To ask and answer questions, choosing and using parts of stories and other sources to show that they know and understand key features of events.
- To understand some of the ways in which we find out about the past.

Expected outcomes
- All children can make a model telephone switchboard from the past.
- Most children can use their switchboards as they were used in the past.
- Some children can use the correct vocabulary to describe exchange switchboards.

Resources
Media resource 'Manual telephone exchanges, 1890s and 1950s' and photocopiable page 131 'How to make a model telephone switchboard'; a pre-made model switchboard; for each pair of children: a printout of the photocopiable instruction sheet, two large cereal boxes covered in white or cream card with backs taken off and sides reinforced with tape from inside, scissors or hole-punch (or make holes before the lesson), hole-reinforcement rings, string, straws, adhesive tape, card circles and card strips to make headphones, bendy straws for the mouthpiece, colouring pens and pencils

■SCHOLASTIC
www.scholastic.co.uk

2: A class telephone exchange

Introduction

● You could either set up the telephone exchange area out of class time for the children to use in subsequent lessons or put it together with the children in an earlier session.

● Introduce the children to their telephone exchange and call area in the classroom.

● Discuss with the children what features have been included in it, such as their model switchboards on tables in a row; chairs and the bells/musical sound for telephone bells to alert the person being called.

● Point to the telephone call section next to the exchange and highlight the telephones with a chair for each one.

Whole-class work or Group work

● Demonstrate how to use the telephone exchange for role play.

● The role play could be set up in a variety of ways depending on how simple or sophisticated you want it to be. One example is:

  ● The children work in groups of three with a caller, the person being called and the operator. They use one of the model switchboards on a table with a bell/ringer by the side of the board and two phones with one bell/ringer for the caller.

  ● The child who plays the caller decides which number out of the given nine numbers they would like to be and which of the other numbers or three emergency names they want to ring.

  ● The caller picks up their phone, rings their bell and calls out their telephone number. The operator then puts a plug in the right numbered hole jack on the home switchboard and asks the caller for the number they want to connect to.

  ● The operator then puts the other end of the plug in the right hole and rings their bell, calling out the number or emergency name.

  ● The child being called hears the bell and picks up the phone to be connected.

  ● The caller and the receiver then have a role-play conversation.

● Encourage the groups to work together to write out their telephone dialogues.

● Remind the children that this is a telephone exchange from the past, so their dialogue storylines need to be in keeping with a time in the past, such as the 1930s or the Second World War.

● As the children use the telephone exchange, encourage them to make comparisons with how we connect to people by telephone today and discuss why there are not many manual exchanges in the world today.

● Have pictures and photographs of telephone exchanges through the ages on display nearby for reference and, if possible, taped oral accounts for the children to listen to.

Differentiation

● Support: supervise the groups as they use the switchboards and telephone call area; organise mixed-ability groups to play on the switchboards.

Review

● Ask the children what they enjoyed about the role play and what they learned about how telephones were used in the past. Was it quick and easy to connect callers, or slow and complicated compared with instant connections today? Use questions that will encourage the children to give full answers and explain their meanings.

Lesson objectives

● To develop an awareness of the past, using common words and phrases relating to the passing of time.

● To identify similarities and differences between ways of life in different periods.

● To use a wide vocabulary of everyday historical terms.

● To ask and answer questions, choosing and using parts of stories and other sources to show that they know and understand key features of events.

● To understand some of the ways in which we find out about the past.

Expected outcomes

● All children use role play to know how an old-fashioned telephone exchange worked.

● Most children use role play to know what telephone callers, operators and receivers said in the past.

● Some children can identify why manual telephone exchanges have been replaced by automatic exchanges.

Resources

A space in the classroom; tables and chairs; some or all of the children's switchboard models; a table with a range of telephones and a chair for each; bells/ringers for each switchboard and telephone; display of pictures and photographs of exchanges through the ages; recordings of oral accounts from telephone operators

Week 5 lesson plans

This week, the children investigate the UK telephone box to see how it has changed in design and use within living memory. In the first lesson, the children use their research skills to create information posters about one of the five major telephone box designs since 1922. In the second lesson, the children discuss the changes in how to make a call in a box and create a telephone box instruction poem. The children become aware that the use of telephone boxes is now uncommon and can explain why.

1: Telephone box posters

Lesson objectives
● To develop an awareness of the past, using common words and phrases relating to the passing of time.
● To show where people and events they study fit within a chronological framework.
● To identify similarities and differences between ways of life in different periods.
● To use a wide vocabulary of everyday historical terms.
● To ask and answer questions, choosing and using parts of stories and other sources to show that they know and understand key features of events.
● To understand some of the ways in which we find out about the past.

Expected outcomes
● All children know that telephone boxes have changed in design in recent history.
● Most children can compare telephone boxes over the years.
● Some children understand the changes in the function of a telephone box over the years.

Resources
Photograph of a modern telephone box, preferably local; photocopiable page 'Telephone boxes' from the CD-ROM; photograph of a red telephone box; pictorial and web information on the history of telephone boxes; A1 or A2 poster paper; writing and drawing pens and pencils; glue; scissors

Introduction
● Show the children a photograph of a modern telephone box and ask what it is called and what it used for. Confirm that it contains a public telephone that anyone can pay to use if they are not at home or in the days when home phones were not common. Share any of the children's experiences of using a telephone box.

Whole-class work
● Display a photograph of a traditional red phone box and say that these were once all over the UK and are still seen as a symbol of Britain.
● Ask the children why they think it is red. (To stand out to make it easily recognisable, as all phone boxes were the same colour.)
● Explain that the first red phone box was called K2 and made in 1928 after a design competition. Explain that the K stands for *kiosk*.
● Ask: *What would a well-designed telephone box need?* List suggestions and prompt other ideas, such as: room to stand; easy-to-read sign; dryness; can be seen clearly; ventilation; quiet inside; windows.
● Explain to the children that they are going to investigate one of the telephone box designs used since 1922.

Group work
● Organise mixed-ability groups and give each group an enlarged version of one of the boxes from photocopiable page 'Telephone boxes' from the CD-ROM, along with A1 or A2 paper.
● Have other text and pictorial sources available to help the children to find out more about their allocated design of phone box.
● Ask the groups to work on a poster about their design, to present to the class. As they work, ask them about the information they have found. How they are going to present it on the poster and who is doing what task?

Whole-class work
● Once the groups have completed their poster reports, ask each one, in chronological order, to present their findings to the class.
● Display the posters in chronological order on a board in the classroom for the children to read and study.

Review
● Draw attention to the display and discuss similarities and differences between the telephone boxes. Note the development of design. Which design do the children prefer?
● Ask: *Why are telephone boxes not used much now? Do you think they will still be used in 20 years from now? Why?*

2: Telephone box instruction poem

Introduction

● Display a photograph of a modern payphone kiosk. Discuss how people can use money, credit cards or phone cards to make a call in telephone boxes, but, in the past, people could only use money in the form of coins. Ask: *Why have the telephone boxes changed from just coins?*

● Ask the children to imagine going into an old red telephone box and not knowing how to use it. What would be useful to have near the telephone to help them? (Instructions.)

● Highlight how all telephone boxes still have simple instructions. With the children, write on the board simple instructions for a telephone box that just takes coins.

● Highlight typical instruction features such as an imperative verb to start, simple vocabulary, numbered steps.

Whole-class work

● Suggest the children create a fun telephone instruction poem on making a telephone call from a phone box. Display the photocopiable page 'Telephone box nonsense poem' from the CD-ROM and read it out to the children.

● Highlight the imperative verbs and the telephone-call vocabulary used in the poem.

● Encourage the children to think of someone unusual or fun that they might like to call from a phone box. It could be an alien, as in the poem, or a cowboy, the Queen, a pop star, an elephant... and work together to write out a class version using the same structure.

Paired work or Independent work

● Let the children work in pairs or independently to create their own telephone box poems using a framework similar to 'Telephone box nonsense poem'.

● Encourage the children to use telephone instruction words as used in the class poem.

● Make sure that when the children have completed their poems, they have read them through and checked the spelling and use of capital letters. Let them know that they will be writing it out again neatly.

● Give the children photocopiable page 'Telephone box template' from the CD-ROM.

● For the inside of the telephone box, let the children write their poem out in their best handwriting.

● The children can then decorate their telephone boxes. When they have finished ask them to cut around their telephone box.

Differentiation

● Support: prompt children if they struggle for ideas, or scribe if they need help with writing.

● Challenge: encourage children to add more lines to their poem, use interesting imperative verbs and make it as fun as possible.

Review

● Encourage volunteers to read out their telephone instruction poems. Check that the children have remembered that callers in old telephone boxes could only pay with coins.

● Display the telephone boxes in a place where children can read the poems.

Lesson objectives

● To identify similarities and differences between ways of life in different periods.

● To use a wide vocabulary of everyday historical terms.

● To understand some of the ways in which we find out about the past.

Expected outcomes

● All children know that telephone boxes have instructions inside to explain how to make a call.

● Most children know that telephone boxes in the past only took coins.

● Some children understand why modern telephone boxes have changed their instructions.

Resources

Photocopiable pages 'Telephone box nonsense poem' and 'Telephone box template' from the CD-ROM; writing and colouring pens and pencils; pictures of red telephones boxes and a modern payphone

Week 6 lesson plans

In the first lesson, this week the children discuss how telephones can be used to get help in an emergency. They role play an emergency in present times and then discuss what would happen without telephones. In the final lesson, the children investigate unusual telephone designs of the past and design and present a telephone for the future.

1: Telephone emergency services

Lesson objectives
- To identify similarities and differences between ways of life in different periods.
- To use a wide vocabulary of everyday historical terms.
- To ask and answer questions, choosing and using parts of stories and other sources to show that they know and understand key features of events.
- To understand some of the ways in which we find out about the past.

Expected outcomes
- All children know that UK telephones have offered an emergency service for over 75 years.
- Most children understand what to do and when to use the telephone emergency call service.
- Some children can understand how the invention of telephones has improved emergency situations.

Resources
Large space for drama; film clip about emergency services (try local emergency services websites)

Introduction
- Ask the children how the telephone could be used to get help. Does anyone know the number to dial in an emergency? Explain that 999 is the world's oldest telephone emergency call service. It started around 75 years ago in 1937, for the main emergency services such as firefighting, police and ambulance.
- Mention the different emergency services that could be called on the telephone today – coastguard, lifeboat service and mountain rescue – in addition to the three main services.

Whole-class work
- If possible, show a short film clip about emergency services and discuss what is showed.
- Give the children an emergency scenario, such as someone getting badly hurt or smoke seen coming out of a building.
- Go through the dialogue that would take place when ringing the emergency services for this scenario. Stress the need to stay calm and give clear information about who and where you are and what you know about the emergency.
- Focus on what the 999 operator would say and why their voices have to be clear and calm. You may want to link this with the work on telephone operators from Week 4.
- Ask the children why it is wrong to ring 999 as a 'joke' or to see what happens. Emphasise how non-emergency callers could be stopping up the operator from dealing with a real emergency.

Group work
- Give mixed-ability groups different emergency scenarios. Ask them to nominate a child to be the 999 operator.
- Ask the children to act out the emergency scenario and then have one of them ring the emergency services. If possible, offer the children the use of any telephones on display the classroom. The model switchboards could also be used in the role play.
- Once the dialogue has taken place, ask the children to think of how they are going to finish their scenario with a positive ending.
Give the groups space to practise their scenes and work on their dialogue.

> ### Differentiation
> - Challenge: children could write up the scene as a short newspaper report.

Review
- Let each group take turns acting their scenes for the rest of the class.
- After each scenario has been performed and discussed, ask the performing group: *What do you think would have happened if the emergency had taken place long ago before telephones were invented?* (Calls for help would take a long time to get to the people who could help and their help might then be too late for the people in need.)
- Encourage one or two of the groups to re-enact their scenarios, but this time without being able to use the telephone.

■ SCHOLASTIC
www.scholastic.co.uk

Lesson objectives
● To develop an awareness of the past, using common words and phrases relating to the passing of time.
● To identify similarities and differences between ways of life in different periods.
● To use a wide vocabulary of everyday historical terms.
● To ask and answer questions, choosing and using parts of stories and other sources to show that they know and understand key features of events.
● To understand some of the ways in which we find out about the past.

Expected outcomes
● All children can investigate the features of unusually designed telephones.
● Most children can place telephones into chronological order and explain why.
● Some children can use their telephone knowledge and vocabulary to discuss telephone designs.

Resources
A real example or a photograph of a 1950s or 1960s telephone; a range of photographs of unusual telephone designs from the past and present

2: Unusual telephone designs

Introduction
● Show the children an example of a 1950s or 1960s telephone with an unusual design. Let the children share their immediate reactions, then encourage them to use their knowledge and vocabulary of telephones to describe its features.
● Ask the children if they think it is an old or new phone. Encourage them to make a prediction of its age, and then confirm when it was made.
● Highlight that, over the years, telephones came to be used by most households in the country, not just the wealthy, and were seen as an important part of the house. Today, telephones are used by most people every day and are cheap and easily available.
● Briefly discuss how mobile phones have made further changes to the way people use phones. Note that it was only in very recent times that mobile phones were first used.
● Look at the telephone again and ask: *Why would someone want a telephone with this unusual design?*

Group work
● Put the children into groups and give them two examples of unusual or quirky telephone designs from the past and the present.
● Encourage them to study each telephone's features and to discuss what kind of person might have bought and used it. A burger-shaped telephone, for example, might look good in a café or kitchen.
● Let each group report back to the rest of the class. Ask: *Which ones do you think are fun designs and why? Which ones do you like? Which ones don't you like?*

Independent work
● Challenge the children to draw an unusual design for a house telephone or mobile phone that might be used in 50 years from now.
● Encourage them to write labels and several sentences of description about their design, who would use it and how it works.

Whole-class work
● Choose volunteers to show and explain their telephone designs to the rest of the class. What new features have they introduced? Which existing features have they kept?

Differentiation
● Support: mixed-ability groups will help the children to support each other in their discussion and observation of the telephone designs; give prompt questions if the children need extra support.

Review
● Take time to go over the topic with the children and review what they have learned about the history of telephones.
● Focus back on the telephone timelines from the first week and discuss how quickly telephones have changed in the living memory of many people and how important they are in everyday life today.

Lesson objectives
● To develop an awareness of the past, using common words and phrases relating to the passing of time.
● To identify similarities and differences between ways of life in different periods.

Resources
A mixture of photographs showing telephones, telephone boxes and telephone exchanges from the 1900s to the present day

Telephones, exchanges and telephone boxes

Revise
● Organise the children to work in pairs or small groups.
● Recap with the children what they have studied during the topic on telephones: for example, how communication was possible before telephones, the changes in telephones through the ages, Alexander Graham Bell, the use of telephone exchanges, telephone boxes and emergency operators.
● Give the children a mixture of photographs showing telephones, telephone boxes and telephone exchanges used long ago (1900–1950s), in the recent past (1960s–1980s) and in the present day.
● Say the key time vocabulary and the dates as you write them on the board, and then ask the children to repeat them back to you.
● Then ask the children to work together in their pair or group to sort their photographs into the three time groups on the board.
● Encourage the children to discuss with the class how they sorted the photographs. Note how well they are using words and phrases relating to the passing of time.

Assess
● Working independently, ask the children to choose one photograph each of a telephone, a telephone exchange and a telephone box from the past and compare each one with three present-day versions.
● Draw a two-column table on the board for the children to copy with the column headings *Differences* and *Similarities*, or give them a prepared table to fill in for each item.
● Depending on skill, ask the children to draw and label the differences and similarities or to write them as a list.
● Offer support as a writing scribe if needed.

Further practice
● Ask the children to choose one of the telephones or telephone boxes from the past and write a non-chronological report about it and its use.

Lesson objectives
● To develop an awareness of the past, using common words and phrases relating to the passing of time.
● To identify similarities and differences between ways of life in different periods.

Resources
Interactive activity 'Y2 Autumn 1 quiz' on the CD-ROM; plastic cup; thin string about 1m long; used matchsticks

Y2 Autumn 1 quiz

Revise
● Ask children to think and write about what life would be like without telephones. They could also ask parents or grandparents about life without mobile phones.

Assess
● Ask the children to complete interactive activity 'Y2 Autumn 1 quiz' on the CD-ROM. There are ten multiple choice questions that test what the children have learned throughout the topic. They will need to read each question carefully before choosing the correct answer.
● Give children a set length of time (such as 15 minutes) to answer the questions. This can be used as part of a formal assessment or as a fun challenge activity, giving children the opportunity to show what they have learned about the topic.

Further practice
● Review any common misconceptions from the quiz. Link to work in science on 'Sound' by challenging children to make a string telephone. Ask them to write down the messages they receive. The idea is for the children to get a sense of hearing sound in an unfamiliar way – as Bell might have done.

How to make a model telephone switchboard

■ You will need:

cereal boxes	straws	string
hole-reinforcement rings	tape	scissors	pens

1. Make 12 holes on each box – four rows of three holes. Put a hole-reinforcement ring on each hole. Write the numbers 1 to 9 under the holes in the top three rows.

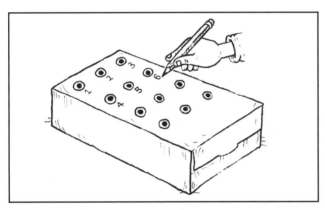

2. Write the words **Doctor**, **Fire** and **Police** under the bottom three holes.

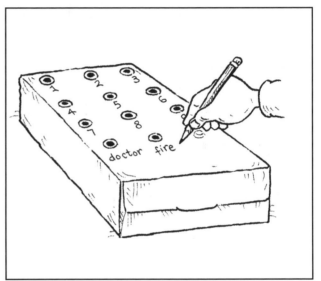

3. Lay one of the cereal boxes horizontally on the table and stand the other one up against the top end of the horizontal box. Tape the two boxes together to make an upright switchboard and home-base switchboard.

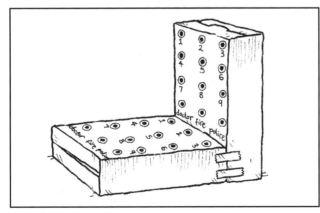

4. Create 12 telephone wires with plugs by attaching a straw at either end of a piece of string. Make sure the string is the right length to be used for both switchboards and that the straw plugs fit into the holes.

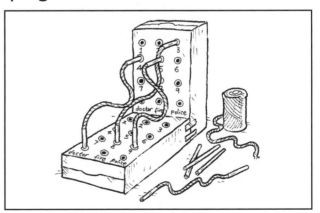

The invention of the telephone

■ Use the wordbank to complete the text about how the telephone was invented.

Alexander Graham _____ worked very

hard to see if he could mix _____ waves

and _____ to invent the first telephone.

In 1875, he met Thomas Watson, who helped him with his

_____ . One day, Thomas Watson went into a

room with one end of the _____ and Alexander

Graham Bell went into another room with the other end. Bell

said into the telephone, "Mr Watson, _____

here. I want to see you." Thomas Watson could

_____ the words clearly. Alexander Graham Bell

had _____ the telephone at last!

Bell	invented	hear	sound	experiment
	electricity	telephone		come

■ On the back of the sheet, draw a picture of Alexander Graham Bell using the telephone.

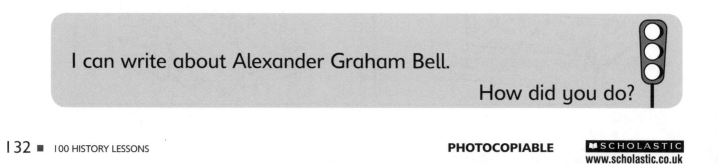

I can write about Alexander Graham Bell.

How did you do?

PHOTOCOPIABLE

SCHOLASTIC
www.scholastic.co.uk

Name: _____   Date: _____

Comparing telephones

■ Draw an old telephone and a new telephone in the boxes.

■ Then write labels for them.

Old telephone	New telephone

■ Make lists of things that are similar and things that are different about the two telephones.

Similar	Different
_____	_____
_____	_____
_____	_____
_____	_____
_____	_____

I can compare old and new telephones.

How did you do?

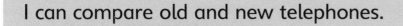
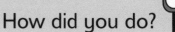

Events beyond living memory: the Gunpowder Plot

The topic of this chapter is the plot to blow up parliament on 5 November 1605. The children focus first on what they know and can relate to – the celebrations of Bonfire Night. Over the years, the reason why we celebrate Bonfire Night, or Guy Fawkes Night, on 5 November and the memory of who Fawkes was, have faded. The topic develops investigative skills so that the children can find out about the reasons behind the plot, those involved and their fate. The children look for clues in pictures and documents, a play scene, reports and information. At the end of the topic, they look at the legacy of the plot.

Chapter at a glance

Curriculum objectives

• Events beyond living memory that are significant nationally or globally.

Week	Lesson	Summary of activities	Expected outcomes
1	1	• Children talk about Bonfire Night. • They learn where and when the plot took place and who was the target. • They use a timeline to establish that the plot was during the Stuart period.	• Can link Bonfire Night to the Gunpowder Plot that took place long ago. • Can find out when and where the plot took place. • Know the plot was during the Stuart period.
	2	• Children identify the reason for the Gunpowder Plot out of a choice of four. • They learn about Catholics and Protestants. • They complete a diary extract.	• Can recognise differences between Catholics and Protestants in Stuart England. • Understand how James I upset Catholics.
2	1	• Children create a biographical information sheet of Fawkes' early life from notes. • They discuss why Fawkes joined the Gunpowder Plot.	• Can use a range of sources to find out who Guy Fawkes was. • Can write a short biography of Fawkes. • Understand why he joined the plot.
	2	• Children discuss the plot and its implications. • They create an order of ceremony for a present-day Opening of Parliament.	• Can find out about the first meeting of the conspirators and their plan. • Know what *parliament* means and what the Opening of Parliament is.
3	1	• Children create a fact card and a portrait for a class mural of the 13 plotters.	• Can study a picture to discuss the image it presents of the conspirators. • Can create a factfile of a plotter.
	2	• Children take turns to go into the hot-seat and are asked, as plotters, questions about their motives and feelings.	• Can find out about the plotters and their motives. • Can debate whether the conspirators were right or wrong.
4	1	• Children look at the Monteagle letter. • They write their own warning letters.	• Know about the importance of the Monteagle letter and its consequences.
	2	• Children listen to the events leading to the capture of Guy Fawkes. • They illustrate a recount of the capture.	• Can use a range of sources to find out what happened on 5 November 1605. • Can recount the event as a pamphlet.
5	1	• Children hear about the battle at Holbeche House. • They write a newspaper front page about how the plotters were captured.	• Know what happened to the conspirators. • Can create a newspaper front page of their capture.
	2	• Children sort pictures and captions of the main events into chronological order. • They to re-enact the plot.	• Can put the events of the Gunpowder Plot into chronological order. • Can work in groups to act out the plot.
6	1	• Children hear about the law passed to remember the 5 November. • They work in pairs to produce a mind map of ways the plot has been remembered.	• Know about the law passed in 1606. • Know why we still celebrate Bonfire Night.
	2	• Children discuss the light and fire features of Guy Fawkes Night. • They write a poem.	• Know that Guy Fawkes Night is a celebration of a past event. • Can compose a Guy Fawkes Night poem.
Assess and review		• To review the half-term's work.	

■ SCHOLASTIC
www.scholastic.co.uk

Expected prior learning

- Children can place people and events in chronological order.
- Children can use a range of primary and secondary sources to find out about the past.
- Children know that events have consequences.

Overview of progression

- The children understand that the Gunpowder Plot took place long ago, during the Stuart period, and that the plot's failure has been celebrated ever since. They make time links with the Great Fire of London. They develop chronological skills by putting the events of the plot in order and re-enacting them. The children also use vocabulary relating to the passing of time when studying 17th century sources, looking at the traditions of the Opening of Parliament and comparing celebrations over the years.
- The children interrogate pictures and portraits and use original and secondary texts to work out what was being planned. They also use hot-seating to interview the plotters about their motives.
- The children discover ways of finding out about the past through sources including paintings and prints from the time as well as a diary account, an old rhyme and modern photographs.

Creative context

- This chapter works well with topics including winter light or fire festivals. Cross-curricular links include:
  - using and developing literacy skills, including the ability to deduce and infer from texts and write information captions, diary recounts, poems, newspaper stories, pamphlets, biographical fact cards and letters; speaking and listening skills, including a hot-seat session;
  - recognising dates and time periods;
  - drawing portraits and studying the style of 17th century engravings;
  - respecting differences between people, discussing what is right and wrong.

Background knowledge

- Gunpowder plot rhyme: Remember, remember, The fifth of November, Gunpowder, treason and plot. We see no reason, Why gunpowder treason, Should ever be forgot.
- In the early reign of James I (1603–1625), Catholic people felt let down and angry. The main religion was Protestantism. Catholics were not allowed to worship openly. Catholic priests often had to go into hiding to avoid arrest.
- Robert Catesby, a devout Catholic, decided to attempt a Catholic coup by killing the king and most of his advisers during the Opening of Parliament. He brought together four other plotters including Guy Fawkes, an explosives expert. On 20 May 1604, they met at the Duck and Drake and hatched a plan.
- Over the next few months, they rented a house near the Houses of Parliament, then hired a cellar directly under the House of Lords. They filled it with 36 barrels of gunpowder and hid them under wood and coal.
- More plotters joined, until there were 13. The date for the Opening of Parliament was announced as 5 November.
- On 26 October, an anonymous letter was sent to Lord Monteagle warning him not to go to parliament. Monteagle sent the letter on to Robert Cecil, the king's main adviser.
- On the early morning of 5 November, Guy Fawkes was arrested as he stood over the barrels of gunpowder. He was tortured for two days in the Tower of London until he confessed the others plotters' names.
- Robert Catesby and a group of other plotters fled to Holbeche House in Staffordshire but were caught and killed. The rest were caught and executed on 30 and 31 January 1606.
- In January 1606, Parliament issued an act for the 'Observance of 5th November 1605' in which everyone had to celebrate the failure of the plot.

Week 1 lesson plans

This week introduces the children to an event that took place over 400 years ago but is still significant today – the Gunpowder Plot of 1605. In the first lesson, the children discuss what happens at a present-day Bonfire Night and then study an old rhyme and pictures to find clues about why we mark the event. The children make connections with other events of the Stuart period. In the second lesson, the children learn about Catholics and Protestants and use a diary extract to find out why some Catholic people were angry enough to plot against the king.

1: Remember, remember, the fifth of November

Introduction

● Show a photograph of a Bonfire Night celebration. Discuss with the children what the event is and when it takes place. Look at its particular features, for example that it takes place in the dark, perhaps with a torch procession, a 'Guy', the bonfire itself and fireworks. Let the children share their experiences of Bonfire Night.

Whole-class work

● Explain to the children that they are going to investigate why we mark Bonfire Night on the 5 November.
● Suggest that they might find a clue from an old Bonfire Night rhyme. Point to the rhyme on the board and read it slowly with the children.
● Focus on the third line and explain what *treason*, *gunpowder* and *plot* mean. Ask: *What does this line tell us about what happened on the 5 November?* Confirm that Bonfire Night is linked to a violent plot or plan.
● Tell the children that they could look at more clues to find out when the plot might have taken place and who it was against.

Paired work

● Organise the children into pairs and give each pair a printout of photocopiable page 'Picture clues' from the CD-ROM. Ask the children to study the pictures closely for clues such as landmarks in the location pictures, the everyday life and clothes giving an indication that it took place *a very long time ago* and features of the portrait to work out who it shows.

Whole-class work

● Let the pairs share their deductions with the rest of the class. Confirm that the place was London and that the plot was against King James I, who ruled in the Stuart period, which was over 400 years ago.
● Display media resource 'The Stuart period timeline' on CD-ROM and ask the children to help you to show when James I reigned and when the plot took place.
● Ask the children if they recognise other events and kings on the timeline, such as the Great Fire of London and Charles II. Explain that Charles II was James I's grandson.
● Tell the children that in the next lesson, they are going to find out *why* there was a plot against James I.

Review

● Look again at the pictures on the photocopiable sheet, and check the children's ability to find and discuss clues. Ask: *When and where did the Gunpowder Plot take place? Why do we hold a bonfire event on the 5 November?*

Lesson objectives
● To develop an awareness of the past, using common words and phrases relating to the passing of time.
● To show where people and events they study fit within a chronological framework.
● To use a wide vocabulary of everyday historical terms.
● To ask and answer questions, choosing and using parts of stories and other sources to show that they know and understand key features of events.
● To understand some of the ways in which we find out about the past.

Expected outcomes
● All children know that we celebrate Bonfire Night on the fifth of November.
● Most children know that James I was king in the Stuart period which was long ago.
● Some children can use clues to find out about the plot against James I long ago in London.

Resources
Interactive whiteboard showing the rhyme 'Remember, remember...' (see Background information on page 135); photograph of Bonfire Night; media resource 'The Stuart period timeline' and photocopiable page 'Picture clues' from the CD-ROM

2: Catholics and Protestants

Introduction
● Point to the old Bonfire Night rhyme, *Remember, Remember, the fifth of November...* on the board and ask the children if they remember it from the last lesson. Read it with the children again.
● Remind the children of what they found out in the last lesson about why we commemorate Bonfire Night on 5 November: because there was a gunpowder plot against King James I in London in 1605 (which was foiled, so giving cause for celebration).

Whole-class work or Group work
● Organise the children into mixed-ability groups of three or four.
● Suggest to the children that now we need to investigate *why* there was a plot to kill the king.
● Explain that you have four possible reasons for the plot, but only one is true. Suggest these four options:
  ● The king has upset the servants with his bad manners.
  ● He has badly treated Catholic people, who worship God differently from Protestant people. (The king was Protestant.)
  ● There has been an argument over a food bill he hasn't paid.
  ● He has taken someone's house to use for himself.
● Give the groups time to debate and decide which one could be right, stressing the seriousness of planning to kill the country's king.
● Once the children have chosen, confirm the real reason – James I's treatment of people who were Catholic.
● Suggest that it would be a good idea now to find out more about Catholic people and Protestant people in the Stuart period.
● Display the photocopiable page 'Catholics and Protestants' from the CD-ROM and use it to help the children to understand each type of faith.

Independent work
● Explain to the children that they are going to read and then complete an unfinished diary extract written by a young Catholic boy in 1605. This will help them to find out what it might have been like to be Catholic during that time.
● Hand out a copy of photocopiable page 149 'Extract from a Catholic boy's diary', to each child. Ask the children to complete the cloze sentences in the extract using the words from the word bank. Point out that then they should answer the question to explain why the boy was angry with King James I.

Whole-class work
● Bring the children together and ask: *Why were Catholics so angry with King James I?*
● Note that in the earlier Tudor period, there were times when Protestant people were treated badly by the Catholic people in power.

Differentiation
● Support: help children read to difficult vocabulary on the photocopiable sheet.
● Challenge: encourage children to find out more about priest holes.

Review
● Ask the children if they can recognise the differences between Catholics and Protestants and understand the reasons why the Catholics were angry with James I.

Lesson objectives
● To develop an awareness of the past, using common words and phrases relating to the passing of time.
● To use a wide vocabulary of everyday historical terms.
● To ask and answer questions, choosing and using parts of stories and other sources to show that they know and understand key features of events.
● To understand some of the ways in which we find out about the past.

Expected outcomes
● All children know that Catholic people were angry with King James I.
● Most children know how Catholic people were treated by James I.
● Some children know key differences between Catholics and Protestants.

Resources
Interactive whiteboard showing the Bonfire Night rhyme 'Remember, remember...'; photocopiable page 'Catholics and Protestants' from the CD-ROM; photocopiable page 149 'Extract from a Catholic boy's diary'

Week 2 lesson plans

This week focuses on who Guy Fawkes was and the first meeting of the original plotters. In the first lesson, the children look at the early life of Guy Fawkes, which will help them to understand that Fawkes was a real person who lived long ago. They turn notes about his life into a biographical report and make a portrait of him. In the second lesson, the children participate in a short play about the meeting of the five plotters and work out what the plotters planned. They also learn about the Opening of Parliament through present-day photographs.

1: Who was Guy Fawkes?

Lesson objectives
● To develop an awareness of the past, using common words and phrases relating to the passing of time.
● To show where people and events they study fit within a chronological framework.
● To use a wide vocabulary of everyday historical terms.
● To ask and answer questions, choosing and using parts of stories and other sources to show that they know and understand key features of events.
● To understand some of the ways in which we find out about the past.

Expected outcomes
● All children know that Guy Fawkes was born long ago in York.
● Most children know that Guy was Catholic, a solider and an expert with gunpowder.
● Some children understand why Guy Fawkes joined the Gunpowder Plot.

Resources
Portrait of Guy Fawkes; photocopiable page 150 'Who was Guy Fawkes?'; photocopiable page 'Guy Fawkes information' from the CD-ROM; drawing pencils

Introduction
● Ask the children: *What name do we also give to Bonfire Night?* (Guy Fawkes Night.)
● Encourage the children to suggest who Guy Fawkes was. Confirm that he was involved in the plot against James I and that in this lesson they are going to find out more about him.

Whole-class work
● Show the portrait of Guy Fawkes. Explore the details of his clothes and hairstyle, pointing out that these were fashionable during the reign of James I.
● Ask the children to suggest Fawkes' mood in the picture. What kind of person do they think he was? Does he look rich, poor, important or ordinary?
● Keep the picture on display for the next activity.
● Explain to the children that they are going to complete a biographical information sheet about the early years of Guy Fawkes from a given set of jumbled-up notes.

Group work or Paired work
● Put the children into mixed-ability pairs or similar-ability groups. Hand out a copy of photocopiable page 150 'Who was Guy Fawkes?', to each child, and a copy of photocopiable page 'Guy Fawkes information' from the CD-ROM to each pair or group.
● Go through the different sections of the worksheet and advise the children that they need to write their answers in sentences. Point out the space where they can draw a portrait of Fawkes.
● As the children work, encourage them to talk to you about the order of the notes and how they are going to convert them into full sentences.

Differentiation
● Support: children might work better in small same-ability groups with adult support if they need help in reading the notes and writing sentences.
● Challenge: children could create a timeline for the dates of Fawkes' life; this could be added to as the topic progresses.

Review
● At the end of the lesson, bring the children together and encourage them to share what they have discovered about Fawkes. Ask prompt questions such as: *Was Guy Fawkes a Catholic or Protestant? Why did he change his name to Guido? What was he well-known for being good at? Why do you think the people behind the Gunpowder plot would want Fawkes to join them? Why did he join?*

Lesson objectives
- To develop an awareness of the past, using common words and phrases relating to the passing of time.
- To use a wide vocabulary of everyday historical terms.
- To ask and answer questions, choosing and using parts of stories and other sources to show that they know and understand key features of events.
- To understand some of the ways in which we find out about the past.
- To identify different ways in which the past is represented.

Expected outcomes
- All children know that the five plotters planned to blow up the Opening of Parliament.
- Most children understand why the plotters wanted to blow up the Opening of Parliament.
- Some children understand what could have happened if the plot had been successful.

Resources
Portrait of Robert Catesby; four rolled-up message/invitation scrolls; photocopiable page 'The Plot: a play scene' from the CD-ROM; props for the play scene (optional); photographs and information or websites on the modern-day Opening of Parliament ceremony

2: The Gunpowder Plot and parliament

Introduction
- Before the lesson, make four invitation-messages for Guy Fawkes, Thomas Wintour, Thomas Percy and John Wright, with the same text apart from the name, for example: *20th May, 1604. Come to the Duck and Drake Inn on the Strand tonight on the ninth hour. Go to the room at the back. Burn this letter now! Catesby.*
- Display a picture of Robert Catesby. Explain that he was Catholic and very angry with King James I about his treatment of Catholics, and he decided to do something about it.
- Give out the four scrolled messages to four of the children. Ask each one in turn to open their scroll and to read out the message.
- Ask all of the children to imagine that they are in the Duck and Drake Inn listening to the conversation between the five men to find out what they are planning to do.
- Display photocopiable page 'The Plot: a scene' from the CD-ROM on the whiteboard, or give printouts to five children who are good readers. Ask them to read the scene out loud, playing the plotters.
- After the play, ask: *Who are the five plotters? How do they intend to get rid of the king and his advisers?* (By blowing up the House of Lords during the Opening of Parliament.) *Who was in charge of what?*

Whole-class work
- Ask: *Why was the Opening of Parliament seen as a good time to kill the king and his advisers?* (The royal family and the government were all in the same place.) Explain what *parliament* means and that, at that time, it took place in the House of Lords. Say that when parliament starts a new year, a ceremony is carried out to open the parliament for work. Discuss the seriousness of Catesby's plot and what it would have meant if it had succeeded.
- Use photographs or footage to show what happens at a modern Opening of Parliament. List the order of events on the board.

Independent work
- Note that this activity might need to be done in a second session.
- Give each child a sheet of paper and ask them write out a short order of events for a modern-day Opening of Parliament that can be used by those attending, as in the style of a service sheet for a wedding or Christening, for example. Model an example on the board.
- Let the children decorate their order of ceremony with images from the ceremony such as the Queen in her carriage.

Differentiation
- Support: ask prompt questions when discussing the play to encourage less-confident learners to extend their answers and responses.
- Challenge: children might want to add more information to their service sheets.

Review
- Remind the children of the play scene and ask them if they worked out what the plotters planned to do and how they were going to do it.
- Note those children who understand at least some of the implications of what could have happened if Parliament had been blown up on 5 November 1605.

Week 3 lesson plans

During week 3, the children create character profiles of each conspirator. In the first lesson, the children study a woodcut engraving of eight of the plotters. They then work in groups to create fact cards and portraits. These then enable the children to make links between the plotters. In the second lesson, a hot-seat session lets the groups investigate the plotters' feelings and motives about the plot and its possible aftermath.

1: The gunpowder plotters

Introduction

● This lesson might need two sessions. Organise the groups to make sure that all 13 conspirators are covered.
● Put the children into small mixed-ability groups and display the engraving of the eight conspirators on the whiteboard. Ask the children who they think the picture shows.
● Let the children look more closely at the picture and ask: *How do we know who is who?* Direct the children to the names engraved above the plotters.
● Discuss the details of their clothes, such as their hats, capes, tunics and hairstyles.
● Ask the children what the men seem to be doing in the picture. Ask: *Does the picture make them look like men you could trust or do they look like they are up to mischief? Why?*

Whole-class work

● Highlight that although there are only eight men in the picture, there were 13 members of the Gunpowder Plot. Explain to the children that they are going to create a large mural of all 13 plotters, with a fact card about each.
● Hold up a sheet of A3 paper to show the size of figure you would like the children to draw. The pictures could then be painted or decorated with collage materials.
● Work with the children to generate a framework for the fact card, for example with subheadings in a left-hand column: *Name:, Date of birth:, Place of birth:, Religion:, Occupation:, Appearance:, Personality:, When he joined the plot:, Role in the plot:, When he died:.*

Group work

● Give out the cards for facts, paper and craft materials to each small mixed-ability group.
● Show the 13 envelopes and place them in a cloth bag. Explain that information about the plotters is in the envelopes.
● Let a member of each group pick out a plotter envelope and work on their fact card and mural portrait using the given information. Encourage the children to use the information about a plotter's appearance in their portrait.

Whole-class work

● Once the portraits and fact cards are completed, ask each group to talk about their plotter. Then briefly say that each one was eventually executed for his role in the plot.
● Use the drawings to create the mural and add the name of each plotter above his picture. (The fact cards will be needed in the next lesson, but can then be added to the mural.)

Review

● Point to two or three of the conspirators in turn, inviting the children to tell you what they know about him.
● Note those children who can understand why aspects of the plotter's personality or background would make him join the plot.

Lesson objectives

● To show where people and events they study fit within a chronological framework.
● To use a wide vocabulary of everyday historical terms.
● To ask and answer questions, choosing and using parts of stories and other sources to show that they know and understand key features of events.
● To understand some of the ways in which we find out about the past.
● To identify different ways in which the past is represented.

Expected outcomes

● All children know that there were 13 plotters in the Gunpowder Plot.
● Most children can build up a picture of what the plotters were like.
● Some children can make links between the beliefs and backgrounds of the conspirators.

Resources

13 envelopes, with a name of a plotter on each envelope, containing a range of pictorial and textual information about him; an old-style cloth bag; the engraving 'The Gunpowder Plotters 1605'; blank cards; A3 paper; drawing and colouring pens and pencils; paints and collage materials (optional)

Lesson objectives
● To use a wide vocabulary of everyday historical terms.
● To ask and answer questions, choosing and using parts of stories and other sources to show that they know and understand key features of events.
● To understand some of the ways in which we find out about the past.

Expected outcomes
● All children can ask the conspirators questions about the Gunpowder Plot.
● Most children can ask and answer questions about the motives and feelings of the plotters.
● Some children can compare the actions of the plotters to modern day terrorism.

Resources
Space and chairs for hot-seat session; fact cards about the plotters from the previous lesson; information about James I (for teacher role in hot-seat session)

2: Interviewing the plotters

Introduction
● Put the children back into their mixed-ability groups from the last lesson and give them their fact cards about their plotters.
● Tell the children that they are going to take part in a hot-seat drama session during which they will have the chance to ask the gunpowder plotters about their motives and feelings about the plot. Highlight that they are also going to have a chance to interview King James I.
● Explain or remind the class what happens in a hot-seat session and the roles of the interviewers and those in the hot seat.

Group work
● To help the children remember who was who, ask each group in turn to say who their plotter was and to explain their background using the fact cards.
● Allocate to each group one or two of the other plotters and ask them to discuss and agree within their group what questions they would like to ask them.
● Emphasise that they must also think about the feelings and thoughts of the plotters and whether they are aware of the death and destruction they could cause.
● Suggest that they should write down their questions if they can.

Whole-class work
● Bring all the children back together and give each group the opportunity to sit in the hot seats to be interviewed.
● Allow the group in the hot seat to either take turns in answering the questions or nominate a spokesperson to be responsible for giving their group's answers.
● Give each group in the hot seat about five questions to answer, or more if time allows.
● Once all the groups/plotters have been interviewed, put yourself in the hot seat.
● Introduce yourself as James I and explain your views on Catholics. Invite questions from all the groups.
● At the end of the hot-seat session, discuss the children's thoughts about the plotters' motives and James I's reactions to it.

Review
● Discuss whether the conspirators were right or wrong to attempt the plot. Ask: *What would have been less violent?* (Organising a petition, staging a 'sit-in' or demonstration, holding a protest march?)
● Note the questions the children put to other plotters and James I about their motives and feelings about the plot, as well as their responses as plotters to others' questions.

Week 4 lesson plans

This week, the children learn about how the Gunpowder Plot was discovered and Guy Fawkes arrested. In the first lesson, the children look at the anonymous letter sent to Lord Monteagle, warning him about the plot. They then write their own warning letters to family or friends. In the second lesson, the children hear of the events leading up to and including the arrest of Guy Fawkes on 5 November. They write a recount with pictures in the style of the 17th century woodcut engravings.

1: The Monteagle letter

Introduction

● Display the image of the original Monteagle letter on the whiteboard. Ask the children how they can tell it is a letter from long ago. Discuss the handwriting, ink, the colour and quality of paper and old spellings and vocabulary.
● Explain that this letter was sent to Lord Monteagle, a member of parliament, in October 1605, by a mystery sender.

Whole-class work

● Now bring up the transcript of the letter from photocopiable page 'The Monteagle letter' from the CD-ROM. Explain that the original letter was written in English used 400 years ago so is difficult for us to understand now. Emphasise that at times, historians rewrite old documents into modern English. Consider how that would help in historical investigations.
● Read the transcript slowly. Then ask prompt questions such as: *What is the letter telling Lord Monteagle to do on the day of the Opening of Parliament? Who do you think sent the letter?* (Some believe the plotter Francis Tresham might have sent it, as he was married to Lord Monteagle's sister.) *What do you think Lord Monteagle did with the letter, and what would this mean for the plot and plotters?* (He passed it on to Robert Cecil, the head of government, and to the king.)

Independent work

● Encourage the children to write a letter to warn a family member or friend not to go to the Opening of Parliament on the 5 November.
● Discuss what they could include in their letter, such as where else to go on the day or hints of where the gunpowder is.
● Advise the children to draft their letter first, then, once they have read it through and are happy with it, to write it neatly on thicker paper.

Whole-class work

● Encourage volunteers to read their letters to the class.
● Remind the children that the original letter was sent by a mystery person.
● Point to the date of the letter, 26 October, and work out together that it was ten days before the plot. Ask: *Why do you think the plotters were not arrested before the 5 November?*

Differentiation
● Support: children may need help to compose orally and then write their letter; the letter can be two or three simple sentences.
● Challenge: expect quite a long descriptive letter.

Review

● Discuss the letter and its message. Note those children who understand what the letter and its revelation of the plot would mean for the plotters and for King James.

Lesson objectives
● To develop an awareness of the past, using common words and phrases relating to the passing of time.
● To use a wide vocabulary of everyday historical terms.
● To ask and answer questions, choosing and using parts of stories and other sources to show that they know and understand key features of events.
● To understand some of the ways in which we find out about the past.

Expected outcomes
● All children know that an anonymous warning letter was sent to Lord Monteagle about the plot.
● Most children understand that the writer knew about the plot and was close to Lord Monteagle.
● Some children know why a document like the Monteagle letter is important to help us find out about the past.

Resources
Image of the Monteagle letter; photocopiable page 'The Monteagle letter' from the CD-ROM; thick paper (if possible cream-coloured and with 'singed' aged edges)

■SCHOLASTIC
www.scholastic.co.uk

Lesson objectives

Lesson objectives
● To use a wide vocabulary of everyday historical terms.
● To ask and answer questions, choosing and using parts of stories and other sources to show that they know and understand key features of events.
● To understand some of the ways in which we find out about the past.
● To identify different ways in which the past is represented.

Expected outcomes
● All children know that Guy Fawkes was caught in the cellar of the House of Lords on 5 November 1605.
● Most children can recount the events of Guy Fawkes' capture.
● Some children understand why the guards suspected that Fawkes was in the cellar.

Resources
Media resource 'Old Gunpowder Plot pictures' on the CD-ROM; information and pictures about 5 November 1605; pamphlet-style blank booklets (paper folded into a book or bound with string); black felt-tipped pens

2: The arrest of Guy Fawkes

Introduction
● Explain to the children the events of what happened on 5 November 1605, using visual resources to refer to where possible (see Background information on page 135).
● Work with the children to write the events out as a list in chronological order.
● Then ask: *Why do you think the guards thought that a plotter was in the cellar (or undercroft)?* Elicit or remind the children about the letter sent to Lord Monteagle.
● Ask: *Why do you think only Fawkes was in the cellar?* (He knew how to set the gunpowder to explode; that was his task in the plot.) *Where were the other plotters?* (In hiding, or fleeing.)

Whole-class work
● Highlight that, after 5 November 1605, reports and ballads (story poems) were written about the Gunpowder Plot and pictures were created to go with them.
● Display a range of old illustrations of the Gunpowder Plot from media resource 'Old Gunpowder Plot pictures' on the CD-ROM. Encourage the children to study the pictures and discuss the stylistic features, such as black line drawings, simple figures and images.
● Focus on the drawing of Guy Fawkes in the cellar and explain that the artist carved the picture into a woodblock and printed it onto paper using ink. Ask: *How does Guy Fawkes look? Does he come across as a hero or villain?* Remind the children of the engraving of the eight plotters that they examined earlier.
● Ask: *Why do you think Guy Fawkes is the only plotter that we really remember after 400 years?* (He was the man who would have 'lit the fuse'; he was the first plotter seized.)
● Remind the children that when using hand-drawn pictures like these engravings or woodcuts to look at historical events, we need to remember they are not necessarily exactly true and accurate.

Independent work
● Explain to the children that they are going to write a recount of what happened on the 5 November, with their own black and white pictures.
● Ask the children to create a pamphlet with black and white pictures and a sentence or two on each page. Encourage the children to compose their sentences orally before they write them down.
● Let the children use pencil initially for their drawings and then give them the option to go over the lines in black pen.

Whole-class work
● Once the children have completed their work, ask them to share and compare their work with others. Have they included the same events and put them in the same order?
● As an extension, you could have an art session to create woodcut prints. (Use softer materials for the cut.) Let the children design a Bonfire Night picture with it.

Differentiation
● Support: extra adult support might be needed to help children write their sentences for their recount.
● Challenge: encourage children to use time connectives in their sentences.

Review
● Share some of the children's recounts and check their understanding of how hand-drawn images of the past can lead us to interpret facts in a certain way.

Week 5 lesson plans

In the first lesson this week, the children learn what happened to the plotters, particularly the five main ringleaders. Their capture and execution need to be told, but it is advised that, at Key Stage 1, details do not have to be discussed or investigated. The children use their knowledge and vocabulary of the rounding up of the plotters to create a newspaper front page. Then they revisit what they have learned about the plot by creating a chronology of events and performing a re-enactment of the plot.

1: Front page news: the plotters' capture

Lesson objectives
● To use a wide vocabulary of everyday historical terms.
● To ask and answer questions, choosing and using parts of stories and other sources to show that they know and understand key features of events.
● To understand some of the ways in which we find out about the past.

Expected outcomes
● All children know that the Gunpowder Plotters were all killed.
● Most children know that some of the plotters tried to escape and were captured.
● Some children know why the plotters were shot during the siege or executed.

Resources
Illustration of Fawkes' arrest; photographs of the Tower of London and Holbeche House; UK map; information on the siege of Holbeche House (for example, from the Gunpowder Plot Society); news-page template (ICT); drawing pencils

Introduction
● Look together at a picture of Guy Fawkes being arrested and ask the children what is happening: *Why is Guy Fawkes the only plotter in the cellar?*
● Show a photograph of the Tower of London. Explain that Guy Fawkes was imprisoned in the Tower after his arrest, and was tortured so that he would say who the other plotters were. Explain with care what *torture* means and say that Fawkes refused to give in and reveal his colleagues' names for two days.

Whole-class work
● Ask the children to speculate on what the other plotters were doing.
● Display a photograph of Holbeche House and, using a large map of the UK, draw a line with your finger from London to Kingswinford in Staffordshire. Explain that most of the plotters fled from London to Holbeche House. Ask the children how they think the plotters travelled. (On horseback.)
● Tell the children about the siege at Holbeche House, which ended with the deaths of the plotters. Others in hiding elsewhere were taken to the Tower of London.

Paired work
● Ask the children to work in pairs to produce a newspaper front page about the capture of the plotters or the siege at Holbeche House.
● Ensure they recognise the key features of a newspaper. It may be useful to provide a template (on screen if possible), with spaces for a headline, a short article and one or more captioned pictures.
● As they work, review the children's progress and share examples of their work. What do they tell the reader about how the plotters were captured.
● Ask: *Is your article written as if you are against the plotters? Should you show your feelings or just report the facts?*

Whole-class work
● Bring the children together to share their front pages. Then briefly say that eight of the plotters, including Guy Fawkes, were executed on 30 and 31 January 1606. Discuss why the punishment was so severe. (It was a very serious crime to try to kill the king, to serve as a warning and deterrent to others.)
● Tell the children that Catholics in England continued to suffer badly for many years after the plot.

> #### Differentiation
> ● Support: ICT would help all children, by allowing drafting and correcting and encouraging quality presentation.

Review
● Use one or two of the children's news stories to discuss what happened to the plotters and how well this has been presented as a dramatic newspaper front page story.

■SCHOLASTIC
www.scholastic.co.uk

2: A re-enactment of the plot

Lesson objectives
● To develop an awareness of the past, using common words and phrases relating to the passing of time.
● To show where people and events they study fit within a chronological framework.
● To use a wide vocabulary of everyday historical terms.
● To ask and answer questions, choosing and using parts of stories and other sources to show that they know and understand key features of events.

Expected outcomes
● All children can put the events of the Gunpowder Plot in chronological order.
● Most children can recount what happened in the Gunpowder Plot.
● Some children can use a timeline to remember reasons for the Gunpowder Plot.

Resources
Photocopiable page 151 'The Gunpowder Plot'; a short film dramatisation of the plot, if possible; scissors; glue; timelines of May 1604 to January 1606; space for children to rehearse and perform; drama props (optional); video camera

Introduction
● Remind the children that the first meeting of the gunpowder plotters took place in the Duck and Drake Inn on 20 May 1604. Work out together that it took a year and a half to make arrangements and fix the suitable date for their attempt to blow up the king and parliament.
● If possible, show a film clip of the Gunpowder Plot story to remind the children of the details.

Paired work
● Organise the children into pairs and hand out photocopiable page 151 'The Gunpowder Plot', and timelines to each child, along with scissors and glue.
● Ask the children to work together in their pairs to put the events of the Gunpowder Plot shown on the sheet into the right chronological order.
● Advise the children first to cut out all of the pictures and captions and then match them together.
● Then, once they are happy and have checked with each other that they have arranged them in the correct order, ask the children to stick them onto their timeline strips.

Group work
● Now combine the pairs into mixed-ability groups of about six children. Ask them to use their Gunpowder Plot timeline to help them to re-enact the events of the whole plot from beginning to end.
● Encourage the children to discuss and decide who is playing which part. Let them know that some of them might have to perform more than one role.
● Suggest a few ideas of how to perform the plot story, for example: with one or two narrators telling the main story while the others mime or have a few lines; a *Crimewatch*-style reconstruction with a television presenter; a more formal play with a speaking part for everyone.
● If possible, have props available. Also suggest to the children that they can use mime in part of their re-enactments, such as rolling barrels into the cellars and digging tunnels.
● After some rehearsal time, let the children perform their re-enactments to the rest of the class. If possible, film their work so the groups can watch their performances.

Review
● Ask the children how well they felt they remembered the significant events of the Gunpowder Plot. What did it reinforce about their understanding of the plot and its participants?

Week 6 lesson plans

This final week considers why Guy Fawkes Night, or Bonfire Night, is still celebrated on 5 November, over 400 years since the event in 1605. In the first lesson, the children find out that James I passed a law that the failure of the plot and his survival should be celebrated every year, and that the Yeoman of the Guard still maintain a tradition of checking the Houses of Parliament cellars. In the second lesson, the children discover why many other winter celebrations are linked with fire and light and whether this is one reason why Guy Fawkes Night has endured so long.

Lesson objectives
- To develop an awareness of the past, using common words and phrases relating to the passing of time.
- To identify similarities and differences between ways of life in different periods.
- To use a wide vocabulary of everyday historical terms.
- To ask and answer questions, choosing and using parts of stories and other sources to show that they know and understand key features of events.
- To understand some of the ways in which we find out about the past.
- To identify different ways in which the past is represented.

Expected outcomes
- All children know that, since 1605, people have remembered the Gunpowder Plot on the 5 November.
- Most children know the different ways people have remembered the Gunpowder Plot.
- Some children understand why people still remember the Gunpowder Plot as a main event in UK history.

Resources
Images of Yeomen of the Guard searching cellars before the Opening of Parliament; A3 paper; drawing pens and pencils; small pictures of Bonfire Night, and glue (optional)

1: Remembering the Gunpowder Plot

Introduction
- Recap with the children what they have learned about the Gunpowder Plot, making notes on the board.
- Explain that the plot was considered so terrible at the time, that, a few months later, the English Parliament passed a law to say that the 5 November should be commemorated every year to remind people of the plot's failure and to celebrate the king's safety.

Whole-class work
- Discuss the ways that people in the 17th century began to commemorate the 5 November, compiling a list on the board, such as church services, bonfires, ringing of bells, fireworks, processions. Ask the children: *Which of these commemorations do we still follow today?*
- Use photograph references to explain that another 400-year-old tradition that comes from the foiling of the plot is the soldiers checking the cellars of the Houses of Parliament before the Opening of Parliament. Ask the children why that tradition started.
- Explain to the children that they are going to create a mind map to show the different ways in which people remember the Gunpowder Plot. Begin an example on the board with the title *Remembering the Gunpowder Plot* in the centre.

Paired work
- Let the children work in pairs to create mind maps with descriptive captions and pictorial examples if possible. (These could be the children's own drawings or cut-out pictures that could be stuck on.)

Whole-class work
- Invite the pairs to share their mind maps.
- Discuss why people of the time were so shocked and horrified by the plot. Ask the children to consider a plot like that in relation to today's Opening of Parliament and the possible terrible aftermath of a similar act.
- Ask the children to recall why Guy Fawkes is the plotter that everyone remembers. Suggest that, over the years, many people have forgotten or didn't ever realise that he was a real person and instead think it is just a name for the figure that is put on the bonfire. How would the children tell someone briefly about the real man, his co-conspirators and what we celebrate?

Differentiation
- Challenge: children could create a mind map as an individual activity; encourage them to caption each picture.

Review
- Look again at the children's mind maps. Compare them to get a full list of celebration features of Bonfire Night. Ask the children if they can relate them to the original celebrations from the time of King James I.

■SCHOLASTIC
www.scholastic.co.uk

Lesson objectives

● To identify similarities and differences between ways of life in different periods.
● To use a wide vocabulary of everyday historical terms.
● To ask and answer questions, choosing and using parts of stories and other sources to show that they know and understand key features of events.
● To understand some of the ways in which we find out about the past.
● To identify different ways in which the past is represented.

Expected outcomes

● All children know that main features of Guy Fawkes Night are the fire and light of fireworks.
● Most children know that there are other winter celebrations of light and fire.
● Some children can link Guy Fawkes Night to traditional fire festivals in winter.

Resources

Photographs of a recent Bonfire Night (local or national); photographs of other winter light or fire festivals such as Diwali, Hanukkah, Loi Krathong and Yi Peng, Christian Advent or Up Helly Aa; white and black paper; writing and drawing pencils and pastels

2: Fire and light poems

Introduction

● Show the children a few photographs of a recent Guy Fawkes Night/Bonfire Night and encourage the children to share their own experiences.
● Talk about what they can see in the photographs and what they remember seeing, hearing and feeling. Focus on the bright fireworks, the light and warmth of the bonfire and enjoyment of hot food and a warm drink on a cold and dark winter's night.

Whole-class work

● Tell the children that during the winter months there are other commemorations and festivals that also use and celebrate light and fire.
● Encourage the children to talk about any that they know, and look at some examples in more detail, such as the Hindu festival of Diwali, Jewish Hanukkah, Loi Krathong and Yi Peng festivals in Thailand, Christian Advent or Up Helly Aa in Shetland.
● Ask the children: *Why do you think light and fire festivals are common in winter?* Elicit appreciation of the long, dark, cold nights of the past when there was no heating or electric light and therefore the comforting and joyful effects of light and warmth of fires (large and small).
● Highlight that some fire and light festivals are linked to people asking their gods or saints for help or giving them thanks for making it safely through the winter.
● Go on to ask: *Do you think these aspects could also be a reason why Guy Fawkes Night, with its warm bonfires and bright fireworks, has continued to be celebrated for over 400 years?*
● Suggest that the children write a Bonfire Night poem that focuses on the light and warmth of the bonfire and fireworks.
● Work with the children to write a range of effective nouns, verbs and adjectives on the board that they could include in their poem.

Independent work

● Let the children begin writing their Bonfire Night poems. Once they have completed their first draft and are happy with their poem, let them write it out neatly in a bonfire or firework design. Ideas could include a shape poem in the form of fireworks or a bonfire or a picture on black paper with the text written in bright colours.

Whole-class work

● Encourage the children to share their poems with others in the class.

Differentiation

● Support: a framework could be used or an acrostic idea using the words 'fire' or 'light'; ICT would also be useful to encourage those with good ideas but less skill in writing to experiment with presentation.
● Challenge: encourage more-able learners to write slightly longer poems and/or create an imaginative presentation layout.

Review

● At the end of the lesson, ask the children why there are many light and fire festivals or celebrations during winter.
● Ask: *Do you think the Gunpowder Plot is an event that is still important to remember? Do you think it will continue to be celebrated for years into the future?*

Lesson objectives
● To know where the people and events they study fit within a chronological framework.

Resources
Picture of King James I; interactive activity 'The Gunpowder Plot quiz' on the CD-ROM; computers, laptops or tablets

People and events of the Gunpowder Plot

Revise
● Show a picture of King James I to the children and ask them who he was.
● Elicit what we call the period of history when he and his family were the kings of England – the Stuart period.
● Ask the children which group of people were angry with him when he was king, and why.
● Say the bonfire night rhyme, *Remember, Remember, the fifth of November...* with the children and discuss what that rhyme is about.

Assess
● Introduce interactive activity 'The Gunpowder Plot quiz' to the children.
● The quiz can be held with different group options, such as the whole class using the interactive whiteboard, or in small groups, in pairs or individually, using computers, laptops or tablets.
● The quiz assesses the children's knowledge of the people and events of the Gunpowder Plot, and the order in which the events took place.
● After the quiz, encourage the children to write their own rhyme about the Gunpowder Plot.

Further practice
● Ask the children to work in pairs or small groups to write extra multiple-choice questions for the quiz. Encourage them to put their questions to the rest of the class or to another pair or group.

Lesson objectives
● To develop an awareness of the past, using common words and phrases relating to the passing of time.
● To identify similarities and differences between ways of life in different periods.

Resources
'Remember, remember...' poem; interactive activity 'Y2 Autumn 2 quiz' on the CD-ROM

Y2 Autumn 2 quiz

Revise
● Take a look back at the 'Remember, remember...'poem. Get the children to make up a new poem, song or rap in remembrance of the Gunpowder Plot.

Assess
● Ask the children to complete the interactive activity 'Y2 Autumn 2 quiz' on the CD-ROM. There are eight multiple choice questions that test what the children will have learned throughout the topic. They will need to read each question carefully before choosing the correct answer.
● Give children a set length of time (such as 15 minutes) to answer the questions. This can be used as part of a formal assessment or as a fun challenge activity, giving children the opportunity to show what they have learned about the topic.
● Less confident readers may need adult support to read the questions aloud.

Further practice
● Review both of the quizzes completed during the 'Assess and review' sessions. Address any misunderstandings about the sequence of events and review what the children know about the Plot and its place in history.

Extract from a Catholic boy's diary

■ Complete this page from a boy's diary written at the time of the Gunpowder Plot.

Dear Diary,   22 May 1604

This morning, I woke up very early

for _____ in our secret family

_____. The hidden door is getting stiff and

has begun to make loud creaking sounds. Both Eliza and I

are scared that one of the servants will find out that we

are _____ and we will get arrested.

      I wish we could just be Catholics and not be picked on.

We can't go to _____ any more or worship

_____ in the way we like. Father thinks

that our priest may be in danger so he has made a special

hiding place in the wall where the _____

can hide. We call it our priest _____.

I am so angry with _____ James. He is

cruel to Catholics and picks on us. It is not fair!

Henry

chapel	Catholics	priest	hole	King	God	mass	church

I can say why there was a plot against King James I.

How did you do?

Who was Guy Fawkes?

■ Answer these questions about Guy Fawkes' early life.

1. When was Guy Fawkes born? _____

2. Where was he born? _____

3. Why did he become a Catholic? _____

4. What did he do as a job? _____

5. Where did he fight as a soldier? _____

6. What new name did he give himself? _____

7. What was he an expert in? _____

8. Any other information? _____

■ Draw a portrait of Guy Fawkes.

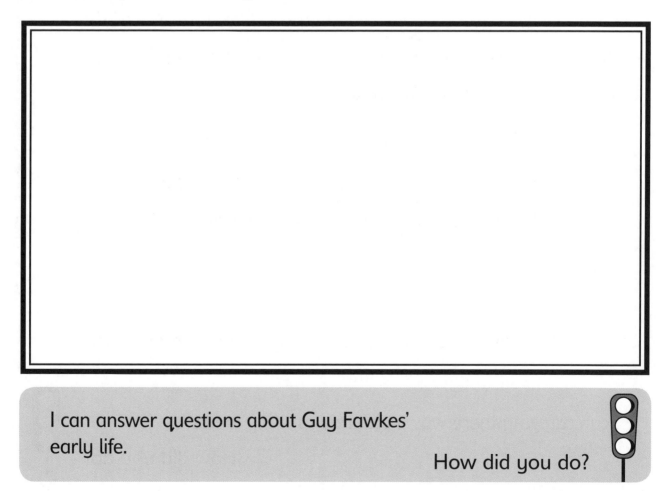

I can answer questions about Guy Fawkes'
early life.

How did you do?

PHOTOCOPIABLE

SCHOLASTIC
www.scholastic.co.uk

The Gunpowder Plot

- Cut out the pictures and captions.
- Match them together.
- Then put them in the right order on your timeline.

The plotters have a plan.	The plotters are executed.
Guy Fawkes is arrested in the cellar.	The plotters store gunpowder in a house.
The other plotters are captured.	A warning letter is sent.

The lives of significant individuals in the past: Rosa Parks and Elizabeth Fry

This chapter looks at the lives of two women who made significant differences to other people's lives – Rosa Parks and Elizabeth Fry. The lessons on Rosa Parks allow the children to find out about international events and changes that happened within recent memory. The life and actions of Elizabeth Fry took place 100 years before Rosa Parks' and was initially centred in the UK. The final week brings the two women together and lets the children compare their many similarities and their differences. Throughout the topic, a main focus is learning and using a range of historical vocabulary in the appropriate way.

Chapter at a glance

Curriculum objectives

- The lives of significant individuals in the past who have contributed to national and international achievements.
- Changes within living memory. Where appropriate, these should be used to reveal aspects of change in national life.
- Events beyond living memory that are significant nationally or globally.

Week	Lesson	Summary of activities	Expected outcomes
1	1	• Children find out who Rosa Parks was and when and where she lived. • They complete a cloze activity about Rosa's early life and draw a picture of her.	• Can use sources to find out who Rosa Parks was and when and where she lived. • Can complete a biography of her childhood.
	2	• Children learn about US racial segregation. • Groups create a display about segregation.	• Can use media sources to understand what segregation is and how it was used in the USA.
2	1	• Children learn about segregation on the bus. • They hear a recount about the events on 1 December 1955.	• Can understand a story about Rosa Parks' actions on 1 December 1955. • Can explore how the bus was set out and the rules implemented.
	2	• Children work in groups to interview 'black' and 'white' passengers on the same bus as Rosa Parks.	• Can create TV or radio interviews to get different viewpoints about what happened on the bus.
3	1	• Children learn about the bus boycott. • They write a short protest letter.	• Know about the Montgomery Bus Boycott and write protest letters.
	2	• Children look at a timeline of Rosa Parks' life to find out what she did after the boycott. • They look at her life is commemorated. • They design their own memorial and write a passage about why we should remember her.	• Know what happened to Rosa Parks later in life. • Can create a memorial to her.
4	1	• Children study and draw a portrait of Elizabeth Fry to establish that she lived long ago. • They listen to an account of her life and put events onto a timeline.	• Know who Elizabeth Fry was and when she lived. • Can make a timeline of her life events.
	2	• Children study the image on a £5 note of Elizabeth Fry at a prison. • They imagine the scene as a prison visitor.	• Can imagine what prison was like in the early 19th century. • Can write reports as prison visitors.
5	1	• Children learn about Elizabeth Fry's committee of Quaker women. • They draw items for a sewing bag for the prisoners.	• Know how Elizabeth Fry helped the female prisoners. • Can list items that could be given to the prisoners.
	2	• Children find out how Elizabeth Fry helped female convicts being transported to Australia. • They learn about the Rajah Quilt. • They make their own paper patchwork quilt.	• Can listen to the story of the Rajah Quilt. • Understand how female convicts created the quilt on the voyage to Australia. • Can create their own paper patchwork quilts.
6	1	• Children review what they have learned about Rosa Parks and Elizabeth Fry.	• Can compare the ways Rosa Parks and Elizabeth Fry made a difference to other people.
	2	• Children plan a way to make a difference to the lives of others.	• Can report plans on how they would like to make a difference to other people.
Assess and review		• To review the half-term's work.	

■SCHOLASTIC
www.scholastic.co.uk

Expected prior learning

● Children can use sources to determine when in the past people lived and events took place.
● Children recognise similarities and differences between the way people lived, their views and where and when they lived.
● Children can identify different ways in which the past is represented.

Overview of progression

● In the first lessons on Rosa Parks and Elizabeth Fry, the children use clues to decide whether they lived in recent times or long ago.
● The children use comparison skills on three levels. First, they compare ways of life within each period studied, then they make comparisons of life in those two periods with today, and finally, they compare the qualities and achievements of Rosa and Elizabeth.
● Throughout the chapter, the children learn quite advanced vocabulary, such as *segregation*, *equality*, *boycott*, *Quaker* and *reformer*.
● The children use a wide range of resources to piece together how and why Rosa Parks and Elizabeth Fry became famous.
● By looking at different aspects and attitudes of the societies that Rosa Parks and Elizabeth Fry lived in, the children extend their understanding of how events and actions of others in the past can be seen in different ways.

Creative context

● This chapter works well with citizenship-led areas. Cross-curricular links include:
  ● creating television or radio news interviews;
  ● learning about their own and other people's feelings, being aware of the views, needs and rights of others, respecting differences and similarities;
  ● drawing portraits, examining pictures, creating wall displays, designing and making memorials, making a patchwork quilt;
  ● recognising time measurements and 2D shapes in patchwork;
  ● locating places such as the state of Alabama and Australia.

Background knowledge

● **Rosa Parks** was born in Tuskegee, Alabama on 4 February 1913. She died on 24 October 2005. She grew up on a farm with her mother, grandparents and brother near Montgomery. In 1932, she married Raymond Parks, a member of the NAACP. Rosa returned to college to get her high school diploma. They had no children. In 1943, Rosa became secretary of the NAACP in Montgomery. On 1 December 1955, Rosa refused to give up her bus seat to a white passenger, as was law at the time. From 1876, the southern states of the USA had Jim Crow laws, which segregated African Americans. Everything was affected, including toilets, hospitals, schools, theatres, shops, buses, water fountains and waiting rooms. The bus driver was verbally abusive and called the police to arrest her. She was bailed the next day. In response to Rosa's actions and arrest, many African Americans boycotted the buses to protest against segregated seating. For nearly a year, the protesters walked, took cabs or shared cars until the bus company finally gave in and the US Supreme Court changed the segregation laws in 1965. One of the young leaders of the protest was Martin Luther King.
● **Elizabeth Fry** was born in Norwich on 21 May 1780 to a wealthy Quaker family. She died on 12 October 1845. In 1800, she married Joseph Fry, a banker and also a Quaker. They had eleven children. She visited Newgate Prison for the first time in 1812. From 1816 onwards, she made regular visits with 12 other Quaker women. She set up a chapel, school and Bible readings as well as sewing classes so the women prisoners could sell their work for more food and bedding. She organised the women prisoners and children to be separated from the men and looked after by women matrons. Elizabeth improved conditions for female convicts being transported to Australia, set up night shelters and soup kitchens for the homeless, improved conditions in mental asylums, hospitals and workhouses and set up the first nursing school.

Week I lesson plans

The topic starts with Rosa Parks and her life and actions. During the first week, the children find out where and when she lived and about her early life. They use time phrases to discover that she lived in *recent times*. In the second lesson, the children are introduced to the concept of racial segregation by learning about segregation in the southern US state of Alabama. Through pictures, photographs and videos the children examine different examples of segregation used from the 1930s to 1950s.

I: Rosa Parks' early life

Lesson objectives
● To develop an awareness of the past, using common words and phrases relating to the passing of time.
● To show where people and events they study fit within a chronological framework.
● To use a wide vocabulary of everyday historical terms.
● To ask and answer questions, choosing and using parts of stories and other sources to show that they know and understand key features of events.

Expected outcomes
● All children know when and where Rosa Parks lived.
● Most children know that Rosa Parks was an African American.
● Some children know about Rosa Parks' early life and its main events.

Resources
Photographs of Rosa Parks and where she grew up in Alabama; footage of or about Rosa (try the BBC or biography.com); world map; photocopiable page 167 'The early years of Rosa Parks'; drawing pencils

Introduction
● Tell the children that they are going to learn about an important famous person called Rosa Parks. Talk about what is meant by a *famous person*. Can the children suggest some people who are famous today?
● Show the children a selection of photographs of Rosa Parks at different times in her life. Briefly explain what Rosa Parks is famous for and why she is remembered (see below).

Whole-class work
● Tell the children that Rosa Parks died only recently, in 2005, when she was 92 years old. Help the children to understand how long ago the year 2005 was by relating it to the ages of the children's family members or major events.
● Explain that Rosa Parks was born near the beginning of the last century, in 1913, and was involved in many changes in her lifetime.
● Tell the children that Rosa Parks was born in the state of Alabama in the USA. Look at a world map together to show the children the location of where Rosa was born. Note that it is in the southern part of the USA.
● Tell the children about the early childhood and teenage years of Rosa Parks, using a range of sources such as photographs and film clips.

Independent work
● Give each child a copy of photocopiable page 167 'The early years of Rosa Parks'.
● Make sure that photographs of Rosa as a young woman and girl as well as pictures of where she lived are on display.
● Let the children complete the cloze sentences on the sheet using the vocabulary from the wordbank.
● Then encourage the children to draw a picture of Rosa Parks as a girl and decorate the frame.
● Provide biographical details so that the children can add her birth and death dates on the frame (see Background information on page 153).

Differentiation
● Support: help children with reading the text and picking out suitable words from the wordbank.
● Challenge: ask children why Rosa Parks' childhood might have been quite hard for her at times.

Review
● Go through the cloze-sentence work on the photocopiable sheet.
● Note those children who understand that Rosa Parks was born in recent times, in the USA during a time of segregation.

■SCHOLASTIC
www.scholastic.co.uk

Lesson objectives
- To develop an awareness of the past, using common words and phrases relating to the passing of time.
- To show where people and events they study fit within a chronological framework.
- To identify similarities and differences between ways of life in different periods.
- To use a wide vocabulary of everyday historical terms.
- To ask and answer questions, choosing and using parts of stories and other sources to show that they know and understand key features of events.

Expected outcomes
- All children know that the black community was once treated badly by the white community in parts of the USA.
- Most children know how people were segregated in parts of the USA until recently.
- Some children understand why racial segregation is wrong.

Resources
A range of photographs and age-appropriate video clips showing segregation (try BBC online); media resource 'Racial segregation' and photocopiable page 'Person template' from the CD-ROM; A4 or A3 paper; drawing pencils

2: Racial segregation in the USA

Introduction
- Note: This lesson may require sensitivity for your class.
- Read out this quote from Rosa Parks about her bus journeys to school as a child:

'I'd see the bus pass every day... The bus was among the first ways I realised there was a black world and a white world.'

- Explain that in the southern part of the United States, when Rosa Parks was a girl, people with black or dark skin were treated differently from the people with white skin.
- Tell the children that laws were passed by people who had white skin, to make sure that the people with black skin did not mix with people with white skin. Introduce the term *segregation*, relating it to separation and setting someone apart.
- Explain that long ago, southern states of the USA used to allow people with white skin to have people with black skin as slaves, and once slavery was stopped, many white people refused to accept them as equals. Stress that not all white people felt that way, especially in other parts of the USA.

Whole-class work
- Display media resource 'Racial segregation' on the CD-ROM and, if possible, show footage of US segregation from the 1930s to 1950s.
- Go through the different ways that the black people were treated differently to white people.
- Focus on the faces and body language. Ask: *How do you think the people who had black skin felt? Why do you think it was difficult for them to try to change the laws so that they were treated more fairly?* (The people who made the laws were the white people who wanted segregation.)

Group work
- Working in groups of four, help the children to create a class wall display to show examples of how black people and white people were segregated.
- Give each group one example of a segregation law, photocopiable page 'Person template' from the CD-ROM and two sheets of drawing paper.
- Ask two children to use the template to draw one white person and one black person. Let the other two children draw two examples of their segregated object or place, for example two toilet doors, two sets of waiting-room chairs. Remind them to add the *black* and *white* signs. Keep media resource 'Racial segregation' on view for reference.
- Once the children have drawn their people and images, encourage them to write a title, such as: *The segregation of a doctor's waiting room*.

Whole-class work
- At the end of the lesson, emphasise that today there is no longer legal segregation in America. People call themselves 'American' or note the country where their family originated, such as 'African American', 'Italian American' or 'Irish American'.

Differentiation
- Challenge: let children research different types of racial segregation and write two or three lines of information to go with the display.
- Support: give children time to study the display to learn more about segregation.

Review
- Check children's understanding of what segregation was and how it came about in the southern USA. Ask: *Why was it wrong and unfair?*

Week 2 lesson plans

This week focuses on Rosa Parks' famous action against segregated seating on a Montgomery Bus on 1 December 1955. In the first lesson, the children learn how the buses were segregated. They then use a recount by Rosa Parks to find out why her actions helped to stop segregation. In the second lesson, the children create TV interviews to investigate how one event seen by lots of eyewitnesses can be recalled in very different ways.

I: Rosa Parks and the bus incident

Introduction

- Show a photograph of the type of Montgomery bus that Rosa Parks took on 1 December 1955. Look at the features and ask the children how they can tell it was a bus from the past and also that it was not British.
- Explain that it was the type of bus that was used 60 years ago in Montgomery, when Rosa Parks was about 40 years old.

Whole-class work

- Remind the children of the racial segregation in the southern US and use media resource 'The bus layout' on the CD-ROM to explain the rules of where 'black' and 'white' people could sit.
- Invite a volunteer to click on different parts of the bus to show the segregation rules. Discuss the rules. Ask: *Where would the people with black skin have to go if all the seats are taken by the people with white skin? Do you think it was fair?*
- Highlight that Rosa Parks also thought it was unfair and did something about it.
- Read photocopiable page 'The bus incident' from the CD-ROM, then discuss it with the children. Ask: *Many people think Rosa Parks was brave. Why? Why do you think her actions encouraged others to stand up to the laws about segregation?*
- Highlight that due to Rosa Parks' life-changing action and similar actions of others after her, a law was eventually passed in the USA to make sure that all people of different skin colours and races were treated fairly and equally.
- With the children, write up short sentences to say what Rosa Parks did, such as: Rosa Parks said 'no' to being treated badly. Rosa Parks was very brave. Rosa Parks changed the lives of many people. Rosa Parks was a hero. Rosa Parks helped others to be brave.

Independent work

- Give each child photocopiable page 'Montgomery bus template' from the CD-ROM.
- Encourage the children to draw a mix of black and white faces in the windows to show that people are now treated the same.
- Let the children choose one of the sentences from the board, or one of their own, and write it as a slogan along the side of the bus.

> **Differentiation**
> - Challenge: children could draw their own diagram of the inside of the Montgomery bus with labelled captions for the rules of each section, or write a list of bus rules.

Review

- Let the children show their buses to the rest of the class and explain why they chose their sentence for their bus. Encourage them to say how they feel about Rosa Parks.
- Check children's understanding of the unfair treatment of segregated passengers and the importance and bravery of Rosa Parks' actions on 1 December 1955.

Lesson objectives

- To develop an awareness of the past, using common words and phrases relating to the passing of time.
- To identify similarities and differences between ways of life in different periods.
- To use a wide vocabulary of everyday historical terms.
- To ask and answer questions, choosing and using parts of stories and other sources to show that they know and understand key features of events.
- To understand some of the ways in which we find out about the past.

Expected outcomes

- All children know what Rosa Parks did on 1 December 1955.
- Most children understand that passengers on the Montgomery buses were segregated.
- Some children understand the importance of Rosa Parks' actions on 1 December 1955.

Resources

Information on Rosa Parks; media resource 'The bus layout' on the CD-ROM; photographs of the Montgomery bus, people in a segregated bus, Rosa Parks in the bus; photocopiable pages 'The bus incident' and 'Montgomery bus template' from the CD-ROM

■SCHOLASTIC
www.scholastic.co.uk

Lesson objectives
● To develop an awareness of the past, using common words and phrases relating to the passing of time.
● To use a wide vocabulary of everyday historical terms.
● To ask and answer questions, choosing and using parts of stories and other sources to show that they know and understand key features of events.
● To understand some of the ways in which we find out about the past.
● To identify different ways in which the past is represented.

Expected outcomes
● All children know that the bus passengers reacted to Rosa Parks' actions.
● Most children can imagine what different passengers saw and thought about Rosa Parks' actions.
● Some children understand that people can see and report the same event in different ways.

Resources
Photocopiable page 'The bus incident' from the CD-ROM and/or a film clip of the event; recording equipment for television or radio interviews, with additional adult support; example television or radio interview clips

2: Media interviews at the bus stop

Introduction
● Recall with the children what happened on the Montgomery city bus on 1 December 1955. If needed, re-read the recount on photocopiable page 'The bus incident' from the CD-ROM or play a film clip of the event.
● Highlight that we know what Rosa Parks felt and why she did not stand up in the bus; but what did the other passengers feel about what happened?

Whole-class work
● Discuss with the children what the other black Americans on the bus might have thought, and list on the board words that describe the emotions, for example: *admiration, fear, tearful, joy, amazement, pride*.
● Do the same with what the white passengers might have thought, perhaps: *anger, confusion, fear, admiration, horror, worry, pleased*.

Group work
● Ask the children to imagine that a local television or radio station has turned up at the bus stop and they want to interview different passengers to find out what happened on the bus and how they feel about Rosa Parks.
● Put the children into mixed-ability groups and ask them to work together to create two television or radio interviews – one of a black passenger and one of a white passenger.
● If necessary, let the children watch or listen to a news report and interview to appreciate the structure and style.
● Encourage the children to decide on a set of questions that they can ask both passengers, noting these down on paper if they want to.
● Once they have thought of and agreed on the questions, let the children decide on the answers.
● Advise the children that they need to work out who are the interviewees and who are the interviewers and then practise the dialogues.
● If possible, set up resources such as microphones and a video camera so that the groups can record their interviews.

Differentiation
● Support: if appropriate, help children practise speaking into a microphone.

Review
● Once all the interviews have been recorded, play them back to the class and discuss what each interviewee said.
● Highlight how this activity shows how one event, in this case Rosa Parks' bus protest, can be seen in a different ways depending on the person watching or listening and what they believe. Note that when we find out about the past, we need to be aware that people witnessing the same event might experience and explain it differently.
● Ask the children to consider the possible immediate reactions to Rosa Parks' actions by the different passengers on the bus. For example, might a black passenger be frightened and run away from the scene?

Week 3 lesson plans

During this week, the children look at the effects of Rosa Parks' stand against segregation. In the first lesson, the children find out about the subsequent Montgomery Bus Boycott and investigate what happened, who was involved, what changes they wanted and whether it worked. They use this knowledge to write a short protest letter. The final lesson for this section on Rosa Parks looks at why she is remembered and revered. The children look at different memorials created for her and design their own along with an epitaph.

1: The Montgomery Bus Boycott

Lesson objectives
● To develop an awareness of the past, using common words and phrases relating to the passing of time.
● To use a wide vocabulary of everyday historical terms.
● To ask and answer questions, choosing and using parts of stories and other sources to show that they know and understand key features of events.
● To understand some of the ways in which we find out about the past.

Expected outcomes
● All children know that many black people stopped using the Montgomery buses in protest.
● Most children know why many people joined the Montgomery Bus Boycott.
● Some children understand how the boycott ended segregation on buses.

Resources
Photograph of Rosa Parks being arrested; a range of photographs of the Montgomery Bus Boycott; photocopiable page 'Person template' from the CD-ROM (optional)

Introduction
● Show the children a photograph of Rosa Parks being arrested after her refusal to give up her seat on the bus.
● Explain that many people from the local black community were upset by this and decided to do something to support Rosa and affirm her actions.
● Display a photograph showing the Montgomery Bus Boycott and ask the children what they think people decided to do.

Whole-class work
● Write the title *The Montgomery Bus Boycott* on the board and explain the terms *boycott* and *protest*.
● Use photographs and/or a video clip to explain the events of the boycott and what was achieved.
● Ask: *Why did so many people from the black community join the boycott? Why do you think some white people also joined the protest?*
● Highlight that in the past, many people could not afford cars, so the bus was their main form of transport. Discuss the different ways people travelled without using the buses. Ask: *Why was it hard for many of the protesters?* (Their shoes wore out; it was very tiring; their days were longer.)
● Make a list of things the protesters wanted the bus companies to change – bus drivers to treat all passengers equally; a first-come first-seated system; no separate sections for 'black' and 'white' people; more non-white bus drivers.
● Explain that some people also wrote letters of protest.
● Ask the children to imagine they have joined the protest and have stopped taking the bus to school and that they want to write a short protest letter to the Montgomery Bus Company.
● Create a letter-writing frame on the board, and model an example, writing out three or four sentences, giving, for example your name and age, why you are sending the letter, what you want changed and how you will walk to school until changes are made.

Paired work or Independent work
● Let the children work independently or in pairs. Encourage them to say their sentences orally first before writing them in their letter.

Differentiation
● Challenge: let children create linked paper-chain figures using the photocopiable page 'Person template' from the CD-ROM to represent the protesters, and add placard signs to one or two of the figures.

Review
● Bring the children back together and ask them to share their letters. Check how well the children understand the meaning of words such as *boycott* and *protest* as well as the reasons why people boycotted the buses and what they did instead.
● Tell the children that, eventually, the boycott was successful and all people could use the Montgomery buses fairly.

■SCHOLASTIC
www.scholastic.co.uk

Lesson objectives

● To identify similarities and differences between ways of life in different periods.
● To use a wide vocabulary of everyday historical terms.
● To ask and answer questions, choosing and using parts of stories and other sources to show that they know and understand key features of events.
● To understand some of the ways in which we find out about the past.
● To identify different ways in which the past is represented.

Expected outcomes

● All children know what a memorial is.
● Most children can design a memorial to represent Rosa Parks' achievements.
● Some children understand why Rosa Parks is a significant person from the past.

Resources

Photographs of Rosa Parks as an old woman and examples of memorials to Rosa Parks; media resource 'Rosa Parks' life' on the CD-ROM; craft materials including, such as air-drying clay, card, collage pieces, paints and pens

2: Remembering Rosa Parks

Introduction

● Show the children a photograph of Rosa Parks as an old woman. Remind the children that she died only recently, in 2005.
● Begin using the timeline in media resource 'Rosa Parks' life' on the CD-ROM to tell the children about what Rosa Parks did after the bus incident on 1 December 1955.
● Read through the significant dates and details on the timeline and ask in what way Rosa still got involved with helping people. Ask: *What different ways was she thanked and remembered?*
● Explain that Rosa Parks was one of the first people of that time to stand up for freedom and ask for people to be treated fairly and equally no matter what colour their person skin or what race they are.
● Emphasise that her actions on the Montgomery bus helped the Civil Rights Movement become a national force for change in the USA and involved other important people like Martin Luther King.

Whole-class work

● Highlight that there are many memorials to Rosa Parks in the USA. Ask: *What is a memorial?* (Something – often permanent and public – to remember a person by.)
● Show examples of different memorials for Rosa Parks, such as a statue, painting, plaque, bench, garden, stamp and coin.
● Ask the children why many of the memorials show her dressed in the clothes she wore on 1 December 1955 or show her standing or sitting on a bus.
● Note that in 2005, on 2 December, over 1000 children marched in a memorial children's walk in the state of Alabama, to remember Rosa Parks' courage and dignity for standing up to segregation and helping to stop it. Highlight that the march was almost 50 years to the day that Rosa Parks sat on the bus.
● Discuss other ways Rosa Parks could be remembered, such as through films, plays, songs, books and poetry.

Independent work or Paired work

● Ask the children to design a special memorial for Rosa Parks. Highlight that it can be anything they want as long as it is connected to Rosa Parks.
● Once the children have designed it, ask them to write a memorial passage, perhaps for a plaque to go on their memorial, about what Rosa Parks did on 1 December 1955 and why we should remember her.
● Give the children time to make their memorials and display them with their memorial passages.

> ### Differentiation
> ● Support: children might need writing support for their memorial passage, or with choosing and using craft materials; ICT could help children put their passage together and choose a suitable font for a memorial text.
> ● Challenge: encourage children to write an obituary for Rosa Parks.

Review

● At the end of the lesson, ask volunteers to show their memorial designs and read out their memorial passages, explaining why they think we should all remember Rosa Parks.

Week 4 lesson plans

This week introduces another woman whose actions and bravery have made a difference to the lives of people unable to stand up for themselves – Elizabeth Fry. The first lesson uses a portrait of Fry to help the children conclude that, unlike Rosa Parks, she lived long ago. The children put the main events of her life on a timeline. In the second lesson, the children learn about prison conditions in the early 19th century and visualise what it would have been like to visit a prison.

Lesson objectives
- To develop an awareness of the past, using common words and phrases relating to the passing of time.
- To show where people and events they study fit within a chronological framework.
- To identify similarities and differences between ways of life in different periods.
- To use a wide vocabulary of everyday historical terms.
- To ask and answer questions, choosing and using parts of stories and other sources to show that they know and understand key features of events.
- To understand some of the ways in which we find out about the past

Expected outcomes
- All children know that Elizabeth Fry lived long ago and is famous for her work.
- Most children are able to put Elizabeth Fry's life story in chronological order.
- Some children know that Elizabeth Fry was famous for helping prisoners and the homeless.

Resources
Portrait of Elizabeth Fry; photocopiable page 'The story of Elizabeth Fry' from the CD-ROM; sentences of key events from the story on separate cards (one set per group); long timeline strips (1780–1850); glue; drawing pencils; short film clip about Elizabeth Fry (optional)

1: The story of Elizabeth Fry

Introduction
- Recap with the children what they learned about Rosa Parks and how she made a difference to the lives of people in the USA.
- Explain to the children that now they are going to find out about a British woman called Elizabeth Fry, who also made a difference to the lives of people who were treated badly.

Whole-class work
- Display a portrait of Elizabeth Fry and ask the children what it tells us about her. Encourage them to focus on her clothes, especially her bonnet and shawl. Ask whether her clothes suggest that she lived long ago or in recent times.
- Emphasise that Elizabeth Fry's clothing and headwear look like they are well-made, but that she is dressed quite plainly. Ask: *What might that tell us about her?*
- Focus on her face and ask the children what kind of person they think Elizabeth Fry might be: kind, gentle, strict, understanding?
- Display photocopiable page 'The story of Elizabeth Fry' from the CD-ROM and read it to the children.
- Afterwards, pick out new vocabulary and check the children understand the meanings of words such as, *Quaker* and *reform*.
- Ask comprehension questions such as: *What kind of work did Elizabeth Fry do? What kind of people did she help? Why did she want to help others?*

Group work
- Put the children into small groups and give each group a shuffled set of cards with sentences from the story, along with timeline strips and glue.
- Invite the children to read the sentences through, supporting them if necessary, and note that they are in the wrong order.
- Encourage the groups to work together to sequence the main events of the story into the right order. Move around the groups, to help them check their sentences against the story shown on the whiteboard.
- Once the children have put the sentences in the right sequence, ask them to stick them onto a long timeline.
- Then give out paper to each child and ask them to draw a portrait of Elizabeth Fry to go with their sequence of events.

Differentiation
- Support: mixed-ability groups would work well in this activity to encourage sharing and support of ideas and suggestions; you could also watch a video about Elizabeth Fry to reinforce the lesson.

Review
- Check how well the children can look for clues in the portrait.
- Do they use time vocabulary when deciding when Elizabeth Fry lived and in what order the events of her life happened?

■SCHOLASTIC
www.scholastic.co.uk

Lesson objectives

Lesson objectives

- To develop an awareness of the past, using common words and phrases relating to the passing of time.
- To identify similarities and differences between ways of life in different periods.
- To use a wide vocabulary of everyday historical terms.
- To ask and answer questions, choosing and using parts of stories and other sources to show that they know and understand key features of events.
- To understand some of the ways in which we find out about the past.

Expected outcomes

- All children know that prison conditions long ago were bad.
- Most children can say what conditions were like for prisoners long ago.
- Some children can use multi-sensory skills to describe what prisons were like long ago.

Resources

One or two £5 notes; the image on the £5 note (such as at the BBC Primary History Famous People website); images of Newgate Prison or similar prisons in the early 19th century; eight fact cards about prisons of the time; photocopiable page 168 'Prison report'

2: Prison conditions in the early 19th century

Introduction

- Let the children take a look at a five-pound note with an Elizabeth Fry image and ask them what it is. Elicit that famous people that have made a difference to the lives of people in the UK are chosen to be on our currency notes.
- Direct the children to the image of Elizabeth Fry. Ask: *Do you recognise this person?* Encourage them to look for clues such as the shawl, bonnet and signature, and confirm that it is Elizabeth Fry.

Whole-class work

- Point at the scene pictured on the left-hand side of the note, and show this picture on the whiteboard too if possible. Ask questions such as: *Which person is Elizabeth Fry? What is she doing?* Look at the light coming through a window. Ask the children where (what place) Elizabeth Fry is.
- Remind the children about Elizabeth Fry's visit to Newgate Prison in London, from the biography they listened to in the last lesson.
- Highlight that long ago in this country, men, women and children were sent to prison for crimes ranging from murder to taking an apple, so some people were imprisoned for minor offences. Women prisoners kept their young children with them while in prison.
- Display images of prison conditions of that time. Give out the eight prison-condition fact cards to eight children and ask them in turn to read out their card out and place it on a display board for everyone to see.
- Next, ask the children to close their eyes and imagine that they are visiting the prison with Elizabeth Fry. Invite them to imagine the sights and smells and how their bodies feel – for example, cold and damp.

Independent work

- After a few minutes, ask the children to open their eyes and discuss with a partner what they saw and felt about what they had seen.
- Give each child a copy of photocopiable page 168 'Prison report', and let them use the framework to write a report and draw a picture of the prisoners.
- Point to the fact cards on display.

Differentiation

- Support: children might benefit from working in small groups with adult support so that they can talk through their ideas and have writing support.
- Challenge: encourage children to write longer descriptive sentences.

Review

- At the end of the lesson, highlight that Elizabeth Fry returned to the prison with warm clothes, blankets and clean straw for the sick.
- Ask: *Do you think Elizabeth was brave to go into the prisons? Why do you think she wanted to help the prisoners?*
- Stress that the prisons were dangerous and prisoners could have attacked Elizabeth. Ask: *Why do you think Elizabeth Fry put herself at risk, like Rosa Parks did in the bus?*

Week 5 lesson plans

This week, the children find out about some of the ways in which Elizabeth Fry made a difference to the lives of female prisoners and the female convicts transported to Australia. In the first lesson, the children learn about the group of Quaker women who helped to improve conditions for the prisoners. In the second lesson, the children learn about the rare Rajah Quilt as an example of how Elizabeth's sewing kits helped female convicts to cope with their harsh transportation. They also get a chance to make a patchwork quilt.

1: How Elizabeth Fry helped the prisoners

Lesson objectives
- To identify similarities and differences between ways of life in different periods.
- To use a wide vocabulary of everyday historical terms.
- To ask and answer questions, choosing and using parts of stories and other sources to show that they know and understand key features of events.
- To understand some of the ways in which we find out about the past.

Expected outcomes
- All children know that Elizabeth Fry made improved the lives of women and children prisoners.
- Most children know what changes Elizabeth Fry made to improve the lives of prisoners.
- Some children understand how Elizabeth Fry's changes made a difference to prisoners.

Resources
Painting of Elizabeth Fry reading to the prisoners at Newgate in 1823; prison-condition fact cards from the previous lesson; photocopiable page 169 'How to help the prisoners'; drawing pencils; scissors; glue

Introduction
- Remind the children of their visualisation of visiting Newgate Prison and the conditions prisoners lived in. Look at the prison conditions fact cards from the last lesson to help the children to remember.
- Recap on Elizabeth Fry's brave visits to the prison and say that after the visits she decided to work hard to improve the conditions for the women and children.

Whole-class work
- Show the picture of Elizabeth Fry reading to the Newgate prisoners. Draw attention to the other women in similar bonnets and shawls. Explain that Fry set up a committee with 12 other Quaker women to help her, called the Association for the Improvement of the Female Prisoners in Newgate. Write the name on the board and explain the terms *committee* and *association*.
- Explain that Elizabeth Fry and her committee met up to plan how to help the women and children in Newgate Prison.

Paired work or Independent work
- Hand out a copy of photocopiable page 169 'How to help the prisoners', paper, pencils, scissors and glue to each child.
- Explain to the children that the committee set of good ideas to help the prisoners have got muddled up with a set of ideas that are not so good.
- In pairs, ask the children to talk about and select the good ideas and then cut and stick them down or write them out in a list on a sheet of paper.
- Encourage them to write the name of Elizabeth Fry's association as a heading.
- Then let the children use the bag shape on the photocopiable sheet to draw and label items the committee could take in to help the women sew or knit, such as wool and other threads, cloth, needles, and thimbles.
- Briefly discuss what would have been sewn or knitted long ago, such as shawls, blankets, patchwork bed covers, vests, tablecloths and curtains.
- Once they have filled the bag shape, ask the children to cut it out and add it to the bottom of their list sheet or keep it as a separate item.

Differentiation
- Challenge: in another session, children could make simple bags and put in them actual items for the women prisoners and children.

Review
- At the end of the lesson, check the children's decisions of what would be good ideas and discuss how these would make a difference to the prisoners, including giving them something positive to do and making them feel valued. Ask: *Why do you think the women did sewing instead of crafts like woodwork?*
- Explain that Elizabeth Fry's improvements were eventually used in most UK prisons and made a difference to the lives of many women and children.

■SCHOLASTIC
www.scholastic.co.uk

Lesson objectives
● To identify similarities and differences between ways of life in different periods.
● To use a wide vocabulary of everyday historical terms.
● To ask and answer questions, choosing and using parts of stories and other sources to show that they know and understand key features of events.
● To understand some of the ways in which we find out about the past.
● To identify different ways in which the past is represented.

Expected outcomes
● All children know that Elizabeth Fry helped women convicts being transported to Australia.
● Most children know that making patchwork quilts helped women on the convict ships.
● Some children understand how making patchwork quilts helped the women to survive the harsh conditions on convict ships.

Resources
World map; image of the convict ship the *Rajah* or similar; calendar; photographs of the Rajah Quilt; picture of Elizabeth Fry with female convicts; patchwork-shape templates; scissors; felt-tipped pens; white or cream paper; coloured and patterned paper; large backing board; glue; sea/sailing sound effects (optional)

2: The Rajah Quilt

Introduction
● Explain that in Elizabeth Fry's time, many women prisoners were sent to Australia because the prisons here were full. Explain that the term for this was *transportation*.
● Discuss with the children how people get to Australia today. Use a world map to emphasise the distance. Explain that today it can take 23 hours to fly by aeroplane to Australia directly. Recall that there were no passenger aeroplanes in the 19th century, only ships.
● Show a picture of a convict ship such as the *Rajah*. Point out that many convict ships during the life of Elizabeth Fry used just sails to power them. Ask: *How long do you think it would have taken to sail from Britain to Australia, long ago?* Tell the children that the *Rajah* left England on 1 April 1841 and arrived in Australia on 1 December 1841. Let the children use a calendar to count the nine months. Ask the children how hard they imagine the voyage would have been.

Whole-class work
● Tell the children that, as well as prisons, Elizabeth Fry also worked to improve conditions for the women on the prison ships. Show a picture of her with the convicts and explain that she would give the women sewing kits and bags of cloth for the long journey.
● Explain how the convict women on the *Rajah* joined together to make one large patchwork quilt during their journey. Show photographs of the Rajah Quilt and look closely at the images and shapes.
● Ask: *How did making the quilt help the prisoners?* (It helped to keep their mind off the long journey and its hardships; it gave them a way of expressing their feelings.)

Group work or Independent work
● Explain to the children that they are going to make a class patchwork quilt from paper shapes.
● Ask them to draw one picture on a white shape about Elizabeth Fry or the lives of prisoners. The rest of the shapes can be made from coloured or patterned paper.
● Organise the groups around tables with a set of patchwork-shape templates, scissors, pens, white or cream paper and coloured and patterned paper.
● Encourage the children to create as many patchwork shapes as possible.
● To add an authentic atmosphere, play sea noises, or encourage the children to use their imagination to tell each other stories of why they are being transported.
● As an extension, in another session, let the children help you to glue their patchwork shapes onto a large board to create a patchwork quilt effect. Include a centrepiece, such as a portrait of Elizabeth Fry. Once the 'quilt' is dry, display it on a wall for all the children to study. The children could write about the Rajah Quilt or create a folk song about it.

Review
● Invite the children to examine the pictures on their quilt. Ask: *How did Elizabeth Fry's patchwork sewing kits help the women convicts during their long transportation voyage? What can we learn about the women from the pictures on their Rajah Quilt?*

Week 6 lesson plans

In this final week, the children look at both Rosa Parks and Elizabeth Fry and get an opportunity to use the knowledge and vocabulary they have learned throughout the topic. In the first lesson, the children watch or listen to recounts of Rosa's and Elizabeth's lives and share their thoughts about the two women. They then investigate the women's similarities and differences. In the final lesson, the children work in groups to plan a campaign or event that would make a difference to others in their local community.

1: Comparing Rosa Parks and Elizabeth Fry

Introduction

● Show film clips of both Rosa Parks' and Elizabeth Fry's lives or tell the children their life events. After each video or recount, establish with the children what Rosa or Elizabeth did that was important and made them famous.
● Encourage the children to use their knowledge and vocabulary to discuss the parts of Rosa's and Elizabeth's lives and achievements that they remember most of all.
● Tell the children that some people did not like Rosa and Elizabeth and were against them and what they did. Ask: *Who do you think these people might have been? Why do you think these people were like that?*

Whole-class work

● Highlight that, even though Elizabeth Fry lived long ago and Rosa Parks lived in recent times, their actions and their bravery helped many people who were treated badly by others.
● Draw a table on the board with the overall heading *Rosa Parks and Elizabeth Fry* and two columns with headings *Similarities* and *Differences*.
● Suggest to the children that, in groups, they think of examples of ways in which Rosa and Elizabeth were similar and ways in which they were different.
● Encourage the groups to talk about their actions, personalities, background, when and where they lived, and so on.

Group work

● Once the children are in mixed-ability groups, ask them to concentrate on either the similarities or differences between the two women (as allocated by you).
● Move around the groups as they discuss and make an oral or written list of the similarities or differences. Prompt them to include aspects that they might not have thought of, such as education, or family (including husbands and children).

Review

● Once the groups have made their list of ideas, bring them together and, taking each group in turn, ask for examples of the similarities or differences.
● Record the examples in the table on the board and encourage the children to explain their choices in depth.
● Use the completed table to make comparisons of the two women. Ask: *What qualities do both women share?*
● Note the children's use of vocabulary and check their skills in comparing the two women's lives and actions.

Lesson objectives
● To show where people and events they study fit within a chronological framework.
● To identify similarities and differences between ways of life in different periods.
● To use a wide vocabulary of everyday historical terms.
● To ask and answer questions, choosing and using parts of stories and other sources to show that they know and understand key features of events.
● To understand some of the ways in which we find out about the past.

Expected outcomes
● All children can see some similarities and differences between Rosa Parks and Elizabeth Fry.
● Most children can compare the lives of Rosa Parks and Elizabeth Fry.
● Some children can make links about how Rosa Parks and Elizabeth Fry were treated by others.

Resources
Film clips about Rosa Parks' and Elizabeth Fry's lives (such as from the BBC's *True Stories* online), or written accounts; the children's work and images from the topic

Lesson objectives
● To identify similarities and differences between ways of life in different periods.
● To use a wide vocabulary of everyday historical terms.
● To ask and answer questions, choosing and using parts of stories and other sources to show that they know and understand key features of events.
● To understand some of the ways in which we find out about the past.

Expected outcomes
● All children understand that they can make a positive difference to others.
● Most children can plan ideas to make a positive difference to others.
● Some children recognise why Rosa Parks and Elizabeth Fry are role models.

Resources
Drawing pencils

2: Making a difference to others

Introduction
● Recap with the children what Rosa Parks and Elizabeth Fry did and why we remember them.
● Write out this inspirational quote from Rosa Parks on the board and read it out loud with the children:
  'Every person must live their life as a model for others.'
● Discuss what she meant and identify what Rosa Parks and Elizabeth Fry each did to be a model for others.
● Discuss with the children how we could try to be like Rosa Parks or Elizabeth Fry and try to make a difference to improve others people's lives.
● Emphasise that it could be something simple or on a bigger scale, such as making a gift for a friend who is unwell, gardening, fundraising for a charity or campaigning for improved access and use of a local park so children with disabilities can also use the play equipment.

Group work or Paired work
● Put the children into small mixed-ability groups or pairs and give them a sheet of paper to write and draw on.
● Explain to the children that, in their groups or pairs, you want them to think of an idea or event that would make a difference to others in their local community.
● Highlight that once they have decided what they would like to do, they need to set out plans of how they could do it and what resources they would need.
● Encourage the children to note down their ideas as they talk, and sketch any designs that they might need to draw up.
● As the children work, move around the groups to check that everyone understands what they should be doing, and ask questions to encourage them to think with focus and detail about their ideas: *Who could benefit from that idea, and how? How could you make it happen?*

Whole-class work
● Towards the end of the lesson, bring the groups together. Let each group come up in turn to present their idea by explaining what it is and how they could carry it out. Ask the rest of the class: *How would this make a difference?*
● As an extension, run a class campaign or event that would make a difference to others, such as fundraising for a charity or big events such as Red Nose Day or Sport Relief. Other ideas could include helping the local community by, for example, inviting a group of elderly people into school for afternoon tea or a class performance.

Review
● Check how well the children participated in the group work and the usefulness of their ideas.
● Ask each child to think of and share one thing they could do to be more like Rosa Parks and Elizabeth Fry.

Lesson objectives
● To identify different ways in which the past is represented.

Resources
Media resource 'Opinions about Rosa Parks and Elizabeth Fry' on the CD-ROM; a picture of Elizabeth Fry and of Rosa Parks for each child; two sheets of paper for each child; multiple sets of descriptive word cards

Characteristics of Rosa Parks and Elizabeth Fry

Revise

● Show the children a picture of Elizabeth Fry and a photograph of Rosa Parks.
● Ask the children who they are and which of them lived long ago and which lived in recent memory.
● Remind the children that, although they contributed great things, people felt differently about the two women and what they achieved.
● Open media resource 'Opinions about Rosa Parks and Elizabeth Fry' on the whiteboard.
● Ask the children to listen carefully to the two points of view about Rosa Parks and her actions. Discuss with the children why the people held those views.
● Do the same for on Elizabeth Fry.

Assess

● Put the children into pairs and give them a set of descriptive word cards, for example: *brave, caring, kind, clever, mean, nasty, selfish, gentle, strong, weak, loyal, bold, gentle, rude, uncaring.*
● Then give each child two sheets of paper and a picture each of Rosa Parks and Elizabeth Fry.
● Ask them to stick one picture in the middle of each sheet so that they have one sheet for Rosa and one sheet for Elizabeth.
● Help them to draw a mind-map circle around each picture.
● Then ask the children to look at the word cards and choose the best ones to describe Rosa Parks and Elizabeth Fry. Advise them that they can use the words more than once. Let them write their choices around each picture, copying the word cards for spellings.
● Encourage them then to write sentences about their own feelings about Rosa Parks and Elizabeth Fry.
● Ask the children which words have been used for both Rosa and Elizabeth.

Further practice

● Create the opportunity for the children to listen to or read different accounts of what people thought of Rosa Parks and Elizabeth Fry during their lifetimes. Have a debate or hot-seat session to question the different viewpoints.

Lesson objectives
● To develop an awareness of the past, using common words and phrases relating to the passing of time.
● To identify similarities and differences between ways of life in different periods.

Resources
Interactive activity 'Y2 Spring I quiz' on the CD-ROM

Y2 Spring I quiz

Revise

● Ask children to take the role of Rosa Parks or Elizabeth Fry and to talk about their lives. Other children could ask questions during this role play.

Assess

● Ask the children to complete the interactive activity 'Y2 Spring I quiz' on the CD-ROM. There are eight multiple-choice questions that test what the children will have learned throughout the topic. They will need to read each question carefully before choosing the correct answer.
● Give children a set length of time to answer the questions. This can be used as part of a formal assessment or as a fun challenge activity, giving children the opportunity to show what they have learned about the topic.

Further practice

● Review children's understanding of both individuals and their importance in history.

The early years of Rosa Parks

■ Use the wordbank to complete this account of Rosa Parks when she was young.

Rosa Parks was born on 4 February, 1913, in _____

in the United States of America (_____). Rosa

spent most of her _____ living with her mother

and _____ on their farm.

She went to a _____ where only

African American children were allowed to go. The school had only

one _____ and did not have enough

money to buy basic things like desks. _____

children went to schools with many classrooms,

desks and lots of _____

and were driven there in a school

_____ . However, Rosa

and her friends had to walk the long

_____ to school every day.

bus	childhood	school	room	grandparents
journey	books	Alabama	USA	White

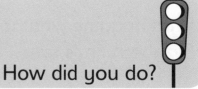

I can complete a text about Rosa Parks.

How did you do?

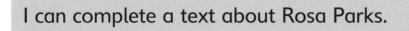

Prison report

■ Write about what you found during your visit to Newgate Prison.

Prison: Newgate Prison, London

What I could see

What I could hear

What I could smell and feel

What I felt about the prison

Picture of the prisoners

I can imagine what a prison was like in Elizabeth Fry's time.

How did you do?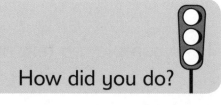

PHOTOCOPIABLE   ■SCHOLASTIC
www.scholastic.co.uk

Name: _____   Date: _____

How to help the prisoners

✂ -

Teach the women how to sew and knit.	Buy them a horse.	Teach the children and women to read.
Teach the children to play the drums.	Separate the men and women prisoners.	Have women guards for the women.
Provide clean clothes.	Start a school for the children.	Have weekly feasts.
Give women sewing and knitting kits.	Give women clock-making kits.	

Events beyond living memory: the Great Exhibition

This chapter looks at a major event during the Victorian period – the Great Exhibition of 1851. The children find out more about Queen Victoria and Prince Albert, and Albert's role in inaugurating the exhibition. They are also are introduced to the abstract term of *empire* and Britain's position in the world then. The children use a wide range of original resources from the Great Exhibition including pictures, photographs, plans, eyewitness accounts, catalogue entries and adverts to help them to find out more about the Crystal Palace building, the exhibitors and exhibits and the experiences of the visitors.

Chapter at a glance

Curriculum objectives

• Events beyond living memory that are significant nationally or globally.
• The lives of significant individuals in the past who have contributed to national and international achievements.

Week	Lesson	Summary of activities	Expected outcomes
1	1	• Children put pictures of Victoria and Albert in time order and draw them.	• Can identify Queen Victoria and Prince Albert. • Can recognise changes in them over time.
	2	• Children create a timeline of Victorian inventions. • They look at a map of the British Empire to find out what countries it included in 1851. • They complete a letter from Prince Albert about his exhibition idea.	• Know about Prince Albert's idea for the first world trade fair. • Understand what an empire is and what it meant for Britain at the time.
2	1	• Children find out about the hall design competition and decide what the hall needed. • They examine pictures to find out about the external features of the hall. • They complete a diagram of the building.	• Can discover how the exhibition space was planned and built and why it was called the Crystal Palace.
	2	• Children work in small groups to create models of the Crystal Palace.	• Can follow images to make a model of the Crystal Palace.
3	1	• Children read an account of the opening of the Great Exhibition. • They write a newspaper report about the day.	• Can use pictures and eyewitness accounts to learn about the opening of the Great Exhibition. • Can write a story for a Victorian newspaper.
	2	• Children study pictures to identify the main features of the exhibition interior. • They make a class edition of the *Illustrated Exhibitor*.	• Know what was in the Great Exhibition halls. • Can create a captioned picture of an exhibit or feature.
4	1	• Children look at a slideshow of British exhibits and identify the exhibition groupings. • They create catalogue entries for exhibits.	• Understand what an exhibit is. • Can identify the range of exhibits from the UK. • Can create their own catalogue entry.
	2	• Children use visual sources to help them design an exhibition stand.	• Can study pictures to look at the wide range of exhibits. • Can design an exhibition stand.
5	1	• Children find out about the international exhibits. • They choose an Indian exhibit and complete a visitor's sheet about it.	• Know where international exhibitors came from. • Understand that for many visitors it was the first experience of anything or anyone from abroad. • Can write about an international exhibit.
	2	• Children find out about the different ticket prices and different classes of visitor. • They create train posters to encourage visitors to see the exhibition.	• Understand that millions of people were able to visit the Great Exhibition due to cheap travel and special ticket days. • Can create train posters for the exhibition.
6	1	• Children listen to recounts from three visitors to the exhibition. • They write their own recounts.	• Are aware of the range of exhibition visitors. • Can imagine the experiences of different visitors.
	2	• Children find out what happened to the Crystal Palace. • They design a new Crystal Palace.	• Know what happened to the Crystal Palace after the exhibition. • Can design a new Crystal Palace for the future.
Assess and review		• To review the half-term's work.	

■SCHOLASTIC
www.scholastic.co.uk

Expected prior learning

● Children can use a range of sources to show that they understand key features and events.
● Children can ask and answer questions about an event to find out more about it.
● Children can identify different ways an event can be represented.

Overview of progression

● The children recall that the Victorian period was beyond living memory. They use clues in pictures of Queen Victoria and Prince Albert to put them in order, and study a Victorian timeline to help them to understand why Victorian Britain was a top industrial nation. The children study the Great Exhibition, starting from Prince Albert's idea and reason for the exhibition through to the planning and building of the Crystal Palace, the opening ceremony, the exhibits and exhibitors, the visitors, and the eventual fate of the Crystal Palace in the 1930s.
● Throughout the chapter, the children enhance their enquiring skills. They find clues to what was in the exhibition halls and what is was like to visit the exhibition. They also create their own stand to reinforce the idea of exhibiting.
● The children should be able to understand how important original 19th century resources are for us to understand more about the Great Exhibition and its importance to British history.
● The children come to understand the big impact the exhibition had on people at the time. Through a range of sources, they investigate the different experiences of different classes of visitor and those who came from different parts of the country and from overseas.

Creative context

● This chapter works particularly well with design and technology learning. Cross-curricular links include:
  ● writing newspaper front pages, information booklets, catalogue entries, a visitor log book, recounts and advertisements;
  ● drawing a diagram of the Crystal Palace, an exhibit, an exhibition stand, a train advertisement; designing a Crystal Palace for the future;
  ● investigating the use of glass and iron as building materials;
  ● using maps to locate the countries of some of the international exhibitors.

Background knowledge

● The Great Exhibition was held in Hyde Park for six months from 1 May 1851. At that time, Britain was a great industrial nation with an empire stretching across the world. It was often called 'the workshop of the world'. Prince Albert wanted to showcase and celebrate Britain's exports and industries as well as invite other countries to exhibit their products.
● Prince Albert and his organisers invited designs for a large and impressive exhibition hall. Out of over 100 designs, the outstanding one was 550m long and 140m wide, made from 300,000 glass panels supported by a highly ornate cast-iron framework. Designed by Joseph Paxton, the parts were delivered to the site in Hyde Park and bolted and slotted into place by teams of builders. Its sparking glass gave it the nickname the 'Crystal Palace'.
● On 1 May 1851, Queen Victoria opened the Great Exhibition after a big procession through London and a special ceremony. Inside the hall were trees from the park, a massive pink glass fountain, statues, food and drink stalls, public toilets and over 100,000 exhibits in stands or display areas on several floors. They included raw materials such as silk and coal, small and large industrial and farming machinery, manufactured products and fine art.
● Over six million visitors came from all over Britain and the world. Many travelled by train. Visitors from all social classes were able to visit thanks to the differently priced tickets and special days.
● In October 1851, the exhibition ended and the Crystal Palace was rebuilt in Sydenham in South London in a specially built pleasure park. It burned down in 1931, but the park still exists.

Week 1 lesson plans

This week reintroduces the children to the Victorian period and to the idea of Britain as a world power through its trade and empire. In the first lesson, the children investigate pictures and photographs to find out about Queen Victoria and her relationship with Prince Albert. In the second lesson, the children create a timeline of major Victorian inventions and are introduced to the concept of *empire*. They study a map of the British Empire during the Victorian era to discover what countries it used to rule. Through this, the children learn about Prince Albert's idea of a world trade fair to show off and celebrate British achievements here and abroad.

1: Queen Victoria and Prince Albert

Lesson objectives
● To develop an awareness of the past, using common words and phrases relating to the passing of time.
● To show where people and events they study fit within a chronological framework.
● To use a wide vocabulary of everyday historical terms.
● To ask and answer questions, choosing and using parts of stories and other sources to show that they know and understand key features of events.
● To understand some of the ways in which we find out about the past.

Expected outcomes
● All children know that Queen Victoria and Prince Albert were married.
● Most children know that Prince Albert died at a young age.
● Some children understand that Prince Albert helped rule Britain with Queen Victoria.

Resources
Large photograph of Queen Victoria in her coronation gown; large wedding portrait of Victoria and Albert; a range of illustrations and photographs of Victoria and Albert over the years and a couple of Victoria as a widow, shuffled out of chronological order

Introduction
● Tell the children that they are going to learn more about a famous queen and her husband from long ago: Queen Victoria and Prince Albert.
● Show the coronation portrait of Victoria and ask the children if they recognise her. Confirm that it is Queen Victoria when she was crowned in 1838, when she was only 18.
● Ask: *Who can remember what we have learned about Queen Victoria?* Take the children's feedback, then confirm that Victoria was queen for 63 years and this block of time is the Victorian period.

Whole-class work
● Show a picture of Victoria and Albert's wedding in 1840. Look at the picture for clues to work out the special event captured. Ask: *Do you think the people look happy?*

Group work
● Explain to the children that they are going to study some pictures of Victoria and Albert. They have been jumbled up so the children's task is to sort them out into time order, using what is in the pictures as clues.
● Give each small group (mixed ability for support) a shuffled set of pictures, including two of Victoria in her widow's 'weeds'.
● Once they have ordered the pictures, ask them to discuss whether they think Victoria and Albert had a happy marriage. How can they tell? Ask: *Why don't the last two photographs include Albert? How does Queen Victoria look in these two pictures?*

Whole-class work
● Bring the groups together and go through the pictures and the correct order.
● Share thoughts about the pictures. Ask: *Why is the Queen dressed in black in the last pictures?*
● Confirm that they were very happy and that Albert helped Victoria to govern the country. Tell the children that he died when he was only 42, and that Victoria mourned him until her own death, 40 years later.
● Ask the children to choose their favourite picture of Victoria and Albert and to draw their own version of it.
● Then let them draw a frame and add the names and birth and death dates of Victoria and Albert.

Review
● Show the children a few of the photographs again and encourage them to explain what clues they used to put them in time order.
● Ask: *What might we able to tell about Victoria and Albert from these pictures and photographs?*

■SCHOLASTIC
www.scholastic.co.uk

Lesson objectives
● To develop an awareness of the past, using common words and phrases relating to the passing of time.
● To show where people and events they study fit within a chronological framework.
● To identify similarities and differences between ways of life in different periods.
● To use a wide vocabulary of everyday historical terms.
● To ask and answer questions, choosing and using parts of stories and other sources to show that they know and understand key features of events.

Expected outcomes
● All children know that Prince Albert had the idea for the Great Exhibition.
● Most children know that Britain was behind some important inventions in the Victorian period.
● Some children understand what *empire* means and how it made Britain powerful and rich.

Resources
Large timeline from 1838 to 1901; date cards for a range of major Victorian inventions; media resource 'British Empire map from 1850' on the CD-ROM; picture of Prince Albert; photocopiable page 185 'Prince Albert's idea'

2: Victorian Britain

Introduction
● Remind the children that Queen Victoria was queen for 63 years and that this block of time is known as the Victorian period.

Whole-class work
● Tell the children that, during the Victorian period, there were many new inventions and changes.
● Suggest that the class make a timeline to show the inventions during the Victorian period.
● Display a timeline on the board. Point out that the start date is the year Queen Victoria was crowned and that the end date is the year when she died (and so the end of her reign).
● Display the invention cards in front of the class. Read them out in chronological order and ask volunteers to place them on the timeline. Inventions could include: the pedal bike (1838); postage stamps (1840); Christmas cards (1843); Morse Code (1844); sewing machine (1846); concrete (1849); ice cream (1851)...
● Note significant inventions that came from Britain and their importance, such as the railway, the spinning frame, the postage stamp and the steam engine.
● Highlight that, in the Victorian period, Britain took over the rule of many other countries in the world. Show media resource 'British Empire map from 1850' on the CD-ROM to the children.
● Point to Britain coloured in red, and work with the children to name some of the other countries also coloured in red, such as India, Australia, South Africa, Canada, Jamaica and Singapore. Explain what the term *empire* means and that these countries were part of the British Empire.
● Highlight that Britain became rich and powerful from using and trading many of the goods that were found in these countries, such as tea and silks from India, timber and wheat from Canada and diamonds from South Africa.
● Now show a picture of Prince Albert and ask the children if they remember who it is. Explain that he wanted to think of a special way to celebrate Britain's achievements, such as its inventions and trade routes.
● Ask the children to talk with a partner to think of an idea that might be suitable for Prince Albert. Make a list of the children's ideas and encourage them to explain their thoughts.
● Help the children to understand the word *exhibition*, and introduce Albert's idea of a world trade fair called the 'Great Exhibition'.

Independent work
● Give out a copy of photocopiable page 185 'Prince Albert's idea', to each child. Explain that it is a letter from Prince Albert to the prime minister of Britain, suggesting the Great Exhibition idea.
● Let the children use the wordbank to add the missing words to the letter.
● Then ask the children to draw a picture of a Victorian train or a postage stamp with Victoria's face on it and a steam train in the background, as an example of an important Victorian invention.

Differentiation
● Challenge: children might be able to colour and label world maps to show the British Empire of the Victorian period.

Review
● Go through the photocopiable sheet, pausing for the children to add the missing words as you read.
● Check the children's understanding of the term *empire* and why Britain's was so important.

Week 2 lesson plans

During the second week, the children focus on the design and building of the exhibition hall or the 'Crystal Palace'. In the first lesson, the children decide what features could be needed for a good exhibition hall. They then look at pictures of Joseph Paxton's design and its features to investigate why it was chosen. They complete the lesson by finishing a labelled drawing by Joseph Paxton. In the second lesson, the children work in small groups to make models of the Crystal Palace.

1: Features of the Crystal Palace

Introduction

● Remind the children about Prince Albert's plan for a world trade fair to be called the Great Exhibition. Check understanding of the words *exhibition* and *exhibit*.
● Explain that Prince Albert invited many architects to send in design ideas for the exhibition hall. Ask the children to suggest what would be needed for the hall: wide, long and tall spaces for the exhibits; lots of room; to be light and attractive. Make a tick list on the board of the children's ideas.

Whole-class work

● Display the media resource 'The Great Exhibition Hall of 1851' on the CD-ROM. Focus first on the pictures of the exterior of the hall. Explain that this was the building design chosen by Prince Albert. Ask: *Why do you think it was chosen? What does it remind you of?* Say that it was designed by Joseph Paxton, who had just built a huge greenhouse for a duke.
● Encourage the children to examine the pictures to discuss the hall's external features, such as the shape, the glass panes, the white-painted iron frame, the arches, columns, three tiered levels, glass arched roof and the many flags along the top.
● Tick off the ideas that the children suggested for a good design against what they see in the pictures.
● Tell the children that the length of the building was about the size of five football pitches and it had to be built around some of the trees in the park where it was sited.
● Point to the pictures of the exhibition hall being built. Highlight that 300,000 glass panes and an iron frame were made in factories and brought to the site ready-made. Discuss why that was a good idea.

Paired work and Independent work

● Hand out a copy of photocopiable page 186 'The Crystal Palace' to each child. Explain that it is an unfinished design drawn by Joseph Paxton. Ask the children to draw in the missing parts and to use the wordbank to label them.
● They should also add the building name and the name of the designer.

Whole-class work

● Bring the children together and explain that the hall was given the nickname the 'Crystal Palace'. Ask: *Why? What would you have called it if you were looking at it for the first time?*

Differentiation
● Challenge: children could include longer captions to go with their labelled drawing.

Review

● Check the children's use of the images to discuss the different features and needs for the hall design as well as their work on their labelled design drawing.

Lesson objectives
● To use a wide vocabulary of everyday historical terms.
● To ask and answer questions, choosing and using parts of stories and other sources to show that they know and understand key features of events.
● To understand some of the ways in which we find out about the past.

Expected outcomes
● All children can recognise different features of the Great Exhibition hall.
● Most children know why the hall design was chosen and who designed it.
● Some children know how and why the Crystal Palace was created.

Resources
Media resource 'The Great Exhibition Hall of 1851' on the CD-ROM; photocopiable page 186 'The Crystal Palace'; drawing paper

Lesson objectives
● To use a wide vocabulary of everyday historical terms.
● To ask and answer questions, choosing and using parts of stories and other sources to show that they know and understand key features of events.
● To understand some of the ways in which we find out about the past.

Expected outcomes
● All children know what the Crystal Palace looked like.
● Most children can create a model of the Crystal Palace.
● Some children can show detailed features on their model of the Crystal Palace.

Resources
Media resource 'The Great Exhibition Hall of 1851' and photocopiable page 'Crystal Palace model template' from the CD-ROM on A3 card; for each group of three: three base boxes, three slightly smaller boxes, three smallest boxes, one card for curved roof; materials and/ or colours to create a glass effect; blunted matchsticks or cocktail sticks; paper for small flags; decorating materials such as paints or felt-tipped pens; scissors; glue; adhesive tape; a pre-made example model; flags of the world as reference (optional)

2: Models of the Crystal Palace

Introduction
● Display media resource 'The Great Exhibition Hall of 1851' on the CD-ROM for all the children to see.
● Focus the children's attention on the shape of the hall, with the two main ends and the main exhibition hall going across them. Note the three tiers and the curved roof of the middle section.

Whole-class work
● Explain to the children that they are going to work in groups of three to create their own models of the Great Exhibition Hall, or Crystal Palace. Discuss first, for example, what materials they could use to re-create the effect of all the glass panels; perhaps silver foil, silver paper, cellophane, or blue colouring.
● Show an example of a model you have already made and explain how you created it using boxes, card and sticks (see below).

Group work
● Put the children into mixed-ability groups of three, with extra adult support if possible, and give each group three boxes and card for the sides.
● Advise the children to have one of the three sections of the hall each and to draw and decorate their own glass and iron frames onto the card to go around the boxes' sides.
● Let them stick their three different-sized boxes on top of each other, referring to the poster on display for the correct shape and orientation.
● For the children creating the central main hall section, help them to create a curved arch roof on top of their boxes.
● The children can then make small flags of different countries to add to their model, using paper and sticks or straws.
● Once the three sections have been made, help the children to stick them together into the shape of the Crystal Palace.
● For a smaller and simpler model, copy the photocopiable page 'Crystal Palace model template' from the CD-ROM onto A3 card and let the children decorate the templates.
● Once they have finished, and cut out their templates, the children can use tape or strong glue to stick the side tabs together to make the model.
● As an extension, the children could add small Victorian figures and a park base.
● Another idea would be to create a class 2D mural of the Crystal Palace showing the full length of one side.

Differentiation
● Support: children many need extra support with visualising how to put together their part of the model.

Review
● Bring the class together and review the models that they have made. Discuss how the design of the building, such as the shape and glass and iron framework, would work for the exhibitors and visitors.

Week 3 lesson plans

During week 3, the children focus on the interior of the Great Exhibition building. In the first lesson, they use an eyewitness account of the opening ceremony and an original sketchbook of the exhibition halls to find out more about the exhibition. In the first lesson, they listen to an eyewitness account and examine a picture to ask and answer questions about the opening ceremony. From this, they create a simple newspaper front page. In the second lesson, the children study original pictures to investigate the different features of the halls and create their own edition of the *Illustrated Exhibitor*.

1: The opening ceremony: a newspaper report

Introduction

● Explain to the children that the Great Exhibition building and exhibits were ready by the end of April 1851. On 1 May, there was a royal ceremony when Queen Victoria and Prince Albert opened the Great Exhibition.
● Discuss examples of modern-day royal ceremonies such as the Opening of Parliament, Changing of the Guard, the Queen's Jubilee or royal weddings.
● Encourage the children to share any memories of the ceremonies they might have seen, such as the many people cheering at the sides of the roads, or a procession of horses or cars.
● Highlight that in 1851, cars had not been invented, so Queen Victoria and Prince Albert went by carriage to the Great Exhibition in Hyde Park.

Whole-class work

● Tell the children that you are going to read the eyewitness account of someone who was invited to the opening ceremony. Check that the children know what an eyewitness account is.
● Display photocopiable page 'The opening ceremony' from the CD-ROM and read the text to the children. Draw attention to the picture at the end of the account.
● Ask, for example: *Why do you think so many people came to see the procession and ceremony? Do you think Prince Albert was pleased with the ceremony? How did the great blue and silver canopy stay up?*

Paired work

● Ask the children to imagine that they work for a Victorian newspaper and have been invited to report the ceremony. Ask the children to work in pairs to produce a newspaper front page about the day.
● Revise key features of a headline story. It may be useful to provide a template, with spaces for headlines, a short recount and pictures.
● Discuss possible ideas for headlines and what the story will focus on: for example, the procession and the people outside, or the indoor ceremony.
● Give each pair a printout of the photocopiable sheets and display or hand out other pictures of the ceremony for the children to use as reference.
● Afterwards, let the children share their newspaper reports with other pairs.

> ### Differentiation
> ● Support: the use of ICT would help all children, by allowing drafting and correcting and encouraging good-quality presentation.

Review

● Review the children's newspaper reports and encourage them to talk about their work. Have they got the events of the day in the right order? Can they understand why it was an important day?

Lesson objectives
● To develop an awareness of the past, using common words and phrases relating to the passing of time.
● To use a wide vocabulary of everyday historical terms.
● To ask and answer questions, choosing and using parts of stories and other sources to show that they know and understand key features of events.
● To understand some of the ways in which we find out about the past.
● To identify different ways in which the past is represented.

Expected outcomes
● All children know that Queen Victoria and Prince Albert opened the Great Exhibition.
● Most children know that the opening ceremony was a big event, watched by many people.
● Some children know why the opening ceremony was a very important occasion.

Resources
Photocopiable page 'The opening ceremony' from the CD-ROM (plus a printout for each pair); pictures of the opening ceremony (optional); example of a newspaper front page; newspaper template (optional); drawing pencils

Lesson objectives

● To use a wide vocabulary of everyday historical terms.
● To ask and answer questions, choosing and using parts of stories and other sources to show that they know and understand key features of events.
● To understand some of the ways in which we find out about the past.
● To identify different ways in which the past is represented.

Expected outcomes

● All children can recognise different features inside the Great Exhibition.
● Most children know that some Great Exhibition features were eye-catching.
● Some children recognise how important the *Illustrated Exhibitor* is as a historical record.

Resources

Pictures of different aspects of the interior of the Great Exhibition; page examples from the *Illustrated Exhibitor* of 1851 (try the Victorians section of the British Library Learning website); a blank booklet for a class version of the *Illustrated Exhibitor*; ICT access

2: Inside the Great Exhibition

Introduction

● Explain to the children that they are going to use pictures drawn during the Great Exhibition to investigate what the Great Exhibition hall looked like inside.

Paired work

● Put the children into pairs and give them a picture of the interior of the Great Exhibition. The pictures could be the same for each pair, or examples of different views.
● Ask the pairs to study their picture closely and to work together to make a written or oral list of what they see. Encourage them to examine the picture for details such as lighting and seating.

Whole-class work

● Bring the class together and display each picture. Invite the pairs to talk about what they found, such as statues, a fountain, the tree, flowers and shrubs, signs, flags, banners and exhibit stands.
● Give them extra information about the features, where possible, such as the elm trees and the crystal fountains.
● Highlight how big and light the space is and the many people there are in the pictures.
● Explain that there were also places to buy food and drink and, for the first time in a big public place, public toilets. Ask: *Why do you think these were needed?*
● Explain that there was so much to see that a magazine of pen and pencil sketches with captions of the different exhibits and features was printed every week for three months.
● Show an example of an exhibition feature from the *Illustrated Exhibitor* magazine. Note the titles and the caption sentences that explain what they are.
● Ask the children: *How can the* Illustrated Exhibitor *help us to know more about what was in the exhibition?*
● Explain to the children that they are going to create a class edition of the *Illustrated Exhibitor*.

Independent work

● Ask the children to choose one feature from the Great Exhibition pictures they have looked at (fountain, statue, exhibit, and so on) and to draw it in pencil.
● Remind them to write the name of their feature and a caption of one or two sentences to explain it.
● Once the children have completed their work, stick the sketches into the class booklet to make the magazine. Let volunteers design the front cover using ICT.
● Keep the booklet available for the children to look at and read in the classroom.

Differentiation
● Support: extra adult support will be needed for those who need guidance with their drawings or caption writing.
● Challenge: encourage children to find out more about their features and write longer captions about them.

Review

● Look through the class version of the *Illustrated Exhibitor* with the children and encourage discussion and observation of the pictures.
● Note those who understand the importance of the *Illustrated Exhibitor* as a historical record.

Week 4 lesson plans

This week, the children find out more about the range of exhibits shown at the Great Exhibition and how they were organised and displayed for the many visitors. In the first lesson, the children focus on examples of British exhibits, which made up half of the 100,000 total. They then create entries for their own creations for the exhibition catalogue. In the second lesson, the children study pictures of the exhibition stands and design their own stand for a particular exhibit.

1: Exhibition catalogue

Lesson objectives
● To develop an awareness of the past, using common words and phrases relating to the passing of time.
● To identify similarities and differences between ways of life in different periods.
● To use a wide vocabulary of everyday historical terms.
● To ask and answer questions, choosing and using parts of stories and other sources to show that they know and understand key features of events.
● To understand some of the ways in which we find out about the past.

Expected outcomes
● All children know that Britain had many exhibits in the Great Exhibition.
● Most children know that there were four main groups of exhibits at the exhibition.
● Some children understand how important the Great Exhibition catalogue was for visitors.

Resources
Photocopiable page 187 'Exhibition catalogue'; internet access and printed sources for ideas for Victorian exhibits

Introduction
● Remind the children of the main reason behind the Great Exhibition – to celebrate Britain's achievements at home and around the world. Highlight that there were over 100,000 objects and inventions from all over the world, with over half coming from Britain and the countries it ruled.
● Emphasise that the exhibition was a bit like a huge interactive museum, with room after room of displays.

Whole-class work
● Explain that the exhibition was arranged in four groups: machinery, fine art, manufactured goods and raw materials.
● Talk about other exhibits, such as an envelope-making machine, a medal-making machine, carriages, unusual umbrellas, stained glass, fashion pieces, farming and steam machines.
● Remind the children how big the Great Exhibition was and ask: *How could the exhibits be organised to make them easier for the visitor to find?* Share ideas and confirm that the exhibits were either put together as groups of the same type or in special halls or rooms linked to a country or town.
● Ask: *If the exhibition was so big, how could the visitor find the stand or section that they wanted to see?* (Exhibition plans, signs and information booklets.)

Independent work
● Explain to the children that information books at exhibitions are called catalogues. They have pictures and information about the exhibits and the stand numbers.
● Give a copy of photocopiable page 187 'Exhibition catalogue' to each child, and ask them to create four of their own exhibition catalogue entries. These should cover the main groups: machines, fine art, manufactured goods, and raw materials.
● Ask them to write a description of each exhibit in the space below the drawings and to include the exhibits' names.
● Emphasise that they can create anything, such as strange machines, designer hats, unusually shaped cutlery, statues – as long as it would be suitable for the Victorian period.

Differentiation
● Support: children might benefit from working in small groups with adult support, allowing them to share their ideas and vocabulary.
● Challenge: children could have one sheet of paper per exhibit, so there is space for more detailed illustrations or longer sentences.

Review
● Invite the children to share their exhibit designs with the class. Encourage them to explain their ideas.

SCHOLASTIC
www.scholastic.co.uk

2: Designing a Great Exhibition stand

Lesson objectives
● To develop an awareness of the past, using common words and phrases relating to the passing of time.
● To identify similarities and differences between ways of life in different periods.
● To use a wide vocabulary of everyday historical terms.
● To ask and answer questions, choosing and using parts of stories and other sources to show that they know and understand key features of events.
● To understand some of the ways in which we find out about the past.

Expected outcomes
● All children understand that many exhibits were shown on exhibition stands.
● Most children can design a stand for the 1851 exhibition.
● Some children understand why exhibition stands needed to be eye-catching.

Resources
A range of pictures showing the stands and exhibition spaces at the Great Exhibition; drawing pencils

Introduction
● Show the children a range of pictures that show exhibits being displayed as well examples of the stands that would have been used to present them. Discuss the different styles, such as the displays on the small stands, objects in open spaces, large machinery in operation, and decorative features of the stands, such as lights, cloth background drapes and table covers.
● Ask the children: *Which stand would you want to visit? Why? What do you like about the way the exhibits are displayed?*

Whole-class work
● Explain to the children that you would like them to work in pairs to design a small stand for an exhibit at the Great Exhibition. Highlight that you will be giving them the exhibit idea.
● Briefly discuss what they need to think about, such as how they are going to display their exhibit, what is needed on the stand, such as a glass case, or a table. How is it going to be decorated so it attracts people? What wording and design would be on the stand's sign?

Paired work
● Put the children into their pairs and give them an exhibit idea each, such as a set of gold and silver plates, embroidered fans, unusual umbrellas, a Victorian toy, a gadget for squeezing lemons.
● Give the pairs paper for rough designs and then paper for the finished stand design. As they work, discuss design and layout ideas with the children, reminding them that it should be eye-catching and suitable for presenting their exhibit in an attractive way.
● Ask prompt questions to encourage the pairs to think and talk further about their design and its potential impact.
● When they have drawn their final design on paper, ask the children to label the different areas. Check that that they have included a sign above their stand.

Whole-class work
● Join pairs together and let them practise presenting their stand designs and ideas.
● As an extension idea in another session, the children could turn their designs into exhibition stands within the classroom for role play as visitors to and exhibitors at the Great Exhibition.

Differentiation
● Support: mixed-ability pairs would work well for this activity; have pictorial resources and information about the stands and exhibit styles available for the children to use as reference.

Review
● Invite the pairs to present their stand designs and the ideas behind them to the class. Note how appropriate their stand is to their allocated exhibit, and how well they incorporate Victorian ideas into their design.

Week 5 lesson plans

In the first lesson this week, the children find out more about the international exhibits at the Great Exhibition by studying original prints of the international halls. They focus on one exhibit from the Indian hall and create an information log sheet. In the second lesson, the children find out how people from all social classes could go to the exhibition thanks to the differently priced tickets and ticket days. They design a train poster to encourage visitors to use the train to get to the exhibition.

1: Describing an international exhibit

Lesson objectives
- To identify similarities and differences between ways of life in different periods.
- To use a wide vocabulary of everyday historical terms.
- To ask and answer questions, choosing and using parts of stories and other sources to show that they know and understand key features of events.
- To understand some of the ways in which we find out about the past.
- To identify different ways in which the past is represented.

Expected outcomes
- All children know that exhibits at the Great Exhibition came from all over the world.
- Most children know that international exhibits were popular with the visitors.
- Some children know that many British people had not seen objects or the exhibitors from other countries before.

Resources
Large world map; list of exhibitor countries (source online); pictures of international exhibit halls at the exhibition, particularly the Indian and Chinese halls; photocopiable pages 'International exhibit log sheet' from the CD-ROM; drawing pencils; magnifying glasses

Introduction
- Remind the children that other countries – not ruled by Britain or part of the empire – were also invited to take part in the exhibition.
- Use a world map to show where some of the international exhibitors (colonial and non-colonial) came from.

Whole-class work
- Explain that each country was given an area or hall at the Great Exhibition to present their products. Show some pictures of different country displays, such as those from India, China and Tunisia.
- Look at the displays and exhibits in detail. Ask: *What are they showing? Which exhibit would you have wanted to look closely at?*
- Highlight that, for many of the British visitors, this was the first time that they had ever seen something from another country or met someone from another country.
- Ask the children to imagine that they are visiting the Great Exhibition and have been given a review sheet at the door to fill in.
- Display photocopiable pages 'International exhibit log sheet' on the whiteboard. Note the title and explain that it is a sheet to record information about one exhibit in the Indian hall.
- Go through the features of the log, such as the area to draw a quick sketch with labels, where to describe the exhibit, where to colour in the map to show where the exhibit came from, what the exhibit might be used for and what they like about it.

Paired work
- Put the children into pairs and give them a picture showing exhibits in the Indian hall. Give a copy of photocopiable page 'International exhibit log sheet' from the CD-ROM to each child. Ask the pairs to choose one of the exhibits in the pictures and to work together to complete their log sheets about it.
- If the picture is quite small, give the children magnifying glasses to help.
- As the children work, help them with their vocabulary where needed or write key words on the board.

Differentiation
- Support: pairs might benefit from joining to form small groups to encourage sharing of ideas and vocabulary.
- Challenge: encourage children to write longer sentences with more extensive vocabulary.

Review
- Once the children have completed their log sheets, encourage them to share their information with another pair.
- Ask the children how seeing international exhibits and exhibitors would have changed many British visitors' ideas about the world.

■ SCHOLASTIC
www.scholastic.co.uk

Lesson objectives
● To identify similarities and differences between ways of life in different periods.
● To use a wide vocabulary of everyday historical terms.
● To ask and answer questions, choosing and using parts of stories and other sources to show that they know and understand key features of events.
● To understand some of the ways in which we find out about the past.
● To identify different ways in which the past is represented.

Expected outcomes
● All children know that exhibition tickets were different prices and used on different days.
● Most children know that many working class people were able to visit the exhibition.
● Some children know that cheap train fares and entry tickets were two reasons why the exhibition was a success.

Resources
Four Victorian visitor cards and four matching Great Exhibition tickets (one pound, season ticket, two shillings and six pence, one shilling); pictures of: trains from 1840s to 1850s, the Crystal Palace building, inside the Great Exhibition, Victorian people; poster paper; drawing pens and pencils; old-style train advertising posters (optional)

Introduction
● Before the lesson, create visitor cards for four Victorian people:
  ● My name is Louisa Parkinson. I live in a big house with my mama and papa in London.
  ● My name is Lord Henry March. My grandfather is a friend of Prince Albert and we go to the Great Exhibition all the time.
  ● My name is Mary Rice. I live in Birmingham. My father is a watchmaker and is taking me to look at his watches.
  ● My name is Stan Brown. I live in Devon on a farm. I work on the fields. It is hard work and we do not have much money.
● Begin the lesson by explaining to the children that the Great Exhibition was for everyone, not just the rich and powerful. Ask for four volunteers to come to the front of the class. Say that they are all Victorian people who plan to visit the Great Exhibition. Give each volunteer a card to read out to the class which explains who they are and where they come from.
● Then give out the four pre-made Great Exhibition tickets to four other children in the class. Ask them to read out what is on their tickets. Briefly explain that a shilling was a coin worth 12 pennies in Victorian times.
● Encourage the rest of the class to match the tickets with the four Victorian visitors.

Whole-class work
● Highlight the different ticket options of the exhibition and how people who did not earn much money could go on 'shilling days'. Many came from towns and villages all over Britain. Ask the children: *How do you think they got to London?* Discuss ideas, such as by train, coach, cart, barge, boat, horse, and walking.
● Note that the owners of the trains and travel companies wanted people to travel by train to the Great Exhibition and offered cheap tickets as well.
● Show pictures of trains from the 1850s. Explain that trains were still quite new and not many people would have travelled long journeys on one.

Independent work
● Ask the children to design an advertising poster from a Victorian train company to encourage people to take a return day trip on their trains to visit the Great Exhibition.
● Write vocabulary on the board that the children might want to use, such as: *Great Exhibition, Crystal Palace, Hyde Park, London, exhibits, shilling day, three shillings.*
● Let the children work on their text for the poster, and keep pictures of the Crystal Palace, and Victorian people, available for reference.

Differentiation
● Support: display examples of old train posters and other travel posters to help the children with design ideas and layout.

Review
● Display the posters and ask volunteers why they chose their images and text to encourage people to come to the Great Exhibition.
● Highlight that, by the time the Great Exhibition closed, over six million people had visited it.
● Ask: *If trains had not been invented or were too expensive and entry tickets were too expensive for most people, do you think the Great Exhibition would have still been a success?*

Week 6 lesson plans

In the first lesson of this week, the children use their knowledge and learned vocabulary to imagine that they are visiting the exhibition and write recounts of their experiences. They discuss how recounts can help them to find out about the different experiences of visitors and exhibitors. In the second lesson, the children discover what happened to the Crystal Palace after the exhibition closed. They find out that some people would be able to remember it today. The topic ends with designs for a new Crystal Palace for the future.

1: A day at the Great Exhibition

Lesson objectives
● To develop an awareness of the past, using common words and phrases relating to the passing of time.
● To use a wide vocabulary of everyday historical terms.
● To ask and answer questions, choosing and using parts of stories and other sources to show that they know and understand key features of events.
● To understand some of the ways in which we find out about the past.
● To identify different ways in which the past is represented.

Expected outcomes
● All children know that rich and poor people visited the Great Exhibition.
● Most children know that people came from all over the UK to visit the exhibition.
● Some children understand that some people visited the exhibition for a specific reason.

Resources
Photocopiable page 'Recounts of the Great Exhibition' from the CD-ROM; a range of pictures of the Great Exhibition and its exhibits; video and/or audio accounts of visiting the exhibition; drawing pencils

Introduction
● Remind the children of the train trips to the Great Exhibition and the different tickets and ticket days for the visitors, such as the shilling days.
● Consider the different types of people who could have visited the exhibition, including factory and farm workers, villagers and farmers, and school children, as well as people living in London.
● Discuss what it must have been like for each of these people going to Hyde Park and seeing the many exhibits in the Great Exhibition.

Whole-class work
● Tell the children that you are going to read out three short recounts from children who visited the Great Exhibition. Ask: *How can these children's recounts help us to find out more about the exhibition and its visitors?*
● Read out photocopiable pages 'Recounts of the Great Exhibition' from the CD-ROM to the children. Then discuss each one. Ask: *Where did this person come from? What ticket did they use? What did they think of the Crystal Palace when they first saw it? What was their favourite exhibit?*
● Highlight that the Koh-i-Noor diamond was a huge Indian diamond owned by Queen Victoria.
● Note the structure of the three recounts and how they tell us about what happened and what the writers saw, in chronological order.
● Model another recount orally, using time words, such as: *In the morning, I went on the large train to go to London... Then... The first thing we saw was...*

Paired work or Independent work
● Display a set of pictures of the Great Exhibition or give them out to the children.
● Ask the children to use their knowledge of the Great Exhibition and the pictures to write a recount of a trip to the Great Exhibition, illustrating their favourite exhibit if they have time.
● Highlight that they can be anyone they want to be and need to decide how they will get to Hyde Park.
● Once the children have completed their recounts, let them share their work with a partner. Encourage the pairs to ask each other questions about their recount to prompt more details and experiences.

Differentiation
● Support: children could work in small groups with adult support, allowing them to share their ideas and vocabulary.
● Challenge: children could write longer sentences with more specific and wider vocabulary.

Review
● Invite volunteers to read their recounts to the class, first introducing what kind of visitor they chose to be, where they came from and how they got to Hyde Park. Check the children's knowledge and understanding of the Great Exhibition and its visitors and exhibits.

Lesson objectives
● To develop an awareness of the past, using common words and phrases relating to the passing of time.
● To show where people and events they study fit within a chronological framework.
● To identify similarities and differences between ways of life in different periods.
● To use a wide vocabulary of everyday historical terms.
● To ask and answer questions, choosing and using parts of stories and other sources to show that they know and understand key features of events.
● To understand some of the ways in which we find out about the past.

Expected outcomes
● All children know that the Crystal Palace was moved from Hyde Park after the Great Exhibition.
● Most children know that the Crystal Palace burned down within living memory.
● Some children understand that the Crystal Palace was used for a wide range of events.

Resources
Photographs of Crystal Palace after 1851; photographs or a film clip of the fire in 1931; map of Greater London; drawing pencils; images of very modern architecture (optional)

2: Designing a new Crystal Palace

Introduction

● Explain to the children that in October 1851, the Great Exhibition closed after the planned six months. Emphasise that it was a huge success, with over six million visitors coming to the Crystal Palace and discovering all sorts of new things invented and produced in Britain and around the world.
● Encourage the children to explain what they think helped to make it successful, such as the stunning Crystal Palace building design, the cheap entry tickets on certain days, pride in the British exhibits, interest in the unusual international exhibits, and ease of transport.
● Ask: *Which part of the exhibition would you have liked to visit or exhibit in? What would you have liked to ask Prince Albert at the end of the exhibition?*
● Tell the children that money made from the exhibition helped to build the Royal Albert Hall and museums such as the Natural History Museum and the Victoria and Albert Museum. Let the children briefly share any experiences of visiting these iconic buildings.

Whole-class work

● Ask the children what they think might have happened to the Crystal Palace once the Great Exhibition was finished. List ideas on the board.
● Go on to explain that in fact it was taken down and carefully rebuilt in a different part of London – Sydenham in south London. Show the Hyde Park and Sydenham locations on a map of London.
● Now show photographs of the Crystal Palace up to the 1930s. Let the children use the photographs to discuss what it was used for: more exhibitions, shows, even a television station.
● Encourage them to compare the building in 1930 with the original 1851 building. Ask: *What has changed?* By 1930, two water towers and two extra wings had been added to the ends, for example; all the roofs are curved; the building is longer; the front is a different design; there are no flags.
● Highlight that at this stage it was a building still within the living memory of some older people today.
● Then show photographs and/or a video clip showing the burning down of the Crystal Palace in 1931. Ask: *How do you feel watching the old building burn down after learning about the Great Exhibition?*

Independent work

● Explain to the children that some people would like a new Crystal Palace to be built. What might it look like? Challenge the children to design a new Crystal Palace for the future. Highlight that it can be any shape or size, but it needs to be able to be used for exhibitions and indoor shows or concerts.
● Hand out paper and encourage the children to work individually to draw and decorate their design for a new Crystal Palace.
● As they work, ask the children what they would call their new building. Would it be still be called the Crystal Palace or would it have another name?
● Ask the children what materials the building would be made from, and encourage them to label the drawing.

> **Differentiation**
> ● Support: children could work in small groups with adult support, allowing them to share their ideas and vocabulary.
> ● Challenge: children could write longer sentences with more specific and wider vocabulary.

Review

● Invite the children to show their designs, and encourage the rest of the class to compare it with the 1930 and 1851 versions of the Crystal Palace.
● Can the children remember what the Crystal Palace was used for after the Great Exhibition?

Lesson objectives
● To understand some of the ways in which we find out about the past.

Resources
A range of primary and secondary resources about the Great Exhibition, such as pictures, photographs, exhibit catalogue entries, pages from the Illustrated Exhibitor, cartoons, transcripts of oral accounts, advertisements, information in books and on websites; photocopiable page 'Sources about the Great Exhibition' from the CD-ROM; writing and drawing pencils

Great Exhibition sources

Revise

● Show the children a range of primary sources used in the topic on the Great Exhibition, such as pictures, photographs, exhibition catalogue pictures, magazine and newspaper cartoons and transcripts of oral accounts.
● Then show examples of secondary sources such as books and information on websites.
● Ask the children what aspects of the Great Exhibition the primary sources helped them to find out about. These could be, for example, what the Crystal Palace looked like, who some of the visitors were and what some of the exhibits were and where they were from.

Assess

● Place different examples of primary sources of information about the Great Exhibition on separate tables around the classroom.
● Give each child photocopiable page 'Sources about the Great Exhibition' from the CD-ROM along with writing and drawing pencils.
● Put the children into groups and let them focus on one table to record the type of source, in writing and/or as a sketch, and how it helps us to find out about the Great Exhibition.
● Either give the groups a set time at each table (about 10 to 15 minutes) or let each child move from table to table at their own pace to complete the photocopiable activity.

Further practice

● Let the children choose one primary source and use it for finding out more about the exhibition, an exhibitor or exhibit, or the type of visitor. They could also use pictorial evidence for storytelling and drama scenarios.

Lesson objectives
● To develop an awareness of the past, using common words and phrases relating to the passing of time.
● To identify similarities and differences between ways of life in different periods.

Resources
Interactive activity 'Y2 Spring 2 quiz' on the CD-ROM

Y2 Spring 2 quiz

Revise

● Ask the children to think what they would include in a Great Exhibition today if they were to plan one on the same themes as in 1851.

Assess

● Ask the children to complete the interactive activity 'Y2 Spring 2 quiz' on the CD-ROM. There are ten multiple choice questions that test what the children will have learned throughout the topic. They will need to read each question carefully before choosing the correct answer.
● Give children a set length of time (such as 15 minutes) to answer the questions. This can be used as part of a formal assessment or as a fun challenge activity, giving children the opportunity to show what they have learned about the topic.
● Less confident readers may need adult support to read the questions aloud.

Further practice

● Ask the children to discuss why they think the Great Exhibition was considered to be a success.

Prince Albert's idea

■ Complete this letter from Prince Albert to the prime minister.

Dear Prime Minister,   3 January 1850

I think we need to show off the many objects and

_____ made in Britain and in the other countries in

our _____ .

Last night, I had a wonderful idea just how to do this.

We can have a very large _____ for people. We

can invite other countries to show their inventions and goods.

A vast building can be built in Hyde Park. It could run for six months

from 1 May _____ .

I suggest that the fair be called the _____

Exhibition of 1851.

Here is an example of a _____ invention that could

be presented at the exhibition.

I hope you like my idea.

Yours faithfully,
Albert, Prince Consort

| Empire | inventions | exhibition | British | 1851 | Great |

I know that Prince Albert had an idea
to celebrate Britain.

How did you do?

Date: _____

The Crystal Palace

■ Draw in the missing parts of the Crystal Palace.
■ Use the wordbank to add the labels and titles.

Name of building: _____

Name of architect: _____

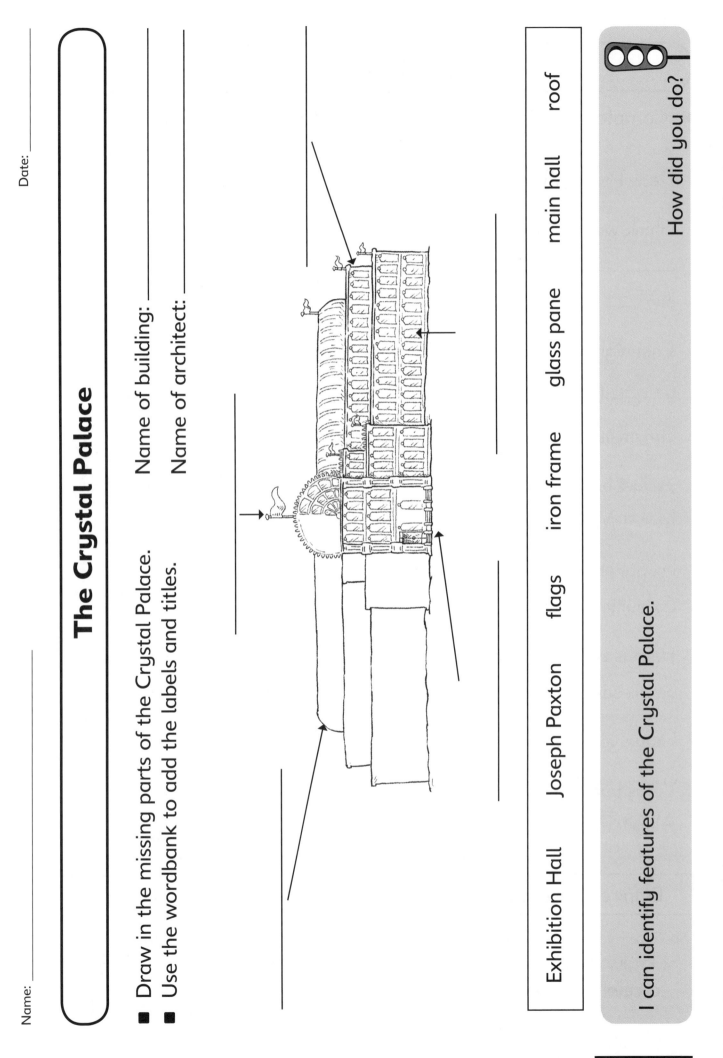

Exhibition Hall   Joseph Paxton   flags   iron frame   glass pane   main hall   roof

I can identify features of the Crystal Palace.

How did you do?

PHOTOCOPIABLE

■ SCHOLASTIC
www.scholastic.co.uk

Exhibition catalogue

- Draw your own exhibits for the four groups.
- Explain what the exhibits are.

Raw material
(coal, metal, precious stones)

Fine art
(paintings, sculpture)

Manufactured goods
(objects that are made)

Machines

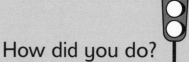

I can design exhibits for the Great Exhibition.

How did you do?

Life as a child during the Second World War

In this chapter, the children find out what it was like to be a child during the Second World War. The topic focuses on food and clothing rationings, air-raid shelters and evacuation. The children are made aware that the war happened in recent memory, allowing them to look at original film clips and photographs as well as listening to experiences of the older generation. Wartime artefacts, such as a gas mask, ration books, evacuee suitcase and recipes, also bring the past to life. If appropriate, use local resources and locations of, for instance, Dig for Victory vegetable plots, shelters, bombings and evacuation stories.

Chapter at a glance

Curriculum objectives

• Changes within living memory. Where appropriate these should be used to reveal aspects of change in national life.
• Significant historical events, people and places in their own locality.

Week	Lesson	Summary of activities	Expected outcomes
1	1	• Children share their knowledge of the Second World War. • They create a timeline of the war. • They create timelines of their own lives.	• Know when the Second World War was and can put it on a timeline. • Know how long the war lasted.
	2	• Children discuss reasons for rationing. • They investigate ration books. • They compare wartime meals with present-day meals.	• Understand what *rationing* means. • Can investigate what was rationed and compare wartime meals with today's meals.
2	1	• Children look at photographs and footage about Dig for Victory. • They plan a vegetable plot for the school.	• Can find out how people used different spaces for growing food and why this was necessary. • Can plan a vegetable plot.
	2	• Children study a range of Dig for Victory posters and design their own.	• Can examine Dig for Victory posters and design their own.
3	1	• Children find out about clothing rations. • They make party outfits, with decorated gas mask boxes, using old clothes and material.	• Understand what clothes rationing meant. • Are aware of the use of gas masks. • Can design an outfit from scraps of material.
	2	• Children study Make-do and Mend posters. • They experience mending or improving a clothing item.	• Can contribute to a Make-do and Mend session. • Can suggest why making-do and mending is a good idea.
4	1	• Children find out about the Blitz and the need for air-raid shelters. • They report on different air-raid shelters. • They draw pictures to show children using a shelter.	• Can use sources to understand why and when air-raid shelters were used.
	2	• Children explore features of an Anderson shelter. • They draw labelled diagrams and answer questions about the Anderson shelter.	• Can identify the features of an Anderson shelter. • Can understand why shelters were built.
5	1	• Children study oral and visual sources to learn about evacuees and the reasons for evacuation. • Groups investigate evacuees' suitcases to find out more about them.	• Can understand the term *evacuation*. • Can investigate a suitcase of artefacts to find out about evacuees.
	2	• Children listen to different diary accounts of evacuation day. • They create their own diary account.	• Understand that children had different views about evacuation. • Can write diary accounts as an evacuee.
6	1	• Children listen to oral accounts of the war. • They listen to a visitor talk about their memories of evacuation and the war as a child, and ask questions.	• Can listen to a visitor who remembers evacuation. • Can ask questions about life as a child in the Second World War.
	2	• Children make props and choose costumes for their re-enactment. • The class act out an evacuation day.	• Can use their knowledge of evacuation for role play and can discuss how they felt during the re-enactment.
Assess and review		• To review the half-term's work.	

■SCHOLASTIC
www.scholastic.co.uk

Expected prior learning
- Children can put events and people within a chronological framework.
- Children can use stories and a range of sources to find out about the past.
- Children can identify different ways in which the past is represented.

Overview of progression
- At the beginning of this chapter, the children create a timeline to show how long the war lasted and understand that this would have been a major part of a child's life. Throughout the topic, the children use time vocabulary for comparison and discussion when using artefacts and sources.
- The children discover differences and similarities between themselves and children who lived during the war. They also become aware of the differences between countryside- and city-living that affected the evacuees.
- The children are encouraged to learn and then use new vocabulary when talking to visitors about childhood experiences of the war.
- The lessons use photographs, film clips, home-front posters, letters, diaries and artefacts; and the children become history detectives to find out about an evacuee from items in a suitcase. They get a chance to carry out tasks that wartime children might have been involved in, such as planning a vegetable plot, helping to make and mend clothes and the experience of being an evacuee. The children extend their understanding of how people can have different accounts of past events, such as the memories of evacuees.

Creative context
- Cross-curricular links include:
  - writing diary recounts, text for posters and explanation texts; extending their vocabulary, listening, asking and answering questions, giving descriptions and explanations; acting in a drama;
  - creating an outfit and using materials in a Make-do and Mend session;
  - drawing pictures, diagrams, posters and plans;
  - using maps to locate places finding out about the differences between the cities and the countryside during the war;
  - using science skills to grow vegetables learning about a healthy diet;
  - using their voices expressively and creatively by singing 1940s songs.

Background knowledge
- **Second World War home-front timeline:** November 1938 – First shelters built. 1 September 1939 – First evacuation of children. 3 September, 1939 – War is declared on Germany. 8 January 1940 – Food rationing starts. June 1940 onwards – Evacuation of children. 3 July 1940 – Cardiff bombed. 7 September 1940 (to May 1941) – the Blitz. March 1941 – Morrison shelters built. June 1941 – Clothing rationing starts. April 1945 – Evacuees start to return. 8 May 1945 – VE day. 15 August – VJ Day; the end of the war.
- **Rationing:** food rationing started in January 1940. By 1943, most foods were rationed apart from home-grown fruit and vegetables, fish, a wholemeal bread called 'national loaf' and game such as rabbit. Food ration books came in three colours: buff for adults; green for children under five, pregnant and nursing women, and blue for children over five. Rationing carried on until 1954. Clothing rations started in 1941. People were given coupons to spend on a list of clothes and shoes. The Make-do and Mend campaign encouraged households to repair and make new clothes from old ones.
- **Air-raid shelters** were set up before the outbreak of war, organised by Sir John Anderson. As well as the Anderson shelters for gardens, there were Morrison shelters for inside the house and also used were cellars, railway arches, caves and tunnels, the Underground and school shelters.
- **Evacuation:** at the beginning of the war, almost three million children, teachers, pregnant women and mothers with young children, the elderly and sick were evacuated from cities to the countryside, or even to other countries. At their destination, billeting officers would allow host families to pick and choose their children. Some evacuee experiences were happy, while some children were badly treated or missed their families.

SUMMER 1 — Life as a child during the Second World War

SCHOLASTIC
www.scholastic.co.uk

100 HISTORY LESSONS · YEAR 2 ■ 189

Week I lesson plans

This first lesson establishes when the Second World War took place and how long it lasted. This allows the children to realise that six years is most of their lives and to appreciate that the war played a significant part in children's lives and why many people have such strong memories of that time. The second lesson starts by asking the children how they would fairly share a tray of food for a week. This demonstrates the idea of food rationing.

I: Second World War timeline

Lesson objectives
● To develop an awareness of the past, using common words and phrases relating to the passing of time.
● To show where people and events they study fit within a chronological framework.
● To use a wide vocabulary of everyday historical terms.
● To understand some of the ways in which we find out about the past.

Expected outcomes
● All children know that the Second World War lasted six years.
● Most children know that many children grew up during the Second World War.
● Some children know that many adults who are over 70 remember growing up during the war.

Resources
Interactive activity 'Second World War timeline' on the CD-ROM; card timeline strips and blank cards; glue

Introduction
● Explain to the children that they are going to find out what it was like for a child to live through the Second World War.
● Talk about what the children know about war and why this one was called the 'Second World War'. Highlight that there was also a 'First World War', which took place 100 years ago.
● Explain gently that many people died in both wars, and link this to Remembrance Day (Poppy Day) in November.
● Ask the children how we might know when the war took place: for example, from accounts, documents, books, film and photographs. Highlight too that the war was in the recent past and that many people still remember it.

Whole-class work
● Suggest that they make a timeline to understand when the war took place.
● Show interactive activity 'Second World War timeline' on the CD-ROM. Ask for volunteers to add the main dates of the war to the timeline.
● Mark the period of the war and discuss how many years the war lasted. Compare this with the six years of their lives.

Paired or Independent work
● Give each child a timeline strip for the first six years of their lives and cards to add to the timelines.
● Suggest they add information about the first six years of their lives to their own timeline, such as their birth date, special events, holidays, nursery and school dates, births of siblings, and so on.
● Model some ideas of your own to demonstrate how the dates can be added.
● Working individually or in discussion pairs, let the children decide what they are going to add and then write simple labels or pictures onto the cards before gluing them on to the timeline.

Whole-class work
● Encourage volunteers to show their timelines and discuss their events.
● Ask the class: *What school year would you be in, six years from now? What do you think you might look like?*
● Highlight that many of the children who grew up during the war would now be in their 70s. Encourage the children to ask older family members if they have any memories of the war.

Differentiation
● Support: children will need extra writing support and prompting for ideas to add to the timeline.
● Challenge: encourage children to write more detailed labels for their timeline.

Review
● Check the children's use of time words and phrases and their ability to put events of the first six years of their life in chronological order.
● Note those who understand that many children grew up during the six years of the Second World War.

Lesson objectives
● To develop an awareness of the past, using common words and phrases relating to the passing of time.
● To use a wide vocabulary of everyday historical terms.
● To ask and answer questions, choosing and using parts of stories and other sources to show that they know and understand key features of events.
● To understand some of the ways in which we find out about the past.

Expected outcomes
● All children know that food was rationed during the Second World War.
● Most children know how food ration books were used.
● Some children understand that meals were different due to rationing.

Resources
Media resource 'Food ration books' on the CD-ROM; world map; photocopiable page 203 'Food rations'; drawing pencils; large tray of food or large photographs of the food with approximate amounts: 225g sugar, 50g butter, 100g margarine, 100g lard, 100g bacon and ham, three pints milk, 450g jam, 50g tea, 50g cheese, one fresh egg, one packet dried egg, 350g sweets and chocolate, £2 worth of meat (perhaps sausages); blank cards for food items; ration book (or photographs); photographs of wartime meals and comparable meals today

2: What was rationing?

Introduction
● Show the children a map of the world and explain that a lot of our food comes from other countries, such as bananas from South America, rice from India and Italy, tea from Sri Lanka, some sugar from the West Indies.
● Use the map to show how Germany stopped many ships bringing in food to Britain during the war. Ask: *Why did they do this?* (To make people hungry and give up their 'fight'.)
● Put out the tray of food. Write the name of each item on a card label as the children identify them. Explain that home-grown vegetables and fruit, as well as fish and wheat-germ bread, were not restricted or completely unavailable, but could be expensive.
● Ask the children to imagine that these are the only food items allowed for the next week. Ask: *How would you make sure the food was shared out fairly? If someone was vegetarian, what could they have more of? Does it look like there is enough for everyone?*

Whole-class work
● Explain that everyone in Britain during the Second World War also had to share their food fairly. Explain that this was called *rationing*, and write the word on the board.
● Show an example of a food ration book and use media resource 'Food ration books' to allow the children to investigate its features and how it was used. Establish why there were three ration books in different colours (see Background information on page 189).
● Draw attention back to the food on the tray and explain that these are weekly rations (along with fruit, vegetables, fish and bread).

Independent work
● Give each child a copy of photocopiable page 203 'Food rations', and ask the children to fill in the missing information on the ration book cover and to make the it the right colour for their age.
● They then use the food words to write and illustrate a list of food items for a week's ration for one.

Whole-class work
● Bring the class together and discuss why certain meals we eat today could not have been cooked during rationing. Highlight that ready-meals and most 'fast food' had not been invented and that food was nearly always home-cooked, or home-prepared, from scratch.
● Show examples of pictures of wartime meals and present-day meals and note the differences.
● Ask: *Why do you think fish and chips were so popular during the war?* (Fish and potatoes were relatively plentiful; it was a filling meal; it was easy and cheap to cook.)
● Explain that to make food last longer, some strange recipes were tried, such as carrot fudge, and potato and chocolate pudding.
● As an extension, you could run a cooking session where the children create a wartime dish from a given recipe.

Differentiation
● Challenge: encourage children to create their own recipes from their rations.

Review
● Go over the photocopiable sheet with the children, identifying the rations for the week. Encourage the children to consider what meals they could make with them.
● Ask: *Why was food rationing necessary during the war?*

Week 2 lesson plans

This week looks at the Dig for Victory campaign. People were encouraged to grow vegetables as a healthy, unrationed food source. In the first lesson, the children study photographs and a wartime information film to find out where people made plots and what vegetables were grown, so that they can plan a plot. If possible, find out if there were Dig for Victory plots in the local area, or ones that still exist in the form of allotments. In the second lesson, the children create a Dig for Victory poster.

1: Growing vegetables during the war

Introduction
- Remind the children about food rationing during the Second World War and that home-grown vegetables were not rationed. Ask the children why.
- Explain that, instead, people were asked to grow their own food. This was a campaign called Dig for Victory, during which people used lots of different spaces, including school fields, to grow fruit and vegetables because the need for food was so important. Show a film clip and photographs of vegetables being grown in, for example, flower beds, tennis courts, golf courses, parks, factory grounds, school fields, allotments, window ledges.
- Ask the children why some people would grow vegetables in window boxes. (People in flats, for example, had no gardens; every available space was used.)
- Ask: *How did growing vegetables help people during the war?* (People could have more food it kept people fit and healthy and let them join in and keep their minds off the bad aspects of the war.)

Whole-class work
- Ask the children to imagine they are children during the war and want to Dig for Victory! Discuss where they could create a vegetable plot in the school grounds.
- Show some of the vegetables that were grown in wartime. Hold up each vegetable and ask: *What is it? Does it grow in the earth or on top of the earth?* Write the names in two lists on the board.
- Highlight that before digging a vegetable plot, a plan needs to be made of what vegetables will be grown where.

Paired work
- Put the children into pairs and give them a large sheet of paper. Ask them to decide on the shape of their plot, what vegetables they are going to grow and where they will grow them.
- Once they have drawn and coloured in their plan, suggest the children add a key with symbols.

Differentiation
- Support: children might need support with creating their plot shape and deciding on which vegetables to use. Advise them to create small, simple plots.
- Challenge: children could create larger plots with more varieties of vegetable and fruit.

Review
- At the end of the lesson, let the pairs show their plans and explain what they are growing and why. How would they feel helping to grow vegetables during the war?
- Discuss how allotments are still popular today. Identify where the local ones are and share any gardening experiences with the children.

Lesson objectives
- To develop an awareness of the past, using common words and phrases relating to the passing of time.
- To identify similarities and differences between ways of life in different periods.
- To use a wide vocabulary of everyday historical terms.
- To ask and answer questions, choosing and using parts of stories and other sources to show that they know and understand key features of events.
- To understand some of the ways in which we find out about the past.

Expected outcomes
- All children know that many people grew vegetables during the Second World War.
- Most children know about the different places where people grew vegetables.
- Some children understand the benefits of people growing vegetables during the war.

Resources
A range of 1940s photographs showing vegetable plots made from flower beds, tennis courts, and so on; a 1940s Dig for Victory film clip (for example, from 'WW2 Dig for Victory techniques' at www.thebigworld.co.uk); 'wartime' vegetables such as brussels sprouts, cabbage, carrot, cauliflower, dwarf and broad beans, globe beet, kale, lettuce, marrow, onion, parsley, parsnip, potatoes, radish, runner beans, spinach, sprouting broccoli, swede, tomatoes, turnip; large sheets of paper; rulers

SCHOLASTIC
www.scholastic.co.uk

Lesson objectives
● To develop an awareness of the past, using common words and phrases relating to the passing of time.
● To use a wide vocabulary of everyday historical terms.
● To ask and answer questions, choosing and using parts of stories and other sources to show that they know and understand key features of events.
● To understand some of the ways in which we find out about the past.
● To identify different ways in which the past is represented.

Expected outcomes
● All children know that there were Dig for Victory posters during the Second World War.
● Most children know that the Dig for Victory posters encouraged people to grow vegetables.
● Some children recognise the messages in Dig for Victory posters.

Resources
Dig for Victory posters, plus individual copies (optional); poster paper and draft paper; drawing pencils; decorating materials; ICT access (optional)

2: Dig for Victory posters

Introduction
● Remind the children about the Dig for Victory campaign and tell them that posters were put up to encourage people to join in and grow vegetables.
● Show a range of Dig for Victory posters for the children to study in detail. Ask prompt questions about each poster, such as: *What is shown on the poster? Why is a box of vegetables shown? Why is a spade shown? Who could the person on the poster be? What are they doing? What do they look like? What does it say on the poster? How does the poster make you want to grow vegetables? Do the posters make you want to eat vegetables? Why would growing and eating vegetables help Britain at war?*
● Explain that many posters were often used in the Second World War to give people information or encourage them to do things to help the country through the war.

Whole-class work
● Explain to the children that they are going to design and draw their own Dig for Victory posters to encourage people to grow their own vegetables as part of the war effort.
● Highlight the large letters on the poster slogans and that the slogans are mainly only three or four words.
● Write the main slogan *Dig for Victory* on the board and ask the children for any other key words they might want to use in their posters, such as *food, vegetables, grow, healthy, garden.*

Independent work
● Hand out paper, pencils, and an example poster. Using sketch paper first, encourage the children to write down the slogan they want to use and draw a rough design of their poster.
● Once they are happy with their design, let the children draw and decorate their poster, making sure their slogan is prominent.
● Once they have completed their posters, let the children share them with others and explain how they have tried to put across their message of the benefits of growing vegetables for the war.
● Display the posters on a wall for all the children to see and study throughout the topic.

Differentiation
● Support: you might want to allow children to use ICT to design their posters.
● Challenge: let children look at the posters and hear songs of Potato Pete and Doctor Carrot, which were used to encourage children to eat their vegetables; let the children create another vegetable figure and their own accompanying songs.

Review
● Briefly recap the reasons for the Dig for Victory campaign. What messages were the posters putting across? How well do the children's posters replicate this?

Week 3 lesson plans

This week looks at another wartime campaign to do with rationing, Make-do and Mend. In the first lesson, the children consider how people could save their ration coupons by reusing and recycling old clothes and household materials. Having studied some typical clothing of 1940s children, the children design outfits using offcuts and old clothes. The Make-do and Mend theme continues in the second lesson with the chance to mend clothes and household items. These lessons will need advance preparation of resources and extra adult helpers.

1: Wartime clothing designs

Lesson objectives
● To develop an awareness of the past, using common words and phrases relating to the passing of time.
● To identify similarities and differences between ways of life in different periods.
● To use a wide vocabulary of everyday historical terms.
● To ask and answer questions, choosing and using parts of stories and other sources to show that they know and understand key features of events.
● To understand some of the ways in which we find out about the past.

Expected outcomes
● All children know that there was a clothing ration during the Second World War.
● Most children know that people adapted old clothing and materials during the war.
● Some children can compare 1940s children's clothing to modern-day clothing.

Resources
Photograph, original or copy of a clothing ration book; wartime public information film about clothing; a range of fabric, old clothes, belts and cords that can be cut up; small boxes for gas masks; photocopiable page 'Person template' from the CD-ROM; long paper for a child's outline; scissors; glue; decorating materials

Introduction
● Write the term *rationing* on the board and ask the children if they remember it, and in what context.
● Explain that as the war went on, there were other things that needed to be rationed, including clothes. Show a photograph or real clothing ration book and explain how it was used.

Whole-class work
● Consider how people might be able to get clothes without using their ration coupons, for example by swapping clothes, passing down outgrown clothes, adapting clothes, or making new clothes from old material.
● Highlight the ways in which clothing styles of 1940s children differed from modern-day styles (and were necessarily simpler, given rationing and reuse), and the fabrics, which tended to be more hardwearing.

Paired work
● Tell the children that they are going to design outfits for a wartime boy or girl to wear to a party.
● Show examples of materials and old clothes and emphasise the need to study them first to work out ways to use them.
● In pairs give each child photocopiable page 'Person template' from the CD-ROM and ask each pair to use the materials to design the outfits for the two templates. Once they have cut and stuck the materials to the outlines, they can label the clothing or material ideas used.

Group work
● In small groups put down a large sheet of paper and ask a child to lie on it, so that an outline can be drawn around them. The children then use old clothing and materials to adapt or cut and stick onto the life-size outline. Put labels and a decorated gas mask box to the side of the outline. Or, children could adapt or cut old clothes and materials to fit onto one of their group who acts as the model for the outfit, as well as decorate the gas mask box. Adult support will be needed for this.

Whole-class work
● If possible, in another lesson, show a 1940s information film about making-do and mending for the children to discuss.

Review
● Present a fashion show, with each group explaining what they have used to create their outfits.

■SCHOLASTIC
www.scholastic.co.uk

Lesson objectives
● To develop an awareness of the past, using common words and phrases relating to the passing of time.
● To identify similarities and differences between ways of life in different periods.
● To use a wide vocabulary of everyday historical terms.
● To understand some of the ways in which we find out about the past.

Expected outcomes
● All children know that people mended their clothes during the war.
● Most children know why people mended their clothing and other items.
● Some children recognise different ways people used to mend their clothes.

Resources
Children's Dig for Victory posters; a range of Make-do and Mend posters; six workstation tables; socks with small holes; wool; blunt darning needles; range of coloured materials; patch template shapes; clothing with holes or worn patches; large buttons; thread; clothing or pockets with missing buttons; pom-pom card shapes; wool for pom-poms; woolly hats and scarves; felt shapes and templates; gloves and hats; fabric pens; squares of white bed sheets; scissors; fabric glue; adult support for work with needles

2: A Make-do and Mend session

Introduction
● Recap with the children that, during the Second World War, people often recycled old clothes and materials to make other clothing.
● Briefly discuss the children's designs from the last lesson and what they were made from.
● Direct the children's attention to their Dig for Victory posters and explain that posters like these were also made to encourage people to sew, knit and mend clothing instead of throwing them away.

Whole-class work
● Display a range of Make-do and Mend posters and help the children to discuss the images and slogans.
● Ask the children what kind of things might need mending, such as holes in socks, tears along seams of clothing, worn-out knees on trousers, loose or lost buttons, new covers for cushions, or adding extra bits to clothing to make them look different and 'new'.

Group work
● Explain to the children that they are going to have a Make-do and Mend session.
● Introduce the six workstations with different activities at each one, for example:
   ● Darning small holes in socks using thick wool;
   ● Cutting material patches to size and sticking them onto clothing;
   ● Sewing large buttons onto pockets;
   ● Making wool pom-poms to go on top of woolly hats or the ends of scarves;
   ● Adding fun felt shapes to cover holes in gloves or hats;
   ● Using fabric pens to decorate white sheet squares for handkerchiefs.
● Go to each workstation and show the children an example of what needs to be done and how it is done.
● Allocate a group to a workstation and let them work on their Make-do and Mend activity.
● Help each group work on their item and encourage them to discuss how useful this would have been in the war, instead of having to use up ration coupons for new items.
● If time, let the groups try out one other activity from another station.

Differentiation
● It might be suitable to allocate more complicated activities to more skilled children, and simpler activities such as handkerchief-decorating or making wool pom-poms to others.

Review
● When all the activities have been completed by the children, let each group show the rest of the class what they have created and how it would have made a difference to damaged or old clothes during the war.
● Highlight that many wartime children were encouraged to help mend their own clothes.
● Discuss that today, many people have started to follow the idea of Make-do and Mend again. Ask why.
● Ask the children how mending or refreshing clothes and household items helped people in the war. Elicit understanding of the feeling of joining in and contributing to the communal war effort as well as the benefit of saving ration coupons.

Week 4 lesson plans

In the first lesson this week, the children find out about the Blitz and the subsequent bombing raids across the UK, before investigating a range of photographs to study different types of air-raid shelter. They learn new terms such as *Blitz*, *air raid*, *air-raid siren* and *air-raid shelter*. Using oral accounts, the children learn about the routine of going into a school shelter when there was an air raid. If possible, investigate local sources to discover where the nearest air-raid shelters were sited and if there are any examples that still exist. In the second lesson, the children investigate the features of an Anderson shelter in order to create an explanation text about it.

1: What were air-raid shelters?

Lesson objectives
● To develop an awareness of the past, using common words and phrases relating to the passing of time.
● To use a wide vocabulary of everyday historical terms.
● To ask and answer questions, choosing and using parts of stories and other sources to show that they know and understand key features of events.
● To understand some of the ways in which we find out about the past.

Expected outcomes
● All children know what an air-raid shelter was.
● Most children know that there were different types of air-raid shelter.
● Some children can empathise with how people felt in the shelters during a bombing raid.

Resources
Media resources 'The Blitz' and 'Air-raid siren' on the CD-ROM; photographs of different air-raid shelters with matching name cards; drawing pencils; oral account about a school shelter (for example, from the World War Two, home front section of www.1900s.org.uk)

Introduction
● Show the children the photographs of the Blitz from media resource 'The Blitz' on the CD-ROM. Ask the children what they think happened. Explain that in September 1940, one year after the start of the war, the German Air Force (the Luftwaffe) flew over London and dropped hundreds of bombs, killing many people and destroying several towns and cities. For the next nine months, some towns and cities all over the UK were bombed *every* night.
● Write the word *Blitz* on the board and explain that this period of bomb raids was called the Blitz, which comes from a German word *Blitzkrieg*, meaning *lightning war*.

Whole-class work
● Play the air-raid warning siren sound from media resource 'Air-raid siren' on the CD-ROM. Explain how the siren warned people that bomber planes were close by. Ask: *Why was it a good way of warning lots of people?*
● Say that these bomb attacks were called *air raids*. Explain that when people heard the siren, they had to stop whatever they were doing and go to air-raid shelters for safety. There were several different types of air-raid shelter.

Group work
● Put the children into groups. Give each group a photograph and name card of one type of air-raid shelter, such as a Morrison shelter, Anderson shelter, school shelter, London Underground shelter, cave shelter and street shelter.
● Let the groups study their photographs to discuss where it could be, who would use it and why it would have been a good place to stay safe during an air raid. Encourage the children to imagine using one. How would the experience have felt?
● Once the groups are ready, let each one come up to share their findings. Add extra information about each shelter.
● Then focus on the photograph showing a school shelter, and read an account of going into one during an air raid.

Independent work
● Ask the children to draw a sequence of six pictures to show the procedure of using the school shelter.
● Confirm the order on the board, perhaps: working in class or playing in the playground, siren sounding and the quieter sound of the aeroplanes, walking in crocodile line to the shelter, sitting in the shelter, coming out after the all-clear siren, back in class or playground again.
● Encourage the children to write brief captions to explain the pictures.

Review
● Ask the children if they can explain the terms *Blitz*, *air raid* and *air-raid shelter*.
● Can they remember the different types of air-raid shelter and where they were used?

Lesson objectives
● To develop an awareness of the past, using common words and phrases relating to the passing of time.
● To use a wide vocabulary of everyday historical terms.
● To ask and answer questions, choosing and using parts of stories and other sources to show that they know and understand key features of events.
● To understand some of the ways in which we find out about the past.

Expected outcomes
● All children know that an Anderson shelter was an air-raid shelter used in the Second World War.
● Most children can recognise the exterior and interior features of an Anderson shelter.
● Some children can imagine being inside an Anderson shelter.

Resources
Interactive activity 'Anderson shelter' on the CD-ROM; oral account of being a child in an Anderson shelter (for example, from www.1990s. org.uk); photocopiable page 204 'Explanation of an Anderson shelter'; writing and drawing pencils

2: Anderson shelters

Introduction

● Display interactive activity 'Anderson shelter' on the CD-ROM, which shows the exterior and interior views of an Anderson shelter.
● Ask the children if they can remember what type of shelter this was and where it was used. Confirm that it was called the Anderson shelter after the man who organised the setting up of air-raid shelters in the UK for the Second World War.
● Explain that, during the war, many households were given the materials and instructions so that they could build their own Anderson shelter in their garden.

Whole-class work

● Focus on the outside of the shelter first and invite the children to help you to drag and drop the correct words to label the different features.
● Discuss why these features were chosen to safeguard people against bombs. For example, the very strong curved corrugated steel panels protected against flying debris and nearby impacts.
● Move on to focus on the inside of the shelter and let volunteers drag and drop the correct words to label the different features.
● Talk about how a child might have felt in the shelter during an air raid. Ask: *Do you think they would have felt safe?*
● Read out a transcript or play an oral account from a child of what it was like in an Anderson shelter.

Paired work or Independent work

● Give a copy of photocopiable page 204 'Explanation of an Anderson shelter' to each child.
● Working in pairs or independently, ask the children to answer the questions about an Anderson shelter.
● Once they have answered the questions, ask the children to draw a labelled diagram of the outside and inside of an Anderson shelter, using the wordbank to help them.

Whole-class work

● Ask the children to think of three things that would not have been good about being in an Anderson shelter, such as the noise, cold in winter, heat in summer, flooding, cramped and smelly conditions.
● Highlight that only people who had gardens would have been able to use an Anderson shelter, which was why the indoor Morrison shelter was more popular.
● As an extension, the children could make models of an Anderson shelter using corrugated card, and fake grass or green paint or, they could create a nearly life-size model for the class to use for role play.

Differentiation
● Support: help children with reading and/or writing on the photocopiable sheet.
● Challenge: encourage children to write an explanation text about the Anderson shelter in their own words, along with the labelled diagrams on a separate sheet of paper.

Review

● Review the children's work on the photocopiable sheet, and check their recognition of the features of an Anderson shelter.
● Recap on where and when an Anderson shelter would have been used, and by whom.

Week 5 lesson plans

During this week, the children are introduced to the terms and words relating to evacuation, including *evacuee*, *billet officer* and *host*. In the first lesson, the children learn about why children from bombed towns and cities had to be evacuated to safer places. They then work as history detectives to investigate the contents of an evacuee's suitcase to find out more about the evacuee and the items they were expected to take. In the second lesson, the children read two diary accounts of evacuees who have very different experiences. Through this activity they use their knowledge and empathy to write their own evacuee diary account.

1: Evacuation

Introduction

● Remind the children of the Blitz. Show the photographs of bombed-out buildings from media resource 'The Blitz' on the CD-ROM, and let the children listen to an oral account of experiencing the bombing.
● Explain that living in cities and towns, where most of the bombs were being dropped, was becoming very dangerous, and it was decided that to keep children safe they would go to live in the countryside away from the bomber planes' targets of factories and important sites in cities.
● Explain that this programme of 'escape' was called *evacuation* and the children who moved away were called *evacuees*. Write both terms on the board and display a range of photographs of evacuees with their suitcases for the children to see using media resource 'Evacuation photographs' on the CD-ROM.
● Suggest that the children become history detectives to find out about four war evacuees by studying the suitcases they are taking with them.

Group work

● Put the children into four mixed-ability groups and give them a gas mask box and a suitcase with items inside for them to investigate. Include something personal for each child, such as a teddy bear and a black-and-white photograph of a family or house, and clues to the evacuee's home-city.
● Point to the four cities you have labelled on a large UK map: for example, London, Liverpool, Cardiff, Coventry or Glasgow and explain that the four evacuees each come from one of these bombed cities.
● Let the children work in their group to look at the different items in the suitcase to find out who the child was, where they came from, where they were being evacuated to and what they were taking with them.
● Give each child a copy of photocopiable page 205 'Evacuee investigation sheet' for them to list the different items, write a few sentences about the evacuee and fill in their destination label.
● Let them use the evacuee photographs from the CD-ROM to draw a picture of their child for their ID card.

Whole-class work

● Bring the children together and ask them to use the suitcase contents to talk about their evacuee.
● Use the UK map to help them to find and label where the child was being evacuated to.

Review

● Look again at the map and note the distances involved. Emphasise that most of the children's parents had to stay behind. Ask the children how they would feel if they had to leave their family behind and live a long way away for quite some time. Discuss their different responses and encourage the children to extend their reasoning behind their thoughts.

Lesson objectives
● To develop an awareness of the past, using common words and phrases relating to the passing of time.
● To identify similarities and differences between ways of life in different periods.
● To use a wide vocabulary of everyday historical terms.
● To ask and answer questions, choosing and using parts of stories and other sources to show that they know and understand key features of events.
● To understand some of the ways in which we find out about the past.

Expected outcomes
● All children know that many children were sent to live in safer places during the war.
● Most children can find out more about what an evacuee took with them.
● Some children can deduce how children might have felt about being evacuated.

Resources
Media resources 'The Blitz' and 'Evacuation photographs' on the CD-ROM; an oral account of the Blitz (for example, TES oral history websites); large UK map with four bomb-target cities labelled; four small suitcases and four small 'gas mask' boxes; items for each suitcase such as clothes, washing kits, ID label with their address and where they are going to, something personal such as a small teddy bear, a black and white photograph of a family member, or a toy; photocopiable page 205 'Evacuee investigation sheet'; drawing pencils

Lesson objectives
● To develop an awareness of the past, using common words and phrases relating to the passing of time.
● To identify similarities and differences between ways of life in different periods.
● To use a wide vocabulary of everyday historical terms.
● To ask and answer questions, choosing and using parts of stories and other sources to show that they know and understand key features of events.
● To understand some of the ways in which we find out about the past.
● To identify different ways in which the past is represented.

Expected outcomes
● All children know that children had different experiences when they were evacuated.
● Most children know what happened when children were evacuated.
● Some children know that letters and diaries written by evacuees can help us find out more about what happened to them.

Resources
Photocopiable page 'Evacuee diaries' and media resource 'Evacuation photographs' from the CD-ROM; drawing pencils

2: Diary of an evacuee

Introduction
● Display the photographs of evacuees from media resource 'Evacuation photographs' on the CD-ROM and recall with the children what was happening during evacuation, and why.
● Recall that each evacuee would have had a different experience of being evacuated. Explain that we know this from the letters and diaries written by evacuated children and from the memories of older people today who were once evacuees. Refer to the photographs again and try to get an idea of how people are feeling from their facial expressions and body language.

Whole-class work
● Explain that you are going to read out two diary entries written by two evacuees on the day they were evacuated.
● Elicit from the children what a diary is and then ask them to listen carefully to both entries to find out what happened.
● Display and read the two diary accounts from photocopiable pages 'Evacuee diaries' from the CD-ROM, which illustrate both a positive and exciting experience, and a frightening experience.
● Discuss the different accounts. Ask questions such as: *What was fun and exciting about the evacuation in the first account? What did the billet officer do? Why did the writer like the countryside compared with the city? Why did they like their host family? In the second account, why was the evacuee so upset at the train station? Why were they scared when they got to their destination? What happened in the hall? Why didn't they like their new home?*
● Ask the children how they would feel if they had to leave home suddenly and were made to live in a totally different place. Would they be excited, scared, brave, sad?

Independent work
● Give the children pencils and paper and ask them to imagine that they are an evacuee, writing their diary about their evacuation day.
● Highlight that they could describe getting on the train, the journey, what the new place was like and their new host family and home.
● Write the date of the diary entry on the board as a model, along with key words and phrases that the children might want to use, such as: *journey, evacuated, countryside, billeting officer, host family*.
● Once the children have completed their diary entry, they could draw a picture to go with it, perhaps of a view from the train window, the billeting hall or their new home.
● Encourage the children to share their diary entries with each other. How different are their experiences?

Differentiation
● Support: children could work in a small group with adult support to help prompt ideas and in writing sentences for their diaries.
● Challenge: encourage children to be more descriptive about how they felt and why.

Review
● Invite children to read their diary entries (aim for both positive and negative experiences). Note the children's use of newly learned vocabulary and their ability to empathise with evacuees.
● Ask: *How do diary entries and letters written by real evacuees help us to understand more about life in Britain during the war?*

Week 6 lesson plans

In this final week, the children consolidate their knowledge and vocabulary of life as a child in the Second World War. They ask questions of a visitor who talks about wartime childhood memories. The children also have the vivid experience of taking part in an evacuation re-enactment. In the first lesson, the children hear a range of childhood memories of the war, helping them to understand that oral accounts and memories of the older generation are important in finding out what life was like in the past. The re-enactment will need two sessions, with the children making props and costumes in the introductory session. Have several adult helpers, including parents if possible, who can also act parts.

1: Remembering the evacuation

Lesson objectives
● To develop an awareness of the past, using common words and phrases relating to the passing of time.
● To identify similarities and differences between ways of life in different periods.
● To ask and answer questions, choosing and using parts of stories and other sources to show that they know and understand key features of events.
● To understand some of the ways in which we find out about the past.
● To identify different ways in which the past is represented.

Expected outcomes
● All children know that some older people remember being a child during the war.
● Most children can listen and ask questions about what life was like during the war.
● Some children understand how memories help us to find out about what the war was like for a child.

Resources
Oral accounts or transcripts of being an evacuee; accounts from local evacuees (optional); a good space for a visitor to talk about wartime memories; audio or video recording equipment

Introduction
● Discuss what has been learned about the children who were evacuees during the Second World War.
● Explain that some children who were evacuated during the Second World War are now adults who remember what it was like being evacuated.
● Suggest that the children listen to some of the memories of older people to find out what it was like being an evacuee and what happened to them.
● Remind them that they need to listen carefully and try to imagine the speaker as a child during the Second World War. Play audio clips (or read transcripts) of evacuation memories.
● Discuss what was heard and encourage the children to think of questions they would have liked to ask the speakers.
● Explain that they are going to meet a visitor soon who has memories about being evacuated or has memories of evacuees, and that, after the talk, they will be able to ask some questions of their own.
● Suggest to the children that they think of some questions to write down for asking during the visit.

Whole-class work
● Invite your visitor to talk to the children. Encourage them to bring in any Second World War artefacts, photographs or mementos that they would like to show to the children.
● Let the visitor introduce themselves and explain how old they were when they were evacuated or met evacuees. Allow them to talk about their memories and experiences of the evacuation programme.
● Then encourage the children to ask their questions.
● You might want to let the visitor and children branch out and discuss other memories of the war, such as food rationing, Make-do and Mend, air-raid shelters and school life.
● Record the question-and-answer session in audio or video format, and, later, let the children listen to or watch the recording.
● Make sure the children thank the visitor for sharing their memories and answering their questions.
● As an extension, set up an area where the children can listen to recorded memories of people who were children during the Second World War. These could be from internet sources, local societies and/or recorded memories of the children's own family members.

Review
● Review together what the children have discovered from the talk and question-and-answer session.
● Discuss how important older people's memories are for finding out about what life was like as a child during the Second World War.

Lesson objectives

● To develop an awareness of the past, using common words and phrases relating to the passing of time.
● To identify similarities and differences between ways of life in different periods.
● To use a wide vocabulary of everyday historical terms.
● To ask and answer questions, choosing and using parts of stories and other sources to show that they know and understand key features of events.
● To understand some of the ways in which we find out about the past.

Expected outcomes

● All children can re-enact being an evacuee during the Second World War.
● Most children can use their knowledge and vocabulary to role-play being an evacuee.
● Some children can empathise with being an evacuee on evacuation day.

Resources

Large space such as the hall or playground; props such as suitcases or pillowcases, gas mask boxes, blank identification labels, railway station signs, register of names; 1940s clothes for the children and adults (optional); sound effects such as media resource 'Air-raid siren' on the CD-ROM, train whistle, train sounds, country animal noises; adult support (staff and parents) in acting roles – teacher, parents of evacuees, station master, billeting officer, host families

2: Evacuation re-enactment

Introduction

● Before the lesson, send a letter home to ask parents if they can support the re-enactment and to help you to dress the children in suitable 1940s clothing, or store up sets of suitable clothing in school.
● In an introductory session, recap with the children what happened during the evacuation of children during the Second World War.
● Take the children through the schedule of a typical evacuation day, from packing their suitcase, leaving home for school, walking from school to the train station, departing, the journey, arriving at their destination, being chosen by a host and going to their new home.
● Explain that you are planning for the class to have a session when they can act at being Second World War evacuees.
● Discuss what props and clothing they would need and have a prop-making session, creating items such as cardboard suitcases and gas mask boxes.
● Give the children identification labels to complete with their personal details.
● Recap the Make-do and Mend sessions to revise what children wore during the war, and encourage the children to suggest ideas of costumes for the drama.

Whole-class work

● In the next session, start the re-enactment as soon as the children come into the classroom, with you and your adult support in role as parents, teachers, billeting officer and evacuation hosts.
● In role as a 1940s teacher, ask each child if they have their suitcases, gas masks and identification tags.
● Put the children into a single 'crocodile' line and walk them to a large area for the embarkation onto the train.
● Read the register and ask the children to say goodbye to their parents and get on the train.
● Use sound effects for the train journey. Remind the children that the journey is long. Sing songs such as 'Ten Green Bottles' to keep the children occupied.
● At the destination, ask the children to walk to a billeting area and sit down for their names to be called out by the billeting officer.
● Explain what the hosts will do and that you will see them at the village school the next day.
● Let the hosts introduce themselves before they choose their group of children and walk away with them.

Differentiation

● Support: make sure all the children are included in the re-enactment; stress that this is a drama re-enactment and not actually happening; make sure that the children are mixed when put into their host groups.

Review

● At the end of the drama session, bring all the children together and encourage them to discuss how they felt. Did they find it easy to imagining being an evacuee? How did it feel? Who enjoyed the acting, and who found it hard? Why?
● Note the children's knowledge, use of vocabulary and dramatic involvement, and their ability to empathise with what it might have been like as an evacuee.

Curriculum objectives
● To use a wide vocabulary of everyday historical terms.

Resources
Multiple sets of cards in which each card features a historical term relating to the five main areas of the topic: timeline of the war, food rationing including Dig for Victory, clothes rationing including Make-do and Mend, air-raid shelters, evacuation; interactive activity 'Second World War terms and definitions' on the CD-ROM

Childhood in the Second World War

Revise
● Organise the children into mixed-ability groups, and give each group a set of historical-term cards and the four subject headings relating to the main areas covered in the topic – *the timeline of the war, food rationing, clothing rationing, air-raid shelters and evacuation.*
● Ask the groups to lay out the subject headings on the table and sort the rest of the cards under the correct headings.
● Encourage the children to read out the different words and phrases under each heading and discuss their meanings in their groups.

Assess
● Let the children work individually or in pairs, on a computer, tablet or laptop, on interactive activity 'Second World War terms and definitions' on the CD-ROM.
● Using the interactive activity, the children read the definitions of significant terms relating aspects of the Second World War.
● Demonstrate that they then need to select the correct term for that definition from a choice of terms given to them via the drop-down box.
● Once the children have completed the interactive activity, ask them to write down in a few sentences about what they think it might have been like to be a child in their local area during the Second World War.

Further practice
● Put the children into pairs or small groups and give them matching sets of historical-term cards relating to just one of the areas covered in the topic. Let them use the cards to play the memory game 'Pairs', with the rule that when a child finds a pair they need to tell the others what the term means.

Curriculum objectives
● To develop an awareness of the past, using common words and phrases relating to the passing of time.
● To identify similarities and differences between ways of life in different periods.

Resources
Interactive activity 'Y2 Summer I quiz' on the CD-ROM

Y2 Summer I quiz

Revise
● Ask the children to select one of themes they have covered, such as food rationing, air-raid shelters and so on, and to prepare a factfile of information.

Assess
● Ask the children to complete the interactive activity 'Y2 Summer I quiz' on the CD-ROM. There are eight multiple-choice questions that test what the children will have learned throughout the topic. They will need to read each question carefully before choosing the correct answer.
● Give children a set length of time (such as 15 minutes) to answer the questions. This can be used as part of a formal assessment or as a fun challenge activity, giving children the opportunity to show what they have learned about the topic.
● Less confident readers may need adult support to read the questions aloud.

Further practice
● Check children's understanding of the Second World War and its impact on childhood. Review any misconceptions.

Food rations

- Write your name and address on the ration book.
- Colour it the right colour for your age.
- Write a list of food items for a week's rations by their pictures.

MINISTRY **MF** OF FOOD

RATION BOOK

Name _____

Address _____

I can understand what rationing was during the war.

How did you do?

Explanation of an Anderson shelter

What is an Anderson shelter? _____

_____

Where was it put? _____

What was it made of?_____

■ Draw a picture of the *outside* of an Anderson shelter and label it.

■ Draw a picture of the *inside* of Anderson shelter and label it.

corrugated steel panels   bunk beds   door   cupboard

I can explain what an Anderson shelter is.

How did you do?

PHOTOCOPIABLE   ■SCHOLASTIC
www.scholastic.co.uk

Evacuee investigation sheet

- Complete your evacuee's label.

Name _____

Address _____

_____

- List the items in your evacuee's suitcase.

_____

_____

- Complete these sentences.

Our evacuee comes from _____

Our evacuee is going to _____

One item in the suitcase that tells us about them is

_____

They have packed it because _____

This is what our evacuee looks like:

I can find out about an evacuee in the Second World War.

How did you do?

Our UK heritage: customs, festivals and fairs

This chapter allows the children to learn about their national and local heritage by exploring UK customs, festivals and fairs. They study events such as well dressing in the Derbyshire/Staffordshire area, the National Eisteddfod of Wales, the Scottish Highland Games and the Notting Hill Carnival in London. The children learn about the historical roots and features of a festival before practical lessons where they make a well dressing, carnival mask and headdress, perform in an Eisteddfod and hold a Highland Games. At the end of the topic, the children hold their own fair, using a local historical event, person, place or industry as its theme. Take the opportunity to include local customs or festivals with historic roots and traditions.

Chapter at a glance

Curriculum objectives

- Significant historical events, people and places in their own locality.
- Events beyond living memory that are significant nationally or globally.

Week	Lesson	Summary of activities	Expected outcomes
1	1	• Children learn what a *custo* is. • They study a photograph of a well dressing.	• Can find out what well dressing is and where and when it takes place. • Can write a report on the custom.
	2	• Children investigate the materials used in well dressing. • They make their own well dressing.	• Can create a well dressing based on an important local event, story, person or place.
2	1	• Children learn about the National Eisteddfod of Wales. • They compare ancient and modern Eisteddfods. • They write and perform poems about their area.	• Can place the National Eisteddfod in Wales. • Can compare ancient and modern festivals. • Can write a poem about local culture.
	2	• Children perform their works at an Eisteddfod to celebrate their local culture. • They follow the custom of naming bards.	• Can perform their cultural poems at a class Eisteddfod. • Can follow the customs of an Eisteddfod.
3	1	• Children locate Scotland on a map. • They look at modern Highland Games. • They speculate on origins of the games. • They suggest reasons for the heavy events.	• Understand that the Highland Games are a tradition in Scotland. • Can speculate about the origins of the games and events.
	2	• Children try events from the Highland Games.	• Can take part in Highland Games. • Understand how the games gives us clues about Scottish heritage.
4	1	• The children find out the West Indian origins of the Notting Hill carnival. • They see the main events of the carnival's history on a timeline. • They create a frieze procession.	• Can identify where and when the Notting Hill Carnival takes place. • Can investigate its origins and put historical events on a timeline. • Can identify features of the carnival.
	2	• Children learn about the Mas Bands and study their costumes. • They create their own carnival masks or headdresses.	• Can design and make a carnival mask or headdress.
5	1	• Children look at photographs of local fairs. • They compare a medieval and modern fair.	• Can investigate the different features and customs of fair days in the UK. • Know how fairs have changed over time.
	2	• Children find out about local history to choose the theme for a mini-fair. • They choose and plan activities for the fair.	• Can organise a mini-fair centred around a piece of local history.
6	1	• Groups prepare activity resources or practise their events for the fair.	• Can create historically themed resources for their mini-fair.
	2	• Children set up, run and pack away the fair. • They review the topic and discuss why customs, festivals and fairs have lasted.	• Can put on their mini-fair for other classes or school visitors.
Assess and review		• To review the half-term's work.	

■SCHOLASTIC
www.scholastic.co.uk

Expected prior learning

● Children are confident in using common words and phrases for the passing of time.
● Children can identify similarities and differences between ways of life in different periods.
● Children can identify different ways in which the past is represented.

Overview of progression

● The children investigate the origins of national and local customs, festivals and fairs, and become aware that events beyond living memory and within living memory have links to present-day celebrations.
● The children study a variety of sources to compare festivals over time. With each practical lesson, the children experience first-hand why such customs are still popular and important to their culture.
● The chapter shows how customs, festivals and fairs can help us to find out about the past, especially when looking at their possible beginnings.
● By the time the children come to this topic, they should understand that there are often many reasons and ideas suggested for why customs, festivals and fairs started, and that each one could have an element of truth.

Creative context

● Cross-curricular links include:
  ● writing skills, such as non-chronological reports, note-taking, and texts for posters and signs; reciting poetry and reading stories;
  ● singing and playing music and listening to different musical styles;
  ● performing country dances;
  ● designing and making a well dressing; making and decorating masks or headdresses; making props and items for a class mini-fair;
  ● naming and locating different places in the UK;
  ● being aware of the local community and the differences and similarities between the customs of people in the UK.

Background knowledge

● **Well dressing** is an ancient custom followed in villages in Derbyshire, Staffordshire and South Yorkshire. Every year, villages have a ceremony where they decorate their wells and springs with colourful pictures made from natural materials and give thanks for their fresh water supply. Some believe the custom originates from an ancient Pagan ceremony, others believe it started at the time of the plague, where villages escaped the disease.
● The **National Eisteddfod** of Wales is a cultural festival held every August to promote the Welsh language and Welsh heritage. The origins are believed to go back as far as 1176, when Lord Rhys invited poets and musicians to Cardigan Castle to compete for the position of best poet and musician and be given a chair at his table.
● The **Highland Games** are held across Scotland throughout the year. They celebrate Scottish heritage through sporting events, music and dance. The modern Highland Games as a festival began in early Victorian times, but one idea of its origin is that Malcolm III in the eleventh century had a competition to choose the best musicians and dancers, fastest runners and strongest men for his court, or there is the idea of friendly competition between clans.
● The **Notting Hill Carnival** is the second largest street festival in the world. Its origins started in the late 1950s, when newly arrived Afro-Caribbean people were struggling against prejudice in London. In 1959, Claudia Jones organised an indoor carnival to showcase Caribbean culture and music. This was so popular that others started up, including a children's street party in Notting Hill in 1964, which turned into a street procession with steel bands.
● Many **fairs** began in medieval times when small towns were given charters to have a fair. This usually fell on a holiday, allowing people to travel to the fairs to buy and sell goods and animals and enjoy the entertainment. Country fairs still retain many customs and traditions such as, maypole dancing, country dancing and crowning of the fair king and queen.

Week 1 lesson plans

In this first week, the children look at the English custom of well dressing. From this example they learn what *custom* means and consider their own local or cultural customs. In the first lesson, the children create a simple poster report about well dressing and its possible origins. In the second lesson, the children create their own well dressing with a picture of something or someone with a local historical connection.

1: The custom of well dressing

Lesson objectives
- To develop an awareness of the past, using common words and phrases relating to the passing of time.
- To use a wide vocabulary of everyday historical terms.
- To ask and answer questions, choosing and using parts of stories and other sources to show that they know and understand key features of events.
- To understand some of the ways in which we find out about the past.
- To identify different ways in which the past is represented.

Expected outcomes
- All children know what a well dressing is.
- Most children understand what a custom is.
- Some children understand how we can find out about the past from our customs.

Resources
Photocopiable page 'Well dressing' from the CD-ROM; photograph showing detail of a well dressing; film clips of well dressing if possible; UK county map; photographs of well dressings; internet access (such as www. peakdistrictinformation.com and www.welldressing.com) and reference books; scissors; glue; drawing pencils; A3 paper

Introduction
- Explain to the children that they will be looking at an old custom that is still carried out in some places in the UK.
- Establish the meaning of the word *custom* as an old, traditional way of doing something special. Think of an example of a custom followed locally and discuss what happens and what makes it a custom.

Whole-class work
- Show a large photograph of a well dressing. Explain what it shows and that the practice is an English custom that started long ago.
- Encourage the children to look closely at the decoration to see that it is made mainly from natural materials such as flower petals and twigs.
- Show photocopiable page 'Well dressing' from the CD-ROM and explain that it is a non-chronological report about well dressing. Discuss why a report like this is useful when learning about new things.
- Help the children to identify the different elements of the report, such as an introduction to what a well dressing is, where and when it is held, why it is done, what happens at a well dressing, and a labelled diagram. Note the length and structure of the text and the use of subheadings and time connectives.
- Highlight that the report is meant to help the reader to know more about an old historical custom followed in the UK.

Paired work or Independent work
- Let the children work in mixed-ability pairs or independently. Explain that you would like them to create their own non-chronological report about well dressing in the same style as on the photocopiable page.
- Hand out paper and pencils and resources such as a UK county map, photographs of well dressings, and access to websites and reference books. Leave the poster on screen, or provide printouts.
- As the children work, ask them about their ideas and choice of report features.

Whole-class work
- Once the report posters have been completed, ask volunteers to present their work to the class.
- If possible, show film clips of well dressing festivals.

Differentiation
- Support: offer typed captions or subheadings for the children to select for their report.

Review
- Ask: *What makes well dressing a custom? Why is it important for those people who do it every year?* (Fresh water is very important to these areas; celebrating and maintaining customs are integral to the culture and keeping history 'alive'; it connects people with their past and local memories.)

■SCHOLASTIC
www.scholastic.co.uk

Lesson objectives

● To ask and answer questions, choosing and using parts of stories and other sources to show that they know and understand key features of events.
● To understand some of the ways in which we find out about the past.
● To identify different ways in which the past is represented.

Expected outcomes

● All children can make a simple well dressing.
● Most children can use a design with a historical local connection.
● Some children can explain why they chose their design for their well dressing.

Resources

Photographs of well dressing; local history information; for each child: small oblong wooden board, matching thin sheet of paper, sharp pencil, ruler, enough clay to cover the board with a 2cm depth, rolling pin for clay, petals (or tissue paper petals), leaves, twigs, beans, eggshells, lentils and other natural materials; protective coverings for tables and clothes

2: Making a well dressing picture

Introduction

● This activity could take place over two sessions. Before the lesson, soak the wooden boards in cold water overnight, so that the clay does not dry out. Make an example well dressing to show the children.
● Show the children a range of photographs of well dressings. Discuss what they are and why they are made every year. Encourage the children to list the different natural materials used to make them. Confirm that the main materials are different-coloured flower petals. Note that the skin of people in the picture can be made from pieces of eggshell.
● Use the photographs to discuss the different picture ideas that have been used in the dressings.

Whole-class work

● Explain to the children that they are going to design and make a well dressing picture of something, someone or an event from the past that is important in their local area. It could be, for example, a castle, an engineer or inventor like Brunel or Whittle, a writer or artist like Thackeray or Hockney, cotton mills or coal mines.
● Show your example of a well dressing picture and emphasise the need to keep the picture simple, without much detail.
● Explain that the picture is on a base of wet clay, which allows the picture to last for a few days. Model the different stages of making the picture:
  ● Roll out the clay onto the board and trim the edges with a ruler.
  ● Place a paper design onto the clay.
  ● Prick out the design outline onto the clay with a pencil.
  ● Take the paper away and fill in the lines with small beans or pieces of twig.
  ● Starting from the bottom, gently press the flower petals and other materials into the clay.

Independent work

● Set aside a drawing area where the children can work on their designs, and have other tables set up for the clay rolling and picture making. Or, make the clay rolling and well dressing in a second session.
● Once the children have completed their designs, encourage them to tell you about their choice of subject, and check that the images are not too complicated.
● As the children create their clay versions, move around the class, and prompt the children to think of colours and textures they could use for different parts of the picture.
● Once the well dressing pictures are completed, the children could design frames for them.

Differentiation
● Challenge: children could write instructions for how to make a well dressing picture.

Review

● After the lesson, create a wall display with a large well and the children's well dressing pictures around it. Add a motif such as, *Thank you for our clean water.*
● Encourage the children to talk about their designs, explaining the meanings behind them and why they chose their focal person or object.

Week 2 lesson plans

This week, the children look at the National Eisteddfod of Wales. In the first lesson, the children find out what an Eisteddfod is and look at the festival held today. They discuss how festivals are important as a way for people to celebrate their culture and community. They then study pictures of a 16th century Eisteddfod and a present-day version. In the second lesson, the children perform in their own mini-Eisteddfod and re-enact the crowing of the bard.

1: The National Eisteddfod

Introduction
● Identify Wales on a map of the UK. Say that every year, for eight days in August, Wales holds its national Eisteddfod. Write *Eisteddfod* on the board and encourage the children to say it with you. Explain that the word is Welsh and means 'a group of people sitting together'.
● Show photographs of a modern Eisteddfod and explain that it is a festival of music, poems, stories and drama in the Welsh language.
● Ask: *Why do you think the Eisteddfod is so important to Welsh people?*
● Discuss any similar local festivals that the children know about and have experienced.

Whole-class work
● Display media resource 'Early and later Eisteddfods' on the CD-ROM. Explain that long ago, Eisteddfods were held by Welsh kings to choose the best musicians, poets and dancers for their courts.
● Encourage the children to study the picture of an old Eisteddfod. Ask prompt questions such as: *Who is the person behind the table? What is the person doing in front of him? What could the chair be for?* Explain what the title *bard* means.
● Then focus on the modern Eisteddfod picture and encourage the children to compare it with the older ceremony. Note the chair, crown, judges, bards and dancers.
● Highlight that new customs have been added to the ceremony in more recent times, such as the crown, but the important focus on the Welsh language, culture and heritage remains.
● Tell the children that they are going to have their own Eisteddfod, where they can read out their own poems about their local area or culture.
● Discuss ideas that could be used in their poems: local landscape, food, clothes, shops, places of historical interest, and so on.

Paired work
● Let the children work together on their poems, which can be in any style or form.
● Encourage them to practise performing their poems to an audience (each other). Another session might be needed to allow the children to complete their poems and perform them to the class.

> **Differentiation**
> ● Support: the class Eisteddfod doesn't have to have just a literacy focus; children could perform music, dance, or drama, or show artwork.

Review
● Note the children's skills at comparing the Eisteddfods between two periods of history.

Lesson objectives
● To develop an awareness of the past, using common words and phrases relating to the passing of time.
● To use a wide vocabulary of everyday historical terms.
● To ask and answer questions, choosing and using parts of stories and other sources to show that they know and understand key features of events.
● To identify different ways in which the past is represented.

Expected outcomes
● All children know that the Eisteddfod is a festival in Wales.
● Most children can make comparisons between Eisteddfods long ago and in present times.
● Some children understand why the Eisteddfod is important to Welsh people and their heritage.

Resources
Media resource 'Early and later Eisteddfods' on the CD-ROM; UK map; photographs of the Eisteddfod today

Lesson objectives
● To use a wide vocabulary of everyday historical terms.
● To ask and answer questions, choosing and using parts of stories and other sources to show that they know and understand key features of events.
● To understand some of the ways in which we find out about the past.

Expected outcomes
● All children know that people performed in Eisteddfods long ago and still do today.
● Most children understand that an Eisteddfod has distinct ceremonies.
● Some children understand why we still celebrate festivals that began long ago.

Resources
A hall or large space for the children to watch and perform their acts; a wooden chair with arms (like a throne); a silver crown; a silver-coloured bucket or pot covered in silver foil; names of all the children in the bucket; video camera; music equipment for music or dance (optional); the children's poems; a well-known local song

2: A class Eisteddfod

Introduction
● Arrange a large space such as the school hall, or create a space in the classroom for the children to perform. Have an adult volunteer to film or take photographs of the event for the children to see at a later date.
● Remind the children of the poems (or other artworks) they wrote in the last lesson and that they are going to perform or present them at their own Eisteddfod.
● Emphasise that in the real festival, artists and writers compete for prizes for work in Welsh. Highlight that here the children don't need to speak Welsh, and it is not a competition, but their Eisteddfod is still going to celebrate their local area or culture.
● If needed, let the children have the chance to rehearse their poems one more time before the event.

Whole-class work
● Lead the children in a procession to where they are going to perform and point out the throne and the crown.
● Explain that at the end of the event, two of the children's names will be pulled out of a silver bucket to be named as bards of the class Eisteddfod. Explain that one child will be named in the Chairing of the Bard ceremony and the other will be named in the Crowning of the Bard ceremony.
● Let the children take turns to introduce and recite (or read) their poems. Encourage the rest of the children to listen attentively as the audience.
● Once all the children have performed their poems, walk forward and pronounce that it is time for the chairing and crowning ceremonies.
● Let an adult helper, or yourself, take one child's name out of the silver bucket for the crowning ceremony.
● Call them out and place the crown on their head and pronounce them a 'Bard of the class Eisteddfod'. Encourage the children to applaud.
● Repeat the 'ritual' for the other child to sit on the throne in the chairing ceremony.
● Close the Eisteddfod with the children singing, and playing, or dancing to a well-known local song.

> ### Differentiation
> ● Support: less confident speakers could choose the lines they feel comfortable with and let a more confident partner say the other part

Review
● In a later session, let the children see the film of their Eisteddfod and discuss each act's connection to a local or cultural link.
● Discuss why customs and festivals that started long ago can still be important to us today.

Week 3 lesson plans

The focus this week is the Scottish Highland Games. In the first lesson, the children find out more about the present-day games with their Victorian origins. Through investigating possible reasons for when and why the games first started and how some of the heavy events became sports, the children gain historical skills in understanding that without exact evidence there are sometimes no definite answers, just likely answers which can be used as links. In the second lesson, the children take part in their own Highland Games and try out heavy events and country dancing.

1: The Highland Games

Lesson objectives
● To use a wide vocabulary of everyday historical terms.
● To understand some of the ways in which we find out about the past.

Expected outcomes
● All children know what types of events are in a Highland Games.
● Most children know that the Highland Games is important to Scottish history.
● Some children understand how the Highland Games can help us know more about Scotland's past.

Resources
Photocopiable page 'Possible reasons for the Highland Games' from the CD-ROM, printed onto cards; photocopiable page 221 'Highland Games heavy events'; drawing pencils

Introduction
● Identify Scotland on the map of the UK. Explain that, every year, the Highland Games are held in Scotland. Ask the children what they think the Highland Games might be and let them share any experiences they have.
● Show footage or photographs of the games and talk about the different events.

Whole-class work
● Tell the children that historians think the first Highland Games might have started long ago, when large Scottish family groups called *clans* would meet up, but they are not sure.

Group work
● Read out each of the four cards from photocopiable page 'Possible reasons for the Highland Games' from the CD-ROM. Then put the children into groups and give each a card.
● Let each group discuss their idea and why it could be a good reason for the games to be held.
● Ask the groups to report back to the class, one at a time.
● Suggest that all of the reasons could be true, that it wasn't until Queen Victoria's time that the games became a more formal yearly festival.

Independent work
● Hand out photocopiable page 221 'Highland Games heavy events' and use an enlarged or on-screen version to point to the pictures of the two heavy events.
● Emphasise the two suggestions about the possible origins of each event under the pictures.
● Highlight that one of the notes is a more likely origin than the other and you want the children to write a sentence saying which one is more likely. Ask: *But why would we say 'likely' instead of 'definitely'?*
● The children could then draw pictures to illustrate their chosen origins next to the modern versions of the events.

Whole-class work
● Ask: *Why do you think many of the heavy events use everyday farming tools or natural objects?*
● Highlight that women can now take part in some of the heavy events. Ask: *Why do you think this did not happen in the past?* (The events were to show off the men's strength; it would not have seemed right or 'proper' for women to do it; they competed in dance and musical events.)

Review
● Encourage the children to share their sentences and explain their choices. Note those who understand that there are no definite answers.

Lesson objectives
● To use a wide vocabulary of everyday historical terms.
● To understand some of the ways in which we find out about the past.

Expected outcomes
● All children know what types of events are in a Highland Games.
● Most children know that the Highland Games are important to Scottish history.
● Some children understand how the Highland Games can help us to know more about Scotland's past.

Resources
Photographs of Highland Game events; playing field or area for sport; recorded music to be played outside (country or Scottish dance music, bagpipe music); for light events: running track, tug-of-war rope, markers for long jump; for heavy events: caber (long paper rolled into a stiff roll), wellies, high jump bar (for throwing over), beanbag attached to rope or thick string; distance markers; measuring equipment

2: A class Highland Games

Introduction
● You will need additional adult support for each of the three types of game.
● Recall with the children the different events in a Highland Games. Use photographs or video footage to remind the children of the three main groups – dancing, light events and heavy events. Briefly go through each event with the children.
● Explain that they are going to have their own mini Highland Games as a class.

Group work
● Take the children to the field and put them into teams. If possible, have bagpipe music playing as they walk onto the field.
● Organise the teams into three groups to focus on the three main events.
● Choose a range of events that would be suitable for the children. For example:
  ● light events – running races, tug of war and long jump;
  ● heavy events – tossing the paper-roll caber, a wellie throw over a bar (sheaf tossing) and throwing a beanbag on a rope (hammer);
  ● country dancing – basic, simple movements.
● Before the children try out each game in the light and heavy events, make sure the adult helper tells them how to play the game and any safety rules to be followed.
● Once the groups have played their games, they can move to another of the main event groups, so that, by the end of the session, all the children have experienced the different Highland Games events.
● If possible, have bagpipe or other suitable music playing between each changeover.

Whole-class work
● Back in the classroom, discuss the children's thoughts and experiences of their Highland Games session.
● Highlight that the Highland Games are also very popular in other countries where Scottish people have moved to live and work. Ask the children why they think that is.
● Ask: *How do the Highland Games help us know more about the Scotland's past?* (It gives us ideas about how people met, what they used for tools, and how they fought.)
● As an extension in another session, let the children create Highland Games posters for the school using Scottish images of the games, such as a set of bagpipes, the Scottish thistle, a Scottish dancer, or a participant tossing the caber. If possible, invite a bagpipe player into school so the children can listen to the music and ask questions.

Differentiation
● Support: use alternative ideas for the heavy events such as creating a lighter caber, a beanbag shot putt, or throwing a shoe a distance.

Review
● Assess the children through their participation in the games and their discussion at the end of the lesson.
● Check their understanding of how the Highland Games have distinct Scottish heritage and help us to know more about Scotland's past.

Lesson objectives
● To develop an awareness of the past, using common words and phrases relating to the passing of time.
● To show where people and events they study fit within a chronological framework.
● To use a wide vocabulary of everyday historical terms.
● To ask and answer questions, choosing and using parts of stories and other sources to show that they know and understand key features of events.
● To understand some of the ways in which we find out about the past.
● To identify different ways in which the past is represented.

Expected outcomes
● All children know that the Notting Hill Carnival began within living memory.
● Most children understand that many Afro-Caribbean people came to live in the UK over 50 years ago.
● Some children understand why the Notting Hill Carnival is so popular.

Resources
Photographs of Notting Hill Carnival; UK map; world map; media resources 'Notting Hill Carnival timeline' and 'Carnival sounds' on the CD-ROM; photocopiable page 222 'Notting Hill Carnival'; long sheet of paper; glue; scissors; colouring pencils; steel band or calypso background music (optional)

Week 4 lesson plans

This week looks at the largest street festival in Europe – the Notting Hill Carnival. This is a good example showing changes in society within living memory. In the first lesson, the children find out how the development of Afro-Caribbean communities in the 1950s and 1960s gave birth to the carnival and how it has changed in the past 50 years. In the second lesson, the children create 'Mas Band' style decorated masks and headdresses. You could also explore the origins of the carnival in freedom from slavery, or learn more about the music.

1: What is the Notting Hill Carnival?

Introduction
● Display photographs of the Notting Hill Carnival and elicit that a carnival is a street festival with processions, dancing and music. Say that this one takes place in London every August. Locate London on a UK map.
● Encourage the children to share experiences of a local street festival or carnival.

Whole-class work
● Explain that the Notting Hill Carnival celebrates the culture of Afro-Caribbean people living in the UK, particularly in London. Point out the West Indies on a world map and explain that, in the 1950s and 60s, many people were encouraged to leave this part of the world to live and work in the UK.
● Consider what it might have been like moving to a very different country. Ask: *What things, along with family and friends, might the people have missed?* (Music, weather, food, traditions.)
● Display media resource 'Notting Hill Carnival timeline' and highlight that many people still remember the 1950s and 1960s. Note main UK events on the timeline, such as the Queen's coronation.
● Point to the photograph of Claudia Jones on the timeline and explain that in 1959 she organised the first Afro-Caribbean festival in London.
● Focus on 1964, when a steel band first played in a children's street festival in Notting Hill. Click on the picture of the steel band and explain what a steel band is and how music is made by beating different areas of different-sized steel pans. Play media resource 'Carnival sounds' on the CD-ROM and ask: *Why would a steel band make the street festival popular?*
● Look at the other points on the timeline and highlight how the carnival has changed in living memory from a small street carnival to a huge procession with millions of spectators. Ask the children why they think this carnival has become so popular since it started over 50 years ago.
● Tell the children that they are going to look at three main features of the Notting Hill Carnival – the Mas Bands, the floats and the music. Use the photographs and sound clip to discuss these features.

Paired work
● Give each child a copy of photocopiable page 222 'Notting Hill Carnival', a long strip of blank paper, glue, scissors and pencils. Ask the children to create their own Notting Hill Carnival procession by cutting out the illustrations and labels and sticking them onto the long strip in the order that they want.
● They can then write a caption to go with each feature to explain what it is.
● Encourage the children to colour in the procession and draw houses for a street backdrop.

Review
● Invite the children to hold up their carnival strips. Look at the vibrant colours and ask the children why the carnival started and has become more and more popular.

Lesson objectives
● To ask and answer questions, choosing and using parts of stories and other sources to show that they know and understand key features of events.
● To understand some of the ways in which we find out about the past.

Expected outcomes
● All children can create a Mas-style mask or headdress.
● Most children know what a Mas Band is.
● Some children understand the importance of the Mas bands in the Notting Hill Carnival.

Resources
Photographs of the carnival Mas Bands; for masks: different-shaped card templates, elastic or string, or sticks to hold the masks; for headdresses: large star or circle card shapes, card headbands; stapler; glue; adhesive tape; scissors; recycled materials; paints; colouring pens; decorative materials such as feathers, sequins and coloured beads; Caribbean carnival music and player

2: Making carnival masks and headdresses

Introduction
● Remind the children of the main features of the Notting Hill Carnival: the music, dancing and processions relating to Caribbean culture.
● Explain that they will be focusing on the Mas Bands in this lesson, who work as a team as they take part in the carnival and are one of the most important aspects of the parade. Look at a range of photographs and video clips showing examples of the costumes, masks, models and music of some of the Mas Bands and discuss the designs, materials and bright colours in detail.
● Highlight that the members of over 100 Mas Bands work all year to create their dances, costumes, masks, floats and models for the Notting Hill Carnival. Note that each band works to a theme idea. If possible, use examples in the photographs to relate these themes to Caribbean culture and history.

Independent work
● Explain to the children that you would like them to create either a decorated mask or a headdress for a class carnival. The theme could be linked to the Caribbean or to another topic area that the children may already be working on, such as animals, flowers or a particular story.
● For the masks, prepare a range of different-shaped card mask templates for the children to draw around, cut out and decorate.
● For the headdresses, create large star or circle shapes out of card which will sit at the back of the head, and card headbands to go around the child's head.
● Let the children use a range of recycled materials, paints, pens and decorative bits and pieces such as feathers, sequins and coloured beads to adorn their masks.
● Before they decorate their masks or headdresses, ask the children to take time to think of *how* they are going to decorate them. Ask: *What bright colours are you going to use? What materials would make your mask or headdress stand out? How does the design reflect the theme?*
● Give out the mask and headdress templates and offer assistance as the children work on their designs.
● Have steel bands or calypso music playing in the background.
● Once the masks and headdresses are finished and dry, help the children to add the elastic or sticks to the masks or attach their headbands to their headdresses. Check the fit and help the children to make adjustments as necessary.

Whole-class work
● Let the children have a procession with their masks and headdresses. Play steel band or calypso music to make the carnival procession feel more authentic.

Review
● Afterwards, ask the children what a Mas Band is.
● Note that some children's Mas Bands in the Notting Hill Carnival do not use costumes, but parade with puppets or artwork on tall poles.

Week 5 lesson plans

During this week, the children begin studying the history of fair days in the UK. In the first lesson, they discuss features of typical fair days using local examples, photographs and their own experiences. They then study a picture of a fair from long ago and compare it with a present-day fair. In the second lesson, the children are challenged with organising and running their own mini-fair with a local historical theme. Working in groups they look at different ideas and vote for the best historical local theme.

1: Fairs past and present

Introduction
● Show the children a range of photographs of fair days from the local area and elsewhere in the UK. Ask the children what they think the photographs are showing. Explain what a fair means in this context – a gathering of people to buy or sell goods as well as enjoying entertainment. Often, fairs are held in the same month every year.
● Using the photographs and the children's own experiences of fairs, list the attractions we might find at a present-day fair, such as floats, stalls, marching bands, sports and games, puppet shows, fancy dress competitions, maypole and country dancing, pet shows, fairground rides and games.

Whole-class work
● Explain that lots of fairs started long ago and were a big event for many people who lived nearby. Bring up interactive activity 'A medieval fair' on the CD-ROM.
● Point out that the picture shows a fair in a town a very long time ago. Ask: *How do we know it was long ago?* Focus on the clothes, buildings and events at the fair.
● Study the different features and invite children to drag and drop the labels to the correct places.
● Highlight that people often went to fairs in the past to buy and sell food, animals cloth, tools and objects they had made, as well as to enjoy the entertainment. The fair was an important day for many families and workers in the villages around the town.

Independent work
● Hand out photocopiable page 223 'Comparing fair days from long ago and today' and ask the children to complete the table of similarities and differences between fairs from long ago and those today.
● Once they have completed the table, encourage them to write about what they would have liked to see at a fair from long ago and at a fair today. Let them draw pictures with their sentences.
● As an extension, look at a historic fair in the local area in more detail, perhaps along the lines of Widecombe Fair in Devon, Scarborough Fair or Heffle Cuckoo Fair in Sussex. You could also invite older local residents to talk about their memories of fair days when they were children.

> **Differentiation**
> ● Support: if possible, let children work in a supported group, so that they can exchange ideas and oral sentences for an adult to scribe.

Review
● Confirm the dates on the photocopiable sheet and invite the children to share the differences and similarities they found.

Lesson objectives
● To develop an awareness of the past, using common words and phrases relating to the passing of time.
● To identify similarities and differences between ways of life in different periods.
● To use a wide vocabulary of everyday historical terms.
● To ask and answer questions, choosing and using parts of stories and other sources to show that they know and understand key features of events.
● To understand some of the ways in which we find out about the past.

Expected outcomes
● All children know what a fair is.
● Most children can compare fairs from long ago and present times.
● Some children know that some features of fairs long ago are still used today.

Resources
Interactive activity 'A medieval fair' on the CD-ROM; photographs of fairs from around the UK; material on fairs local to your area; photocopiable page 223 'Comparing fair days from long ago and today'; drawing pencils

■SCHOLASTIC
www.scholastic.co.uk

2: Planning a historical mini-fair

Lesson objectives

- To develop an awareness of the past, using common words and phrases relating to the passing of time.
- To use a wide vocabulary of everyday historical terms.
- To ask and answer questions, choosing and using parts of stories and other sources to show that they know and understand key features of events.
- To understand some of the ways in which we find out about the past.
- To identify different ways in which the past is represented.

Expected outcomes

- All children can choose a local historical theme for their class mini-fair.
- Most children can explain why their local historical choice should be used in the fair.
- Some children can use their knowledge of a local historical theme to plan their fair.

Resources

A range of resources on significant local events, people, places, industry or objects that could be used as fair theme; sticky notes

Introduction

- Explain to the children that, as a class, they are going to organise a mini-fair that can be held in school. Emphasise that the fair needs to have a theme based on a well-known and significant historical place, event, industry, object or person connected to their local area. Suggest to the children that first they work in groups to look at possible ideas, using a range of resources.
- Note that you will need to keep a record of the events and features that the children decide to organise.

Group work

- Put the children into groups and give each group a selection of resources such as brochures, books and pictures, about different local historical events, people, places, industry or objects that could be used as a fair theme.
- Give the groups time to look through their resources and use sticky notes to mark areas that they think would be a good focus. Remind the children to share ideas as a group, allowing everyone a turn to speak, and making sure everyone listens too.
- When the children are ready, ask each group to present their ideas and explain how their given theme could work for the fair day.

Whole-class work

- Once all the groups have presented their ideas, have a class discussion and agreement, or election, to choose the theme that the fair will have.
- Highlight the need to decide also on what attractions and features the themed fair will have on the day. Emphasise that as it is a mini-fair, it would be best to stick to six to eight main features or events.
- Create a mind map on the board of the different events and features the fair will have.
- Once the children have put all their ideas onto the mind map, work with them to remove certain ideas and keep others, ensuring that the theme is kept in mind.
- Look at the final six to eight events and features; perhaps a craft stall, cake stall, tug of war, maypole dancing, a themed game, fancy dress competition.
- Ask the children what they plan to call their fair. Stress that the theme should be mentioned in the title.

Group work

- Organise the children into groups – one for each of the fair's activities.
- Ask them to plan their event or feature within their group. They should list what is needed and what each person in the group will do.
- Ask them to think carefully when planning. For example, if there is country dancing, what music will be used? Will a maypole be needed? Will the stalls need signs? What are the rules for the games? What cakes or crafts will be made?
- At the end of the lesson, collect the notes and plans for use in the next lesson.

Differentiation
- Support: children can share their skills and ideas in mixed-ability groups.

Review

- Invite the groups to tell the class what activity they are responsible for.
- Discuss the choice of local history focus, and how it can be used as a theme for the fair.

Week 6 lesson plans

In the first lesson this final week, the children create resources and props for their historically themed mini-fair. In the second lesson, they set up, run and then put away their mini-fair. Make sure that there are enough adult helpers to support them during these sessions. Invite families, carers and other classes to the fair. It could have free admission, or you might want to organise it as a small fundraiser. At the end of the second lesson, the children have the chance to review the topic on customs, festivals and fairs and discuss why so many of them have lasted for many years.

1: Creating historical resources

Introduction

● Note that this lesson will need quite a bit of preparation and more than one session to make sure that the children have the materials and resources needed to organise their event for the fair.
● Put the children back into their planning groups from last time. Remind them about their themed mini-fair and its local historical connections.
● Briefly look at the pieces of information the children have highlighted about the historical connection and how it could be used in their fair. Ask: *Why is it a good idea to have a fair based on a local historical connection?* (It makes the fair interesting and fun for the local community; it reflects the historical traditions behind other fairs.)

Group work

● Encourage each group to explain what activity or entertainment they are planning and what they need to make or do.
● Then let each group work on their resources, with adult support. Activities could include:
  ● making small cakes, biscuits or no-cook sweets;
  ● making simple crafts;
  ● writing stall signs;
  ● decorating a tall pole with ribbons;
  ● practising maypole dancing or country dancing;
  ● making rosettes for prizes;
  ● designing posters for the fair;
  ● painting background scenery for funfair games, such as a coconut;
  ● finding or making puppets and puppet theatre;
  ● making animal cut-outs for a pet show;
  ● making bunting with paper flags;
  ● organising costumes and props for a small mummers-style play;
  ● writing rules for games.
● Arrange time, space and adult support to help children who might want to learn and rehearse a dance, and allow several smaller sessions for all the resources to be prepared.

Whole-class work

● Discuss with the children what order the events should be held in and any stall-based activities that can run at the same time. Help the children to write simple programmes with the running order.
● If you have not done so already, encourage the children to write invitations to ask visitors to their fair, such as their families or other classes.

Review

● Run through the order of events with the children. Ask them to think about which fairgoers will like which event or activity.
● Note any children whose posters, fair decorations or invitations mention or reflect the fair's chosen local history theme.

Lesson objectives
● To use a wide vocabulary of everyday historical terms.
● To ask and answer questions, choosing and using parts of stories and other sources to show that they know and understand key features of events.
● To understand some of the ways in which we find out about the past.
● To identify different ways in which the past is represented.

Expected outcomes
● All children can create resources for their historically themed fair.
● Most children understand how their historical theme can make their fair interesting.
● Some children use their knowledge about the historical theme to create effective fair resources.

Resources
Children's planning notes from the previous lesson; information and resources on their chosen local historical theme; a range of art, craft and drawing materials for the fair activities

■SCHOLASTIC
www.scholastic.co.uk

Lesson objectives
● To identify similarities and differences between ways of life in different periods.
● To use a wide vocabulary of everyday historical terms.
● To ask and answer questions, choosing and using parts of stories and other sources to show that they know and understand key features of events.
● To understand some of the ways in which we find out about the past.
● To identify different ways in which the past is represented.

Expected outcomes
● All children understand that customs, fairs and festivals have links to the past.
● Most children understand why many customs, fairs and festivals are important to a country's heritage.
● Some children understand how customs, fairs and festivals help us find out about the past.

Resources
A large indoor space such as the hall, or outdoor space such as a playground or field; the children's fair props and resources; tables and chairs for stalls; music player; scissors; sticky tack; adhesive tape; bowls or boxes for coins as appropriate; decorations; adult support

2: A class mini-fair

Introduction
● Select a suitable time to hold the mini-fair. The children would need time to set it up, run the fair, and tidy up, so a whole morning or afternoon might be needed.
● Put the children into their groups, with adult support for each group.
● Explain to the children that they all need to work together as a class to set up the fair. Stress that when a fair is put on, time is needed to set it up and then tidy away afterwards.
● Let the children collect their items for the fair and go to where the fair will be based. Encourage the children to help you to work out where the stalls and other features could be and then help them to set up and decorate the fair.

Whole-class work
● When the time comes and everyone is ready, open the fair with one or two of the children reading out a proclamation with reference to the local historical theme.
● If money is being handled on the stalls and games, make sure that an adult is with the children to help them to count the change correctly.
● Encourage different children to announce the various events as appropriate.
● At the end of the fair, the children may want to have a prize-giving ceremony for events such as the best fancy dress, the best pet, and so on.
● Once the fair is closed, help the children to tidy up and put things away.
● At the end of the session, or in the next session, discuss the mini-fair with the children and whether the historical theme worked well and was enjoyed. Ask: *Why do you think people have been going to fair days like these for hundreds of years?*

Review
● Briefly look back over the whole topic and discuss with the children what they have learned about other fair days in addition to the well dressing custom, and the festivals in Wales and Scotland and the Notting Hill Carnival.
● Ask the children about the customs, festivals and fairs they have in their local area, or give the children of some examples. Discuss which ones they like and why.
● Ask: *Why do you think some of the customs, festivals and fairs that we have found out about have lasted for many years and are still popular? How can fairs like this help us to find out about the past?* (Elicit reference to the theme of their fair and how visitors will have learned a little about it while enjoying the various events.)

Lesson objectives
● To ask and answer questions, choosing and using parts of stories and other sources to show that they know and understand key features of events.

Resources
Writing and drawing paper and pencils; sources used in the lessons such as pictures, reports and the children's own work; reference books and access to websites

Customs, festivals and fairs

Revise

● Working with the children, create a mind map on the board of the main areas that have been covered in the topic: customs – well dressing; festivals – Eisteddfod, Highland Games and Notting Hill Carnival; fair days.

● Under each heading, ask the children to help you to list the information and concepts that they have learned.

● Go through each section in detail, encouraging the children to impart their learned knowledge and historical vocabulary.

● Discuss the possible historical origins for each custom, festival and fair that they have studied within the topic.

● Remind the children that some customs and festivals have origins from long ago, so it is very difficult to say definitely how they started.

Assess

● Put the children into mixed-ability pairs and allocate them one of the five topic areas.

● Write a set of general instruction questions on the board that you would like the children to answer in sentences on a sheet of paper. The questions could be:

  ● Write the name of the topic area.
  ● What is it? (What happens?)
  ● Where is it held?
  ● Why do you think it started?
  ● Why do you think it is still celebrated today?
  ● Write an amazing fact about it.

● Model an answer sentence or two, such as: *The topic is the Highland Games. They are held in Scotland.*

● Once the children have completed writing their answers, ask one of the pair to draw a picture of the topic area in the past and the partner to draw a picture of what it looks like today.

● Encourage the children to use their written work and other resources to discuss their topic area with another pair who have focused on a different area. This should generate some interesting comparison talk about historical origins and traditions.

● Ask the children to share with the other pairs their thoughts about which part of the topic they found most interesting and would like to know more about.

● Offer writing support to those who might need it.

Further practice

● Encourage the children to work in pairs to look at other UK or international customs, festivals or fairs that have historic origins and long traditions. For example, if they have enjoyed the Notting Hill Carnival work, they might want to research the background to the even bigger carnival in Rio. Suggest they create a non-chronological report about their chosen subject, using ICT or on paper, and present it to the class.

■SCHOLASTIC
www.scholastic.co.uk

Highland Games heavy events

- Look at the pictures of these Highland Games events.
- Tick the most likely idea of where each event came from.
- Write a sentence to say why your chosen idea is better.
- Draw the likely origin next to the picture of the event.

Caber toss

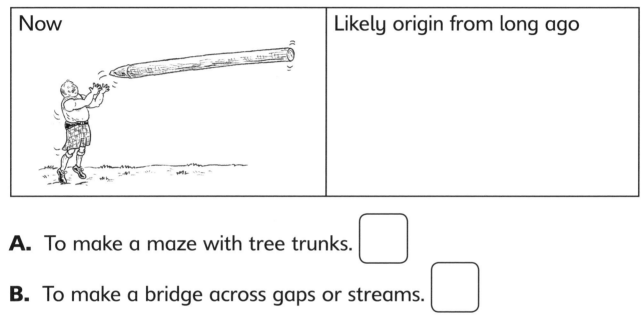

Now	Likely origin from long ago

A. To make a maze with tree trunks. ☐

B. To make a bridge across gaps or streams. ☐

_____ is more likely because _____

Sheaf tossing

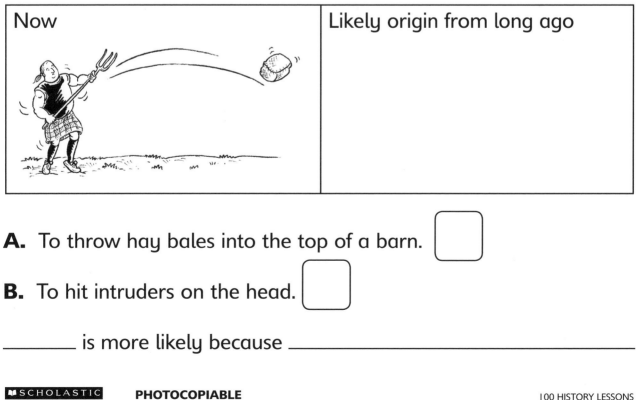

Now	Likely origin from long ago

A. To throw hay bales into the top of a barn. ☐

B. To hit intruders on the head. ☐

_____ is more likely because _____

Notting Hill Carnival

■ Decorate and cut out the pictures.

■ Stick them on a strip of paper to make a Notting Hill Carnival procession.

■ Cut out the labels and put them with the right pictures in your procession.

A steel band	A float
A Mas Band	A children's Mas Band
A calypso band	A float

PHOTOCOPIABLE

■SCHOLASTIC
www.scholastic.co.uk

Name: _____   Date: _____

Comparing fair days from long ago and today

■ Which fair day is from long ago (1400) and which shows a fair day today (now)?

■ Put the dates *1400* and *Now* on the pictures below.

■ What are the differences between the fairs. What is the same?

Differences	Similarities
_____	_____
_____	_____
_____	_____
_____	_____
_____	_____

I can compare fairs from long ago with fairs today.

How did you do?

≜SCHOLASTIC

Fully in line with the new curriculum objectives

Essential support for the 2014 National Curriculum

Plan with confidence with 100 Lessons Planning Guides
Complete planning frameworks with long and medium-term guidance for Years 1-6

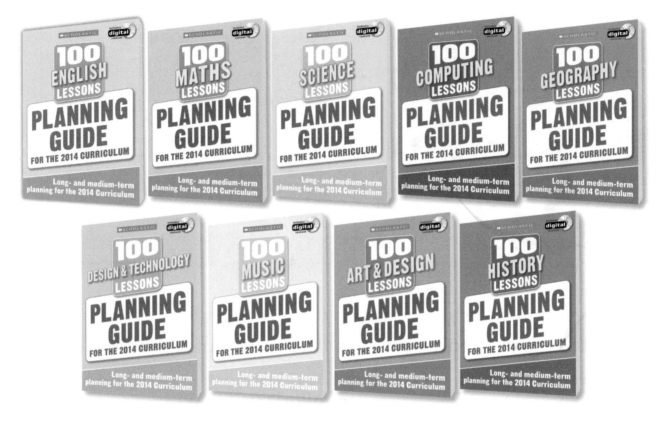

Save time with a whole year's ready-made lessons
100 Lessons matched to the new objectives for Years 1-6

"The 100 Lessons series will definitely help prepare for reaching the higher targets set by Government, and save me time completely re-planning everything."

Steven Gibson, teacher

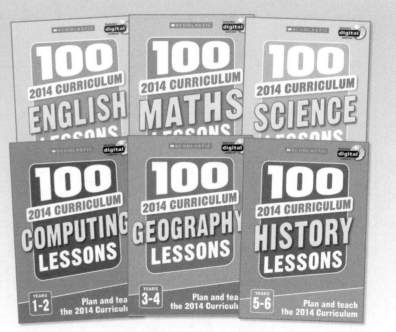

Order at www.scholastic.co.uk/100lessons **or call us on** 0845 603 9091